SUBMARINES
WAR BENEATH THE WAVES
FROM 1776 TO THE PRESENT DAY

SUBMARINES

WAR BENEATH THE WAVES

FROM 1776 TO THE PRESENT DAY

ROBERT HUTCHINSON

TED SMART

This edititon produced for The Book People Ltd,
Hall Wood Avenue, Haydock, St Helens WAll 9UL

In the UK for information please contact:
HarperCollins*Publishers*
77-85 Fulham Palace Road
Hammersmith
London W6 8JB
Great Britain
ww w.**fire**and**water**.com

In the US for information please contact:
HarperCollins*Publishers* Inc.
10 East 53rd Street
New York
NY 10022
USA
ww w.harpercollins.com

First published by HarperCollins*Publishers* 2001

ISBN 0 00 765333 6

Editor: Ian Tandy
Editorial Assistant: Clara Théau-Laurent
Drawings: Tony Gibbons
Design: Rod Teasdale
Origination: Dot Gradations, England

Printed and bound in Spain

Photographs courtesy: Royal Navy Submarine Museum, API, Imperial War Museum,
National Maritime Museum, US Navy, Canadian DoD, BAe Systems Marine

CONTENTS

EARLY DESIGNS

MAN HAS ALWAYS NURTURED TWO SEEMINGLY IMPOSSIBLE DREAMS: to fly in the air like a bird, and to swim underwater - like a fish. In both cases, it was not until the early years of the 20th Century that both dreams were fully realised by powered, manoeuvrable machines. The military value of submarines was grasped far quicker than that of aircraft - despite navies' misgivings about wartime roles and some admirals' pre-occupation with the firepower of heavily armoured capital ships.

Attempts to construct workable submarines also pre-date man's efforts to fly. During the three centuries from 1600, more than 130 designs for submarines were conceived and sometimes built, including the ambitious Maclaine concept for a submersible battleship in 1898, armed with sixteen 12 inch guns, fortunately, perhaps, never constructed, but a forerunner of the ill-fated commerce raiders of the 1930s.

The first true design for a submersible appeared in 1578, when English mathematician William Bourne (c.1535-82) envisaged an enclosed wooden hull, waterproofed by leather hides, that could submerge and surface by the use of air-filled leather ballast tanks, compressed or released by several screws. Oars would provide propulsion underwater.

Bourne, a self-educated man from Gravesend, Kent, had served as a gunner in the English Navy under Admiral Sir William Monson, and in 1567, had published the book, *Certyn Rules for Navigation*. One of his stepsons, James, was a ship's master by 1577. Bourne's boat was never built, but Dutch inventor and alchemist Cornelius Jacobszoon Drebbel, (1572-1633), the son of a prosperous Alkmaar farmer, later modified his design. Already the holder of patents for a pump and a "perpetual motion" clock, and the manufacturer of compound microscopes, Drebbel designed a submersible around 1620, with tubes attached to floats on the surface to provide crewmen with fresh air.

CORNELIUS DREBBEL

Like Bourne's design, the Drebbel boat relied on oarsmen for both surface and sub-surface propulsion, with leather gaskets preserving the integrity of a greased leather-sheathed hull constructed of wood on iron frames. Unlike Bourne, Drebbel's craft was actually built between 1620-1626, and was tested on London's River Thames, reportedly at depths between 12 and 15 feet; although it is more likely that it operated only partially awash. During the first test, it leaked badly.

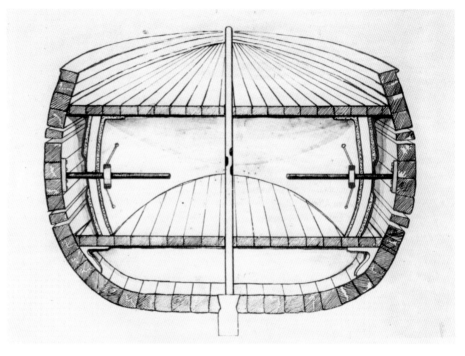

Above: Bourne's design for a submersible boat included screws which compressed leather ballast tanks.

Although there is controversy as to its true nature - was it really a kind of diving bell or a true submarine? - there is little doubt that the boat undertook at least one successful partially submerged trial, lasting around three hours, with twelve oarsmen and a number of foolhardy passengers on board.

Its true significance was the development of an air supply, akin to the modern snorkel, first seen operationally on the German submarine *U 539* in January 1944,[1] although Drebbel is also said to have created a chemical that purified air within the submerged boat. As he had discovered how to produce oxygen from heating potassium nitrate (saltpetre), this may be plausible. If used, the process makes the courage of the 17th Century pioneer submariners even more breathtaking.

State Papers reveal substantial government support for Drebbel's work. In June 1626, (soon after Charles I ascended the English throne), Sir William Heydon, Lieutenant of the Ordnance, issued a warrant to make "four water mines, and water petards…" for experiments involving "underwater explosive machines". The following month, George, Earl of Totnes, issued a warrant signed by the King, to Heydon, for "lodgings and workshops to be provided in the Minories" (in London) for Drebbel and an assistant, Arnold Rotispen, "who are to apply their skill for his Majesty's service," (the Navy). Eleven months later, the King himself wrote to Heydon with instructions to pay Drebble and Rotispen £100 - a considerable sum in the 17th Century - as a reward "for forging divers(e) water engines," almost certainly a reference to the embryo submersible. But this payment

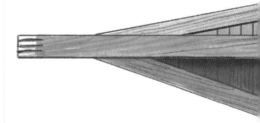

Left: Artist's impression of Drebbel's boat underway on the Thames in the 1620s.

1 UNDERWATER PROPULSION BY DIESEL ENGINES WITH A PIPE TO SUPPLY AIR WAS TRIALLED BY THE DUTCH NAVY IN *O 19* AND *O 20* IN 1938-39.

seems to mark the end of the experiments, and as the British Navy was more interested in Drebbel's expertise in explosives for fireships than in submersibles, the project died, as would others.

MERSENNE & FOURNIER

A number of designs for submarines followed hard on Drebbel's heels. Two French priests, Marin Mersenne (1588-1648) and the Jesuit Georges Fournier (1595-1652), produced a design in the late 1630s for an armed submarine fitted with wheels for mobility on the seabed. It was to have air pumps and some form of phosphorescent system for internal lighting. Another priest, the Italian Abbé Giovanni Alfonso Borelli (1608-79), designed a boat with a hand-operated system for controlling buoyancy by forcing water from leather bottles.

In 1653, a Frenchman called de Son, constructed a submarine in Rotterdam, which for the first time, included mechanical power, and was based on an internal paddle wheel fitted amidships and worked by clockwork. The concept was innovative but the power generated was insufficient to propel the 72-foot long craft through water and it is likely that the boat was never intended to operate other than awash.

In the next century, another design, by an inventor known only as "M.T.", seems to have copied that produced 22 years before, by Nathaniel Symons, a carpenter of Harbeston, near Totnes, Devonshire. This was based on Borelli's system of emptying and refilling air in leather buoyancy bags or bottles. M.T.'s design, published in the English periodical *The Gentleman's Magazine* in 1747, used inflated goats' skins as buoyancy aids.

Then came the ill-fated venture by another Devon ship's carpenter, John Day. Following an unwise bet, he procured the 50-foot sloop *Maria*, constructed a 12-feet long "airtight" cabin in her hold amidships, and roped seventy-five large barrels around the ship as buoyancy aids. Two large weights, amounting to 10 tons apiece and hanging from the keel, were fixed to internal iron rods attached to ringbolts as releasable ballast - with a further 10 tons stowed within the hull. Confident of success, Day furnished his cabin with a hammock, candles, biscuits

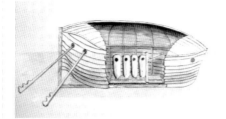

Above: The 17th Century design of Abbe Giovani Borelli.

Right: Bushnell's *Turtle* was fitted with hand-driven vertical and horizontal propellers

and water. He also designed a signalling system to spectators on the surface: the release of a white buoy signified that he was well; red, "in indifferent health"; and black, "in great danger." On June 20 1774, the *Maria* sank in 170 feet of water in Plymouth Harbour, between Drake's Island and the Prince of Wales Battery. She never surfaced. No buoys were released. The hull was probably crushed by water pressure: an important lesson had been tragically learnt.

BUSHNELL'S TURTLE

The next tangible step forward in submarine technology was the design and construction, in the USA, of the pear-shaped wooden *Turtle* in 1775, fitted with flooding water tanks which were cleared by two hand pumps. Although strictly speaking another semi-submersible, it became the first submarine demonstrably to dive, happily to surface, and to attack an enemy warship - albeit unsuccessfully. It also introduced the concept of screw propulsion.[2] The submarine was now tacitly acknowledged as a weapon, not one of defence, but of aggression.

A passionate thread of anti-British sentiment was to run throughout early submarine development and became the driving force behind some designs and much innovation. The *Turtle's* designer was David Bushnell, (1742-1824) a 34-year-old Yale University graduate, who began building the boat in his hometown of Saybrook, Connecticut. The 7-feet long, 6-feet diameter boat, made of tar-caulked oak and reinforced with iron bands (rather like a barrel), was propelled by hand-driven vertical and horizontal

propellers. With slight positive buoyancy, it travelled with around six inches exposed above the surface of the water. The armament consisted of a 150-lb. gunpowder mine, intended to be screwed into the wooden hull of the target warship by using an augur or gimlet attached to the vertical propeller of the submersible. It was be fired by a primitive clockwork flintlock device.

After interesting the leadership of American forces, then fighting a War of Independence against Britain in this new weapon, the *Turtle*, manned by Army Sergeant Ezra Lee, was sent to attack the British warship HMS *Eagle*. This was Admiral Howe's 64-gun flagship, anchored in New York harbour on September 6, 1776. Although the craft manoeuvred into position undetected, the mine could not be screwed into the *Eagle's* hull, probably because of it's curvature - and the attack failed. British soldiers on shore spotted the submersible and a 12-oared boat was sent to investigate. Lee released the charge, the timer primed. The British beat a hasty retreat and the charge exploded near the entrance to the East River. Bushnell mounted a later attack on a British frigate *Cerberus*, between the Connecticut River and New

Left: De Son's mechanical submarine of 1653.

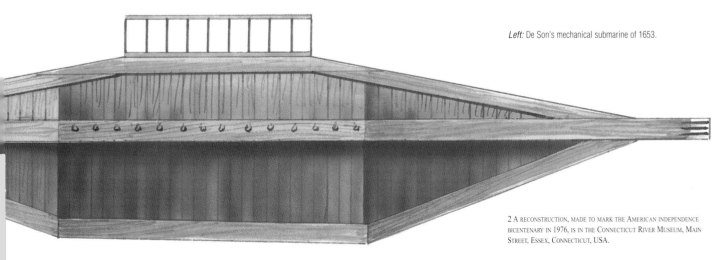

2 A RECONSTRUCTION, MADE TO MARK THE AMERICAN INDEPENDENCE BICENTENARY IN 1976, IS IN THE CONNECTICUT RIVER MUSEUM, MAIN STREET, ESSEX, CONNECTICUT, USA.

London, but this probably involved explosives carried by a whaler rather than the submersible. During the Anglo-American war of 1812, there were (possibly apocryphal) reports of a second Turtle used in an attack on the British warship *Ramillies*, at anchor off New London, but again the mission failed. General George Washington wrote to Thomas Jefferson, whilst Ambassador in Paris, in September 1787:

Bushnell is a man of great mechanical powers - a fertile education - and a master in execution. He came to me in 1776 recommended by Governor Trumbull (now dead) and other respectable characters who were proselytes to his plan. Although I wanted faith myself, I furnished him with money and other aids to carry it into execution.

He laboured for some time ineffectually and though advocates for his scheme continued sanguine, he never did succeed. One accident or another was always intervening. I then thought, and still think, that it was an effort of genius."

In France, American engineer and inventor Robert Fulton (1765-1815) was working on torpedo designs which initially interested both the French and British governments. During the winter of 1799-1800, he turned to submarines and built the *Nautilus*, which was 21-feet 4 inches long, with a copper-sheathed hull, equipped with a mast, bowsprit and two sails for surface propulsion and two hand-cranked screws to travel underwater - one providing vertical motion. The mast was unstepped before diving. Depth was estimated using a barometer and air supplied to the four-man crew by flasks of compressed air on board.

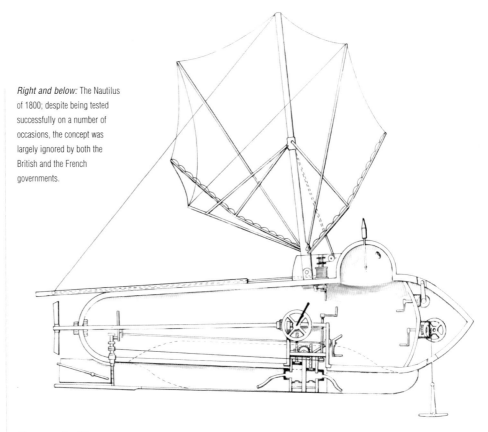

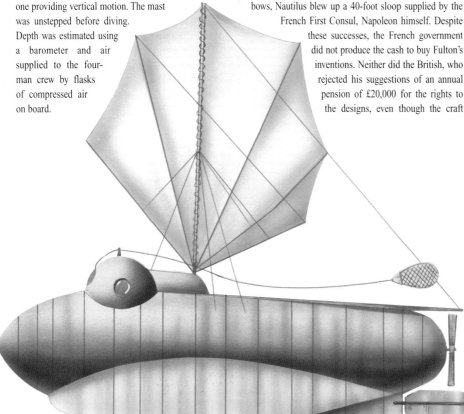

FULTON'S NAUTILUS

The boat was first demonstrated in the River Seine in Paris, between what today would be the Concorde and Alma bridges. Tests to depths of nearly 30 feet were staged within the port of Brest during July 1801, the boat remaining submerged for more than an hour with Fulton and three brave mechanics on board. Using an explosive charge mounted on a spar attached to the submarine bows, Nautilus blew up a 40-foot sloop supplied by the French First Consul, Napoleon himself. Despite these successes, the French government did not produce the cash to buy Fulton's inventions. Neither did the British, who rejected his suggestions of an annual pension of £20,000 for the rights to the designs, even though the craft

was demonstrated to them in October 1805, blowing up a heavy brig, the *Dorothy*, off Walmer Castle in Kent, with 70-lbs. of gunpowder.

Spurned, he returned to the United States in December 1806, where he offered his expertise to the US government in the development of underwater guns. He also worked on a much larger submarine (powered by a steam engine), the 80-feet long, 22-feet wide *Mute,* which began construction in New York. But Fulton died before the project was completed.

Up to the mid-19th Century, experiments continued in submarine technologies, with American shoemaker Lodner Phillips and the French engineer Brutus de Villeroi, among others, improving on Fulton's designs. Phillips designed two submarines, one configured for peaceful operations and the larger one for war; this being a 39-feet long boat with a telescopic funnel to provide air. De Villeroi built two boats in 1832-35, (one with a displacement greater than 30 tons) and another in 1855.

THE BAUER 'BRANDTAUCHER'

In 1850, the former artillery non-commissioned officer, Wilhelm Bauer (1822-1875) built the *Brandtaucher* ('Fire Diver') in Kiel, Germany; an unattractive 27-feet long craft with a short, stubby steel hull, a low conning tower right forward at the bows with two bulls-eye portholes, and a displacement of nearly 39 tons. It accommodated three men. Again, it relied on muscle power to drive the screws, via a large treadmill mounted amidships - after earlier tests with clockwork again failed to supply enough power. The aim was to develop a weapon that would disrupt a Danish naval blockade of northern German ports. It was tested to depths of just over 50 feet but was never deployed operationally after the first test, on February 1 1851, nearly became a disaster.

The boat plunged to the sea bottom, 54 feet below the surface and after more than five terrifying hours, Bauer

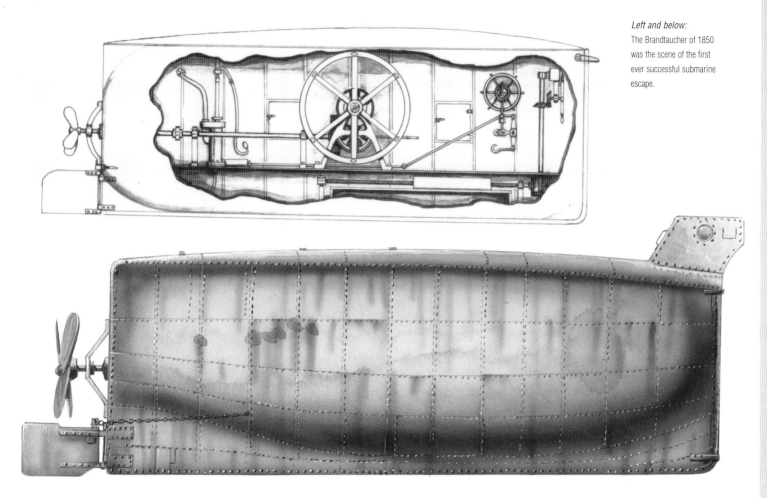

Left and below:
The Brandtaucher of 1850
was the scene of the first
ever successful submarine
escape.

opened the flood valves to equalise the pressure within the hull to allow escape. When the seawater reached the chins of Bauer and his two fellow crewmen, a bubble of air blew the hatch open and all three shot to the surface - to survive. It was the first successful submarine escape.

Brandtaucher was later raised from the bottom of Kiel Harbour in 1887 and renovated. This remains the oldest preserved submarine in the world and can be seen today in the Deutsches Armeemuseum, Neuer Garten, Potsdam, Germany.

Four years later, Bauer built the *Seeteufel* ('Sea Devil') for the Russian Navy, a much larger and more ambitious design, with a steel hull, a 13 man crew, and a small engine for use on the surface. The flat, sausage-shaped hull, launched from the Leuchtemburg yard in St Petersburg, on November 2 1855, was 52-feet long and 12-feet wide. The problem of sub-surface propulsion remained intractable with the *Seeteufel* relying on his earlier, cumbersome system of a treadmill-cranked screw. Water ballast was controlled by a system of hand-pumps. The boat made 133 successful dives, including one at St. Petersburg on September 6 1856 - during the coronation of Czar Alexander II - when it submerged with a number of musicians on board who patriotically played the Russian national anthem. The submarine finally foundered off Ochda, although there are suggestions that it was scuttled.

The limitations of technology in developing a robust propulsion system or adequate manoeuvrability still remained a major inhibiting factor that restricted potential submarine warfare to three basic tactics in attack:

- *Based on the spar-mounted explosive mine originally conceived by Fulton.*

- *A mine attached to the hull of a target warship by mechanical means deployed by the submarine (like the Turtle).*

- *The final, and most hazardous of all for potential submariners, was towing a primitive torpedo fitted with a contact fuze and diving (or ducking) below the target in the hope that the torpedo, following on behind, would strike the hull.*

AMERICAN CIVIL WAR

The American Civil War saw the submarine coming of age as a true weapon of war, intended to destroy enemy shipping. It is hardly surprising that the Confederate states, threatened by a Federal naval blockade, put more effort into building submersibles - by both official and private efforts. Early entrants into the conflict were the Confederate steam-powered semi-submersibles, the so-called 'David' boats, possibly named after the engineer

David Chenowith Ebaugh. These were 40-foot long cigar-shaped hulls, fitted with tell-tale telescopic smokestacks and a spar-mounted explosive charge. These were limited to operating with the smokestack well above the surface of the sea, thus destroying the submarine's major weapon. However, one of the class, captained by Lieut. William T.Glassel CSN, damaged the three-masted USS *New Ironsides* in an attack on October 5 1863. The attack would have been more deadly if Glassel had fully pressed home the attack. Instead, he prematurely tugged the lanyard triggering the 40-lbs. of gunpowder at the tip of the spar. In the subsequent confusion, he and his crew were taken prisoner.

When Union naval forces entered Charleston Harbour in February 1865, they captured nine 'David' boats, tied up alongside, and found a further two stuck in the mud of the Cooper River.

True submarines were also being developed by the Confederacy, spurred by private investment. The *Pioneer*, built by James McClintock and Baxter Watson at the Leeds Foundry in New Orleans, in the winter of 1861/2, received letters of marque to operate as a privateer. The cigar-shaped craft, displacing four tons, was 34-feet long - four feet in diameter, with a quarter-inch thick iron hull, painted black. It was powered by a propeller and cranked by two crewmen, under a commander. The boat was floated in February 1862 and underwent trials in Lake Ponchartrain and reportedly sank two barges and a

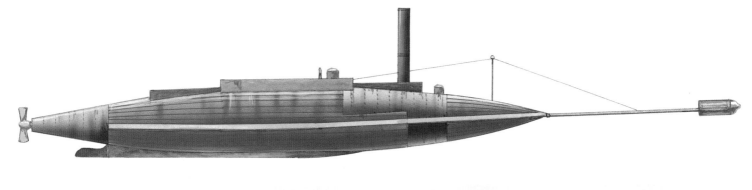

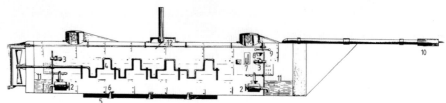

Above and right: The Confederate Hunley, 1863. 1. Rudder, 2. Pumps, 3. Sea cocks, 4. Propeller crank, 5. Cast iron keel, 6. Release bolts, 7. Mercury gauge, 8. Compass, 9. Steering wheel, 10. Spar torpedo, 11. Ballast tanks (open), 12. Air box.

schooner, using towed contact torpedoes. However, later in 1862, Federal forces captured New Orleans and the *Pioneer* was abandoned, and sold for scrap after the war in 1868.

AMERICAN DIVER

McClintock and Watson meanwhile had fled ahead of the Union armies to Mobile, Alabama, and began construction in 1863 of a new, slightly larger boat, the *American Diver*, at the Park & Lyons engineering plant. This also had a quarter-inch thick iron hull, but was built in a square sided design with a wedge-shaped bow and stern. The boat was 36-feet long, three-feet in width and fitted with a 30-inch diameter propeller. Much effort was expended in developing first an electro-magnetic engine, then a steam engine, but all development came to naught and the designers resorted to hand-cranking by four men - a major drawback in any plan to attack Union warships offshore. The *American Diver* was doomed to failure before her first patrol. In February 1863, it was towed off Fort Morgan but foundered in heavy seas.

HUNLEY

McClintock was not deterred. Although by now financially straitened, he and his colleagues bought a second-hand steam boiler, probably from a steamship, which was lengthened into an elliptical craft of 40-feet long. This craft was 4 feet in diameter and fitted with bulls-eye glass in two manhole covers fore and aft on the deck, which were secured by rubber gaskets and bolted from within. The hull was 3/8-inch thick iron, with a keel, and contained water-ballast tanks to raise and dive the boat, via pumps and sea-cocks. Diving was assisted by two lateral fins, five feet long, operated by a lever amidships. The 3½-foot diameter propeller was turned by

hand by eight crewmen, and the boat was reported capable of making four knots in calm seas.

A month after completion, the submarine was taken by railway flatcar to Charleston in August, 1863, fitted out for combat and crewed by Confederate Navy volunteers. Disaster struck in one trial, when the boat unexpectedly dived with manholes open and sank rapidly in 42-feet of water. Five of the crew of nine drowned - Absolum Williams of the CSS *Palmetto State* and Frederick Doyle, John Kelly, Nicholas Davis and Michael Kane, from the CSS *Chicora* - the first submariners to die in history.

The boat was raised and a further crew, this time, civilian volunteers, (including Horace Hunley, Deputy Collector of Customs in New Orleans, and one of the original submarine designers) were brought in to operate the craft. Again, disaster struck, this time apparently caused by the

Below: The Hunley was responsible for the first successful submarine attack against a Federal ship during the Civil War. Using a harpoon, filled with explosive, she sank the sloop USS Housatonic, but failed to return from the patrol.

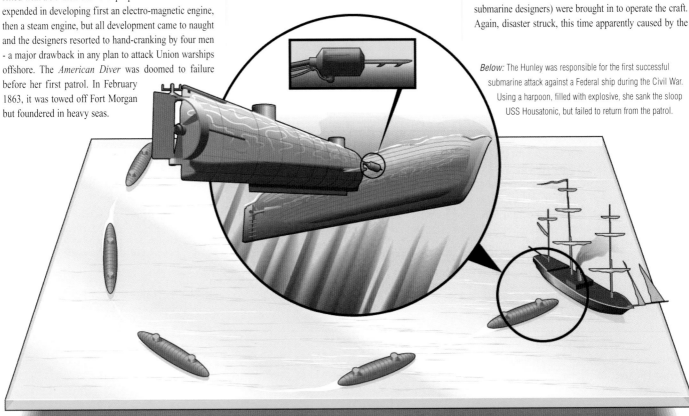

craft's commander, Hunley, failing to adjust the ballast tanks whilst submerged. The boat rammed its bows into the harbour mud at an angle of about 35° and partially flooded, drowning all eight crew.

The hull was raised again and named the *H.L. Hunley* in memory of her dead commander. (Small wonder her nickname became 'The Peripatetic Coffin'.) Astonishingly, a third volunteer crew was assembled from naval personnel as well as one artilleryman, commanded by Lieut. George Dixon, of the 21st Alabama Regiment. Not only is this an indication of the tremendous courage of those involved in the project, but also of the desperate impact the Federal blockade was having inside Charleston.

Hunley performed a number of unsuccessful night patrols off Charleston before setting out on her final and fatal cruise on the moonlit night of February 17 1864. By this time, earlier efforts to tow a mine on a plank had been discarded. The *Hunley* was now fitted with a manoeuvrable 20-25-feet long, two inch diameter iron pipe harpoon, tipped with a 90-lb explosive charge, triggered by the percussion "Singer's torpedo fuze" or more likely, by a lanyard.

The brand new Federal steam sloop USS *Housatonic*, 1,264 tons, armed with 11 large calibre guns, was anchored three miles off the Charleston Bar, on blockade duty. She was a priority target for the *Hunley*, and once submerged, the submarine steered a course for an attack at 8.40 PM. She was spotted by the ship's lookouts about two feet beneath the surface on the starboard side while making three or four knots. The glint of light from her deadlights could be clearly seen. She came under small-arms fire as the Federal ship desperately tried to slip her anchor and go astern. It was too late. The *Hunley*'s explosive charge ripped into the hull a little forward of the mizzen mast, blowing off the stern, and the *Housatonic* sank in just three minutes, taking five of its crew with her. So Ensign E.C.Hazeltine, Captain's Clerk C.O.Muzzey, Quartermaster John Williams, Landsman Theodore Parker and Firemen John Walsh, became the first casualties of a submarine attack.

The *Hunley*, after making the first successful attack on a warship, failed to return to base. All nine crew were lost. Her fate remains a mystery to this day. Four theories remain tenable: she was damaged in the explosion; she was damaged by the explosion's concussion wave; *Housatonic*'s small-arms fire pierced or damaged a vulnerable part of a hull - her commanding officer, Captain Charles Pickering, took special aim with a double-barrelled shotgun at the two protruding hatches; or finally she foundered in the worsening weather that followed the attack. Her hull was located 30-feet down in May 1995, off her base at Sullivan's Island in South Carolina, and it was here that a 3-foot hole was spotted by divers in the side of the wreck. Now raised archaeological investigations will provide new evidence of her fate.

A reconstruction of the CSS *Hunley* is located at the Hunley Museum in Charleston - a fitting memorial to the brave men who forged submarine history in a hull reconstructed from an old steam boiler.

Another Confederate submarine is on display at the Louisiana State Museum in New Orleans - a submersible recovered in July 1878 from a canal leading to Lake Ponchartrain. This is said to be the *Pioneer* but its small size suggests merely a working prototype.

SAINT PATRICK

A further Confederate submarine venture came with the *Saint Patrick*, designed and built by Irish immigrant engineer John P. Halligan at the Ordnance Works in Selma, Alabama. He had been granted exemption from military service in January 1864 for the "purpose of building a submarine torpedo boat." By October, the 30-foot long boat, steam-powered on the surface and hand-cranked underwater, was ready for sea trials.

Before she could enter service there were unseemly wrangles over her command, but within three days of the Confederate Navy finally taking over, she was in action, based in Mobile Bay. In the early hours of January 27 1865 - under the command of Lieut. John T. Walker CSN - *Saint Patrick* made a surface attack on the 10 gun, paddle-wheeled steamer USS *Octorara*, striking the Federal warship aft of the wheelhouse with a charge mounted on a spar. There was no explosion. The attack failed. Subsequently, *Saint Patrick* was relegated to running supplies to isolated Confederate garrisons, the last mission coming in April 1865, to troops based at Spanish Fort.

In 1872, the Royal Navy received a report on McClintock's designs from Capt. F. Nicholson and the chief engineer of HMS *Royal Alfred*, Mr J. Ellis. The report, datelined New York March 4 1872, said: "I have had the opportunity of examining a very ingenious vessel for submarine warfare. I had heard from officers who served in the Confederate services that, what had been thought was a huge fish had been observed by the people on board their vessels on more than one occasion crossing the river just below the surface of the water." The covering letter, from Vice Admiral E. Fanshawe, based at Halifax, Nova Scotia, said: "…it would be very desirable to bring Mr McClintock to England…

"and to afford him all necessary means to construct or superintend construction of a boat of good capacity according to his plans at the public's expense, which would not be great in comparison with the object. He hates his countrymen, Americans, and hopes some day to be a British subject."

The report, and McClintock's hopes of a new career in England, ended up in the Admiralty's perpetual pending tray.

The loss of the *Housatonic* had a major impact on Union naval tactical thinking particularly in blockading strategies and practice, but it failed to accelerate submarine design in the North. The cigar-shaped *Alligator* was the first submarine purchased by the US Navy. It was designed as a mine layer in Confederate harbours and was equipped with two crude air purifiers (based on an oxygen-generating chemical) and bellows to force air through slaked lime. Unfortunately, it sank under tow in April 1863.

THE INTELLIGENT WHALE

The second Union design was the deliciously named *Intelligent Whale*, (alias 'Disastrous Jonah') which Oliver Halstead began building in 1860 and which was tested between 1864 and September 1872. Its length was 28-feet 8 inches, with a beam of 7-feet, and it displaced two tons.

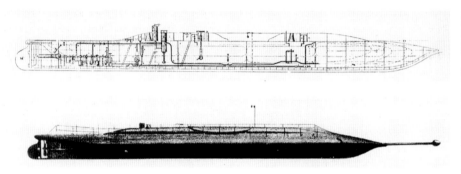

It was designed with an overly optimistic combat endurance of 10 hours. The crew of between six and thirteen hand-turned the propeller. The boat, equipped with water and compressed air buoyancy controls, was steered by horizontal and vertical rudders. An innovation was a wooden door in the hull that released a diver with a mine.

The US Navy bought the *Intelligent Whale* in 1870 but in her only official test in 1872, the submarine suddenly flooded, the crew happily escaping without loss. The Navy refused to commission her and lost all interest in submarines for more than two decades, although the boat is credited with inspiring John Holland to develop his first working submarine in the modern sense. The *Intelligent Whale* remains on display at the National Guard Militia Museum of New Jersey, at Sea Girt in New Jersey.

Below: Nordenfelt & Garratt's fourth boat ran aground in 1880 en-route to Russia.

LE PLONGEUR

Whilst the concept of employing submarines as weapons platforms had now excited interest amongst navies, (particularly after development of the Whitehead torpedo in 1870) the all-important hurdle of a viable method of underwater propulsion had not been resolved.

Across the Atlantic, two French naval officers Capt. S. Bourgois and Commander Charles Brun built *Le Plongeur* for the French Navy at Rochefort, beginning in June 1860. This was designed to overcome the limitations of man-cranked propulsion, by employing an engine breathing compressed air - but they could not construct air tanks big enough to sustain realistic endurance times. The boat, 140-feet long, with a 20-foot beam, displaced 453 tons. Tests began on April 16 1863 and continued for three years, but the craft failed to be adopted by the French Navy. She lived up to her name: a pipe system to move water within the craft to adjust longitudinal stability was slow and inefficient, and the submarine therefore repeatedly plunged during operations.

Steam technology seemed to offer the solution. The Revd. George William Garrett, newly ordained curate at Christchurch in the Manchester suburb of Moss Side, England, had studied the designs of the Confederate submarines in the American Civil War and torpedo boat operations during the Russo-Turkish war of 1877. The British warship *Shah* on May 29 that year had fired the first British torpedo in anger, against the Peruvian rebel ship *Huascar* off Ho, Peru. Here was the ideal weapon system – but the question was how to deliver it from a submarine hampered by inadequate propulsion?

RESURGAM

Garrett first built a one-man 14-foot long ovoid iron submarine - nicknamed the 'Curate's Egg' - with financial support from his father and a group of Manchester businessmen to meet the £232 cost of construction. A flywheel was used to hand-turn the 4 ton submersible's screw and bizarrely, Garret planned to plant the craft's mine himself, using leather gloves fixed to the outer casing of the submarine.

After further experiments, the clergyman heard of the invention of a closed steam engine - patented by Eugene Lamm in 1872 - and this was included in designs for a new submarine, *Resurgam*. Built by a Birkenhead company of shipwrights, *Resurgam* later became the world's first powered submarine, armed with external torpedo tubes. (**See special feature page 20**). Unfortunately, *en route* to trials for the British Royal Navy at Portsmouth, the *Resurgam* foundered off the town of Rhyl in North Wales on February 26 1880, whilst under tow.

Like McClintock before him, Garrett was not deterred by this crushing blow to his hopes, despite his financial

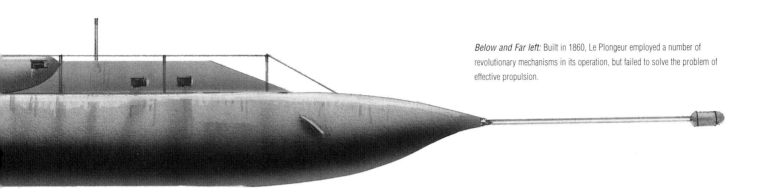

Below and Far left: Built in 1860, Le Plongeur employed a number of revolutionary mechanisms in its operation, but failed to solve the problem of effective propulsion.

problems. Together with the Swedish millionaire machine gun manufacturer Thorsten Nordenfelt, he designed and built new submarines for the navies of Turkey, Greece and Sweden with varying degrees of success.

NORDENFELT BOATS

Nordenfelt I was laid down at Eckensberg, near Stockholm in 1882 and launched in June 1883. It was 64-feet long, had a maximum beam of 9-feet and displaced 60 tons. Unlike *Resurgam*, it had a flattened cigar-shaped pressure hull, fitted with a glass dome amidships on top of a conning tower. Propulsion was by steam, driving a large propeller. It carried a Whitehead torpedo in an externally mounted tube. Despite less than impressive trials off Landskrona in 1885, the Greek Navy bought the boat at the bargain price of £9,000. She was shipped by cargo vessel, and trials in the Bay of Salamis in March 1886 demonstrated the submarine's operational defects. She was laid up to rot at Piraeus.

Garrett and Nordenfelt moved onto a new design, the *Nordenfelt II,* built at Des Vignes on the River Thames at Chertsey, Surrey. It was launched on April 14 1886, but later broke down and shipped in sections for assembly by its purchaser, the Turkish Navy. It arrived on May 17, and was re-fabricated to become the *Abdul Hamid,* 100-feet long, 160 tons displacement, armed with two internal torpedo tubes and two Nordenfelt machine guns mounted on the casing, fore and aft. The second Nordenfelt boat, the *Abdul Mecid,* was launched on August 4 1887 at Chertsey. The first boat was demonstrated off Scutari, successfully staging mock attacks on a steam ship, first on the surface and then dived. Subsequent official trials were disastrous. P.W.

D'Alton, who worked with Garrett and Nordenfelt, wrote later in the *Engineer* magazine:-

She had the fault of all submarine boats - a total lack of longitudinal stability.... The Turkish boat was submerged by admitting water to tanks aided by horizontal propellers and raised by blowing out the ballast once again and reversing the propellers.

Nothing could be imagined more unstable than this Turkish boat. The moment she left the horizontal position, the water in her boiler and tanks surged forwards and backwards and increased the angle of inclination. She was perpetually working up and down like a scale beam and no human vigilance could keep her on an even keel for half a minute at a time.

Once, and only once, she fired a torpedo with the result that she as nearly as possible stood up vertically on her tail and proceeded to plunge to the bottom stern first.

On another occasion, all hands were nearly lost. Mr. Garrett was in the little conning-tower. The boat was being slowly submerged... before a committee of Ottoman officers when a boat came alongside without warning. Her wash sent a considerable quantity of water down the conning-tower, the lid of which was not closed, and the submarine boat instantly began to sink like a stone. Mr Garrett got the lid closed just in time and Mr Lawrie, the engineer, without waiting for orders, blew some ballast water out. It was an exceedingly narrow escape."

After *Resurgam,* Garrett knew all about submarine hatches. Amazingly, the Turkish Navy bought the submarine but experienced great problems in operations. On May 22 1888, Garrett was given the honorary rank of *Binbasi* (equivalent to Lieut. Commander) in order to train Turkish submariners for a month a year at Constantinople. However, the Turkish Navy soon tired of their unpredictable and dangerous submarines and they were left to rust in the mud of Constantinople Harbour. During the First World War, the Turks, with German technical assistance, unsuccessfully attempted to overhaul and refit both boats.

Nordenfelt and Garrett pressed on. A design for another submarine was produced, this time, 125-feet long, 12-feet in diameter, with a flattened hull terminating in sharp, vertical edges at bows and stern. It displaced 245 tons and was fitted with two conning towers, one for the boat's commander. The deck had one-inch thick armoured plating. Two propellers, recessed at stem and stern, would produce speeds of 15 knots on the surface and five submerged - driven by 1200 hp of engine power, utilising a modified Lamm system. *Nordenfelt III* was built at Barrow-in-Furness and launched in March, 1887 and appeared at the Golden Jubilee Naval Review at Spithead on July 23 1887. It was demonstrated to naval representatives from Austria, Germany, Italy, Japan, Spain, Turkey and the USA in trials in the Solent, off Calshot, in December 1887, but the Russians had already expressed strong interest in purchasing her.

The boat set off for Kronstadt in November 1888 but ran aground off Jutland. The Russians refused to buy her, or to pay anything at all.

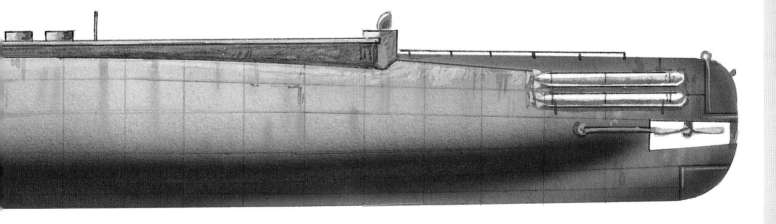

Resurgam - first fully powered submarine

The world's first fully powered submarine, *Resurgam* ('I shall rise again') was built in 1879 at the Britannia Engine Works, Birkenhead, England, by the J.T.Cochran & Sons company of shipwrights, for just £1,538. Her designer, youthful Manchester clergyman, the Revd. George Garrett, sought to solve the problem of submarine propulsion by installing a Lamm closed system steam engine.

Although this involved dampening down the furnace before diving, the system enabled stored latent heat to drive the rod-cylinder engine to turn the single screw underwater, generating a speed of two knots submerged and three knots on the surface. Endurance was estimated at four hours underwater.

Garrett's submarine was a 45-feet long, 9?-feet (amidships) diameter iron craft, fabricated over iron frames and displacing 30 tons with sharp, conical bows and stern. On top, amid a cutwater, was a short conning tower, fitted with a hatch and portholes. An air purification system was installed to extract poisonous carbon monoxide generated by boiler combustion. A method of externally firing two Whitehead torpedoes was also fitted.

The boat was launched by a 50-ton crane into the Wallesey dock on November 26, 1879. Publicity surrounding the trials, involving Garrett, an engineer called George Price and a master mariner, Captain Jackson, in Liverpool Bay was encouraging enough to interest a still sceptical Admiralty which asked Garrett to mount a demonstration at Portsmouth.

Garrett and his two-man crew set off for Portsmouth on the evening of December 10, 1879, the clergyman (optimistically) determined to get there under the submarine's own steam, as a striking demonstration of the boat's capability. After leaving Birkenhead,

Above and below: Rev'd Garrett's Resurgam, the world's first genuine powered submarine, which foundered en-route to Portsmouth in 1880.

Resurgam encountered a sailing ship in Liverpool Bay inbound for the port. Garrett, astride the submarine's conning tower and with waves swirling around the hull, shouted across to the ship's master, seeking his position. In response, the captain asked Garrett's destination and the boat's complement. When told, the captain's now legendary reply was: "You are the three biggest fools I have ever met."

Temperatures of more than 100° F within the hull generated by the boiler, together with fumes from the furnace, no doubt sapped the stamina of the crew and was the reason why *Resurgam* docked in the port of Rhyl, North Wales. Modifications also had to be made while alongside in the port. Despite Garrett's earlier optimism and bravado, this may lay behind the subsequent decision to complete the voyage under tow by the steam yacht *Elfin*, departing Rhyl on the night of February 24, 1880. *Elfin* developed engine trouble early the next morning in increasingly heavy seas, and the submarine's crew, with difficulty, no doubt, later boarded the yacht to help. The problem resolved, the tow continued.

Unfortunately, the tow-rope parted on the morning of February 26, and heavy seas began to pour into the submarine through the open conning tower hatch, quickly flooding it. Garrett was the last to leave as the boat sank under him, The nightmare was not yet over: the yacht sought safety from the heavy weather in the estuary of the River Dee but was rammed by another boat, despatched to provide assistance. It was a horrible chapter of accidents.

Garrett was undeterred by the loss of the *Resurgam* and began work on other designs in partnership with Swedish gun manufacturer Thorsten Nordenfelt producing submarines ordered by the Greek and Turkish navies. The Turkish Navy appointed Garratt a naval commander to assist in training. The last of the designs appeared at the Royal Navy's Royal Jubilee Spithead review in 1887 and was purchased by the Russian Czar. Unfortunately it was wrecked on its delivery cruise off the coast of Denmark's Jutland coast and the Russian Navy refused to pay any money for it.

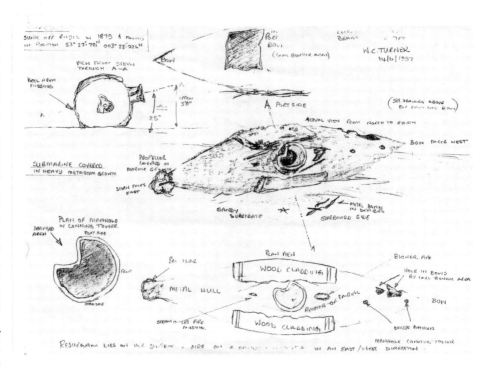

Above: Rev'd Garrett's Resurgam, as sketched on the sea-bed by Bill Turner of 'Malvern Archaeological Diving Unit' (MADU). Since this drawing was done the Resurgam has shifted and is now in a different position. Funding, as yet, has not been made available for the recovery of this historic boat.

That was the end of Garrett's career in submarine design. He left both the partnership with Nordenfelt and the Church and emigrated to the United States. At some stage, he became a visiting tutor in classics, mathematics and the sciences with an address at 466 Lennox Avenue, New York City. That too was unsuccessful and the one-time clergyman joined the US Army in the Corps of Engineers, later fighting in the Spanish-American war of 1898 as a corporal in Puerto Rico. He died penniless in New York aged 50, on February 26, 1902.

The wreck of the *Resurgam* was discovered in November 1995 when the nets of a fishing boat snagged on the hull, off Rhyl, on the north coast of Wales, just 60 feet down. Garrett's great grandson, of New Jersey, USA, who had supported the search for the submarine, dived on the wreck and partially entered the *Resurgam*'s stubby conning tower, left by his great grandfather in February, 1880.

The hull, now lying on its side, had been shifted from its original position and was damaged, probably as a result of a ship's heavy anchor snagging the wreck. There was also a large dent on the port side aft of the conning tower that may have occurred during the foundering of the submarine.

A full-sized replica of the *Resurgam* is on permanent display at Woodside ferry terminal, Birkenhead.

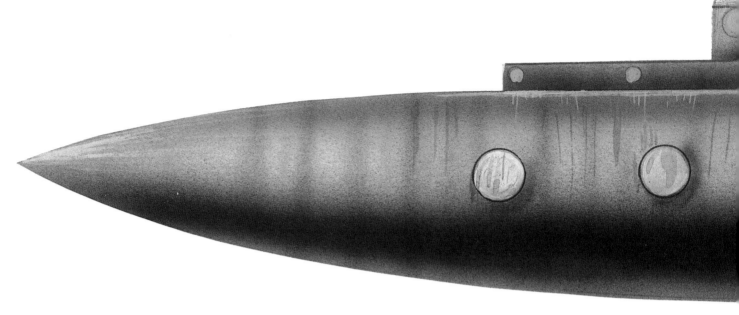

Above and Left: The British Nautilus trialled in 1886 was of all-steel construction and was powered by electric motors. Trials proved less than successful.

NAUTILUS

With advances in battery technology, electric motors looked more viable solutions to the problems of propulsion. Two Englishmen, Campbell and Ash, designed an all-steel cigar-shaped boat, *Nautilus*, built by Wolseley & Lyon, 60-feet long, 50 tons displacement, with twin screws, powered by electric motors. During trials in Tilbury docks in London in 1886, the boat, (warranted "extra special safe,") with the Royal Navy's Chief Constructor Sir William White on board, submerged - but became stuck in mud. An eyewitness, Bennett Burleigh, wrote afterwards:

Below: The Spanish Ictineo of 1889.

She remained invisible for a protracted period, greater, in truth, than those on the dock knew was safe, for she had no air or oxygen storage. ... Finally, to everybody's intense relief, she reappeared. Sir William suggested, when the light was turning blue, as were some faces, moving the crew to the higher end of the craft. It had the desired effect, the boat was lifted from the grip of the mud. Once on top, the engineer undid the manhole and shouted with elation .... that they were going down again. Several of the visitors had had more than enough and the gentleman was pulled down by the legs to make way for those who wished to escape..."

Nautilus disappeared into oblivion.

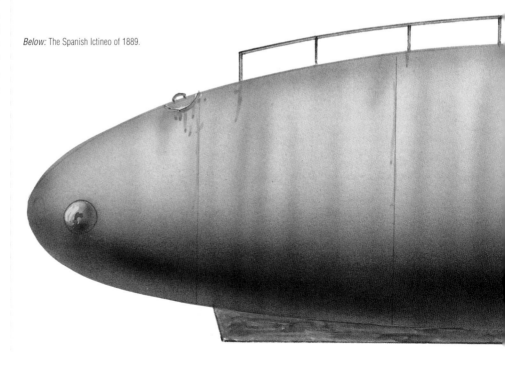

In France, civil engineer Claude Goubet built a short, fat submarine, *Goubet I,* in Paris in 1885. This was only 16-feet long, 11 tons, with a crew of two (sitting back-to-back amidships), and propelled by electric motors, powered by accumulators. Trials in the River Seine in March 1887 were followed by others off Cherbourg between 1889 and 1892, but she proved difficult in handling both on the surface and dived. Goubet built a second larger version but this proved unsuccessful in tests at Toulon in 1899.

In Spain, a young naval lieutenant, Isaac Peral, designed a 87 ton submerged displacement boat, launched at the Arsenal of Caraca on September 8 1888, powered by two 30 hp electric motors and twin screws.[3]

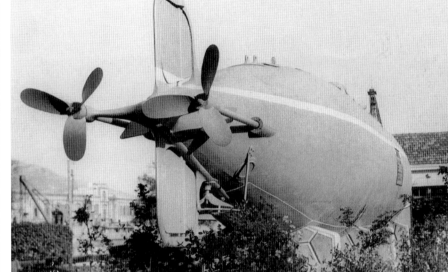

Right: The Spanish Peral, of 1888, now on display in Cartagena, Spain.

3 Spain had previously produced two designs, the *Ictineo I,* just eight tons displacement, launched in July, 1859 and the *Ictineo II,* 65 tons, steam-powered, in October 1864.

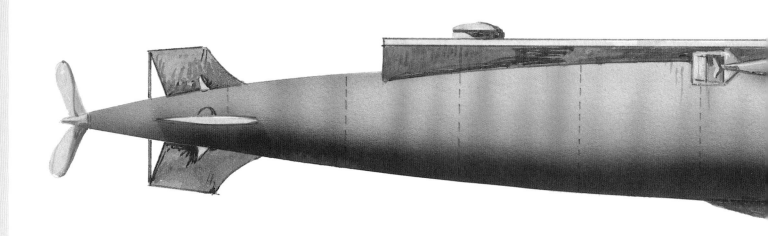

Above and Left: The French designed Gymnote was the first boat to use compressed air to expel ballast and a variable pitch propellor.

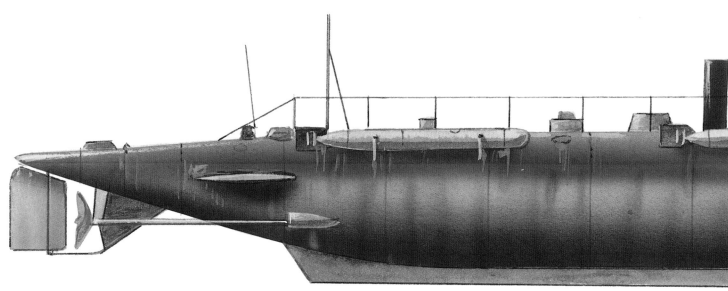

The 70-feet long craft was equipped with a lamp to examine the seabed. Trials performance was encouraging, with a 8-kt surface speed and a maximum diving depth of 100-feet; although it needed a tow to get back into harbour at one stage. The project was quietly dropped, even though Peral was amply rewarded. The submarine is preserved in Paseo del Muelle, in Cartagena, Spain.

All was not lost in France, however. Gustave Zédé, a retired naval constructor, took the designs of Dupuy de Lôme, who had recently died, to produce the 31 ton displacement *Gymnote*, at Toulon, which introduced the major advance of compressed air to expel ballast water. In 1890, the French Navy took her over and later fitted two sets of hydroplanes, a new motor and a variable-pitch propeller. The first viable submarine had arrived.

Another design, produced by Romazotti, Zédé's nephew, began building in 1893. The 266 ton displacement boat, named after his uncle which later became operational with the French Navy. Meanwhile, the French government organised a competition for a submarine design. Out of six submitted, the winner was Laubeuf's double-hulled *Narval* of 1899, 111-feet long, 168 tons displacement, with steam providing surface propulsion and electric motors for dived operations. Together with the *Gustave Zédé*, *Narval* became the parents of France's submarine fleet in the early 1900s.

Across the Atlantic, the US Navy had also changed its mind about submarines.

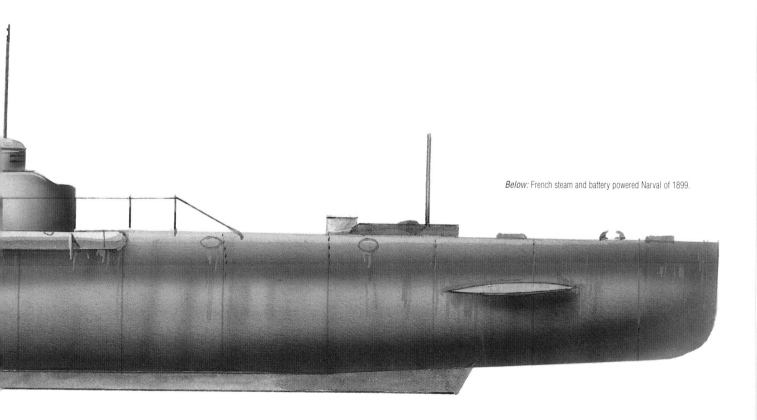

Below: French steam and battery powered Narval of 1899.

THE HOLLAND BOATS

THE SUBMARINE AGE WAS BORN WHEN THE US NAVY, ON APRIL 11 1900, bought the
74 ton *Holland VI*, a later fruit of the imaginative designs produced by the determined
Irish-American inventor, John Philip Holland (1841-1914). The simple 53-feet nine inches
long boat was the forerunner of other submarines purchased soon after by
the British, Japanese and Dutch navies.

Holland, born in Ireland, became interested in submarines in 1869 after reading of the wholly unsuccessful *Intelligent Whale*. He emigrated to the USA in 1873 and became a teacher at a school in Paterson, New Jersey. His younger brother Michael introduced Holland to the Irish Fenian Brotherhood, a society dedicated to freeing Ireland from British rule, who became financial backers for Holland's first three abortive submarine designs.

The first, *Holland 1*, was a tiny iron craft, displacing only 2 tons, built at the Albany City Iron Works, New York in 1877 and ineffectually powered by a 4 hp petrol engine. In May, trials in the Passaic River at Paterson convinced the Fenians to finance a bigger boat and the *Holland I* was scuttled.[1]

Holland II or the *Fenian Ram* was a cigar-shaped iron hull, displacing 19 tons, which began construction on May 3 1879 at the Delameter Iron Works, New York, and was launched in April 1881. The three-man craft was armed with a "pneumatic gun" which fired a torpedo-like projectile from an 11-foot long internal tube up to 50 or 60 yards underwater. A third boat, the *Holland III* or *Fenian Model* was a trials version displacing only one ton with a length of 16-feet 4-inches, built in Jersey City. Following a dispute, the Fenians appropriated both boats in November 1883, towing them by tug up the East River. The *Fenian Model* foundered but the *Fenian Ram* reached New Haven, Connecticut, where she was dragged ashore and abandoned.[2]

Holland then worked with an army lieutenant, Edmund Zalinksi, in the construction of a 50-feet long wooden boat, at Fort Lafayette in 1885 - later transported to Fort Hamilton. Above the casing there was a small dome, with glass bulls-eyes. The boat, powered by a petrol engine, was designed as a platform for experiments involving Zalinksi's terrifying compressed air gun, which fired cartridges filled with volatile nitro-glycerine explosive.

US NAVY COMPETITIONS

The US Navy, fired by French advances in submarine technology, in 1888 staged a competition for "a submarine torpedo boat" that could travel submerged for two hours at eight knots at depths up to 150-feet. A

Holland design won the competition but no contract to build was awarded. Five years later, another US Navy contest for a submarine design was announced.

There was another contender. Simon Lake (1866-1945) built the *Argonaut* in 1894 in New Jersey, fitted with large wheels to move along the seabed. Lake's designs, including the *Protector*, built in 1901, begin to resemble today's submarines, with a periscope (Lake called it the 'omniscope'), free-flooding tanks in *Protector*, diving planes forward of a flat, stubby conning tower and three torpedoes.

In 1893, Holland's work was aided by the formation of the Holland Torpedo Boat Company, with financial support by lawyer Elihu B. Frost. Holland entered the second contest with a new design for the 85-feet long, initially steam-powered, *Plunger*, 168 tons, launched at the Columbia Iron Works, Baltimore, Maryland on August 7 1897. However, it quickly became apparent that the design was a failure and the hull was not completed.

Right: The wooden built Zalinski boat, built in conjunction with John Holland in 1885.

Left: The Fenian Ram, or Holland II was iron hulled with a crew of three with a crude pneumatic weapon.

1 IT WAS RAISED IN 1927 AND IS DISPLAYED AT THE PATERSON MUSEUM, MARKET STREET, PATERSON, NEW JERSEY.
2 SHE IS ALSO AT THE PATERSON MUSEUM.

Left: The Holland I boat, launched in 1877, now on display in a museum in Paterson, New Jersey.

	Holland VI	US 'A' class	British Type 7	Japanese Type 7-P†	Dutch 0-1
Length (ft)	53' 10"	63' 4"	63' 10"	67' 0"	67' 0"
Beam (ft)	10' 3"	11' 9"	11' 9"	11 10"	11 10"
Displacement (tons)					
Surfaced	64	108	110	105	105
Submerged	74	120	123	120	120
Speed (kts)					
Surfaced	8.0	8.0	8.0	9.0	7.5
Dived	5.0	7.0	7.0	7.0	5.0
Armament	1x18" bow tube (2 reloads)	1x18" bow tube (4 reloads)	1x14" bow tube (2 reloads)	1x18" bow tube (4 reloads)	1x18" bow tube (3 reloads)
Engines	45 hp Otto petrol	160 hp Otto petrol	160 hp petrol	180 hp petrol	160 hp Otto petrol**
	50 hp electric	70 hp electric	74 hp electric	70 hp electric	65 hp electric
Range					
Surface	N/K	250 miles at 8kts	250 miles at 8kts	185 miles at 8kts	200 nm at 8kts
Submerged	N/K	20 miles at 7 kts	20 miles at 7 kts	20 miles at 7 kts	24 nm at 6kts
Complement	9	7	8*	8	10

*   One additional crew for training.

** Replaced by 200 hp MAN diesel, 1914. Decommissioned, 1920. Conning tower preserved at Den Helder naval base, Netherlands.

† Reinforced to depth of 125 ft.

Right: The Plunger remained uncompleted, after the realisation that the design would not be effective.

Improved (Holland Type 7 Design) submarines

Boat	Builder	Laid down	Commissioned	Fate
USA 'A' Boats				
Fulton	Crescent Shipyard, Elizabethport, New Jersey	1900 ?	1901	Sank in dock, New Suffolk, Long Island, 12-1901. Sold to Russia as *Madam*, 1904.
A 1 (ex-Plunger)	Crescent Shipyard, Elizabethport, New Jersey	21-05-1901	19-09-1903	Stricken from Navy ship list, 24-02-1913. Experimental target, 1916. Scrapped 26-01-1922.
A2 (ex-Adder) SS-3	Crescent Shipyard, Elizabethport, New Jersey	03-10-1900	12-01-1903	Stricken 16-01-1922
A 3 (ex-Grampus) SS-4	Union Ironworks, San Francisco, California	10-12-1900	28-05-1903	Used as target for US Asiatic Fleet. Stricken 16-01-1922
A 4 (ex-Moccasin) SS-5	Crescent Shipyard, Elizabethport, New Jersey	08-11-1900	17-01-1903	Decommissioned 12-12-1919. Stricken 16-01-1922
A 5 (ex-Pike) SS-6	Union Ironworks, San Francisco, California	10-12-1900	28-05-1903	Decommissioned 25-07-1921. Stricken 16-01-1922
A 6 (ex-Porpoise) SS-7	Crescent Shipyard, Elizabethport, New Jersey	13-12-1900	19-09-1903	Decommissioned 12-12-1919. Target, 1921. Stricken 16-01-1922
A 7 (ex-Shark) SS-8	Crescent Shipyard, Elizabethport, New Jersey.			
	Fitted out, New Suffolk, Long Island, New York.	11-01-1901	19-09-1903	Explosion of petrol fumes while on patrol, Manila Bay, 24-07-1917. 6 crew died. Stricken 16-01-1922
Japan Type 7-P				
No 1	Fore River yard, Massachusetts, reassembled in Japan	N/K	01-08-1905	Stricken 1922
No 2	Fore River yard, Massachusetts, reassembled in Japan	N/K	05-09-1905	Stricken 1922
No 3	Fore River yard, Massachusetts, reassembled in Japan	N/K	05-09-1905	Stricken 1922
No 4	Fore River yard, Massachusetts, reassembled in Japan	N/K	01-10-1905	Sunk following petrol explosion, 14-11-1916. Salved. Stricken, 1922.
No 5	Fore River yard, Massachusetts, reassembled in Japan	N/K	01-10-1905	Stricken 1922.
Britain Type 7				
*Holland No 1**	Vickers, Barrow	04-02-1901	02-02-1903	Sold 1913, sank under tow off Plymouth. Raised 1982. Now in Submarine Museum, Gosport, UK
Holland No 2	Vickers, Barrow	04-02-1901	01-08-1902	Sold 07-10-1913
Holland No 3	Vickers, Barrow	04-02-1901	01-08-1902	Sank in trials, 1911. Sold 07-10-1913
Holland No 4	Vickers, Barrow	1902	02-08-1903	Foundered, 03-09-1912. Salved and used as gunnery target 17-10-1914.
Holland No 5	Vickers, Barrow	1902	19-01-1903	Sank under tow to breakers, 08-08-1912.
Netherlands 'O' class (Type 7-P)				
0-1 (ex-Luctor et Emergo)	K M De Schelde, Flushing	01-06-1904	21-12-1906	Decommissioned 1920. Scrapped 1920s. * Launched without name or number, 02-10-1901.

NOTE

License to build five Type 7-P submarines bought by the Russian government, named *Byeluga, Piskar, Sterliard, Tchuka,* and *Som.* Boats with these names, dating from 1904, reportedly captured by German forces in 1918.

Again, no Navy decision was announced and Holland modified his design and won continued financial backing to build the *Holland VI*, 53-feet 10 inches long, displacing 74 tons, submerged. It was launched on May 17 1897, at Elizabeth port, New Jersey, equipped with a 50 hp petrol engine for surface propulsion with a range of 1,000 miles, and offered for sale to the US Navy.

A series of trials were held for Navy observers in 1898-99, including the firing of 17.7 inch Whitehead torpedoes. At long last, the US Navy purchased the *Holland VI,* for $165,000 and commissioned her as USS *Holland* (later *SS-1*) on October 12 1900. The Holland Torpedo Boat Company was now merged with Isaac Rice's Electric Boat Company.

The *Holland* showed her capabilities during naval exercises off Newport, Rhode Island, in September 1900,

Left: John Holland.

Left: SS-1, USS Holland shown here during trials in 1900.

Left: USS Fulton at its launch in 1901. This, the lead vessel of the A Class boats was later sold to Russia. SS-1, USS Holland cost the US Navy $165,000 in October 1900.

when the submarine came within 100 yards of the battleship USS *Kearsage* and showed a light to indicate that the warship could have been torpedoed.

Living conditions within the *Holland*'s single compartment were basic: bodily waste was held in a bucket and emptied on the deck when surfaced. The crew slept on newspaper or sacks in the battery area. The boat was decommissioned on November 21 1910 at Norfolk, Virginia and scrapped sometime after 1932.

Navy appropriations called for the construction of five submarines in 1900. On August 25, the Navy contracted for six boats of an improved Holland type, the 'A' boats. A seventh boat was ordered and all built in 1900-03.

The prototype for the new class was the *Fulton*, 63-feet 4-inches long, displacing 120 tons, and launched at the Nixon yard at Elizabethport, on June 12 1901. After the 'A' boats were delivered, *Fulton* was sold to the Russian Government and re-commissioned as the *Madam*.

BRITISH HOLLANDS

Britain also was now interested in submarines. The Naval Estimates for 1901-1902 included provision for five improved Holland boats, which were built by Vickers at Barrow-in-Furness, under license, in 1901-03. The first was launched anonymously on October 2 1901, and it was only later that she became known as *No 1*. (She is now on display at the Royal Navy Submarine Museum at Gosport.) Japan purchased five improved Hollands, built at the Fore River yard in Quincy, Massachusetts; knocked down and transported to Japan for reassembly at Yokosuka dockyard.

The de Schelde shipyard at Vlissingen also contracted to build an improved Holland, the *Luctor et Emergo* (later

0-1) launched on July 8 1905, and bought by the Dutch Navy on December 21 1906 for 430,000 Dutch guilders.

What of Simon Lake? He sold the *Protector* to Russia in 1904 and later designed submarines for the German, Austrian and Russian navies, returning to the USA in 1912. After founding the Lake Torpedo Boat Company, he designed and built submarines for the US Navy including the 'N' class, built 1916-17 and the 'G' class, of

which *G 1* set a diving depth record of 256-feet in November, 1912. The company closed in the mid-1920s.

And John Holland? He resigned from the Electric Boat in March 1904 and died on August 12 1914 in Newark, New Jersey. On September 22, the German *U 9* torpedoed and sank three elderly 12,000 ton British cruisers *Aboukir*, *Cressy* and *Hogue* near the Maas light vessel, off Holland.

Above: Royal Navy Holland No.1 submarine, which sank under tow in 1913.

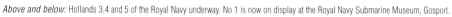

Above and below: Hollands 3.4 and 5 of the Royal Navy underway. No 1 is now on display at the Royal Navy Submarine Museum, Gosport.

PRE-WORLD WAR I DESIGNS

THE STRATEGIC ROLE OF SUBMARINES REMAINED A MATTER OF DEBATE
within western navies in the years leading up to the First World War. Boats were used mainly for
coastal and harbour defence by both the US and Royal Navies. Germany had plans for more significant
deployment, with the design and construction of the ocean hunter, U19 from 1912 onwards,
although the Royal Navy evolved the 'D' class overseas service submarine
which had a wartime role in support of the Grand Fleet.

British 'A' class coastal submarines 1902-1908

The 'A' class, with a short, stubby, conning tower, was the first all-British design submarine to serve in the Royal Navy, entering service in March 1904. It was an unlucky class - only five boats escaped accidents - and, like the 'Hollands,' suffered from low buoyancy reserves. Overall, it marked significant sea-handling improvements and considerably extended experience in dived operations. During World War I, the survivors of the class were used only for training.

Problems with the petrol engines dogged the boats from the very start. *A 1* had to be towed to Portsmouth after completion, and the crew abandoned the craft after sea water penetrated the batteries and chlorine gas filled the boat. *A 5* was damaged in a petrol fumes explosion shortly after refuelling alongside *Hazard,* at Queenstown (now in the Irish Republic) on February 16 1905 - five crew died. It was not until *A 13* that a diesel engine was fitted - the first in any British submarine.

A 10 was fitted with experimental vertical propellers, to assist depth keeping, either at the end of 1915 or early the following year.

	Group 1	A2, A3	Group 2
Length (ft)	103.25 oa	105.04 oa	105.04 oa
Beam (ft)	11.9 oa	12.75 oa	12.75 oa
Displacement (tons)			
Surfaced	190	190	190
Submerged	207	205	207
Speed (kts)			
Surfaced	11.5 kts	10.5 kts	11.0 kts
Dived	7.0 kts	7.0 kts	8.0 kts
Armament	1x18" torpedo tube	2x18" torpedo tubes	2x18" torpedo tubes
	2 reloads	2 reloads	2 reloads
Engines	450 hp petrol	450 hp petrol	550 hp petrol
	87 hp electric	150 hp electric	150 hp electric*
Range			
Surface	500 nm at 11.5 kts	360 miles at 10.5 kts	325 nm at 11 kts
Submerged	20 nm at 5 kts	20 nm at 5 kts	20 nm at 6 kts
Complement	11	11	13

* A 13 fitted with a 400 hp diesel and 150 hp electric motors

Left: A 3 pictured before she was lost after a collision with a submarine tender in 1912.

The conning tower of *A 7* was also fitted with experimental hydroplanes to aid diving and re-surfacing but these did not help when she stuck fast in mud on the seabed, on January 16 1914, during torpedo attack exercises, off Whitsands Bay, Cornwall. All the complement died.

The first 'A' boat's career was short-lived: on March 18 1904, *A 1* was rammed, (holing her conning tower) and sunk by the SS *Berwick Castle* 1 miles off the Nab Tower, off her Portsmouth home base, with the loss of her crew. The sister boat *A 3* was lost in precisely the same way in almost the same position - rammed and sunk by the aptly named submarine tender - HMS *Hazard* - off the Isle of Wight on February 2, 1912, again with all crew lost.

A 4 sank during a signalling exercise off Spithead on October 16 1905, when sea water poured through a ventilator, creating chlorine gas when it saturated the batteries. An explosion followed shortly afterwards. *A 8* sank after developing a bows-down angle just off Plymouth's breakwater on June 8 1905, with the loss of all hands. She was salvaged and re-commissioned into service, and scrapped in 1920.

Below: Raised conning towers were fitted to 'A' Class boats with double hatches to prevent accidental flooding.

British 'A' class coastal submarines

Boat	Builder	Laid Down	Commissioned	Fate
Group 1				
A 1 (ex-Holland 6)	Vickers, Barrow	19-02-1902	18-03-1904	Rammed and sunk by steamship *Berwick Castle*, 18-03-1904, off Nab Tower, Portsmouth. Crew lost. Raised 18-04-1904 and used in experiments to test hull resistance to explosions. Sunk 18-03-1911, raised, but wrecked (without crew) off Selsey Bill, 08-1911. Wreck discovered 1989.
A 2	Vickers, Barrow	19-02-1902	26-03-1904	Wrecked, Bomb Ketch Lake, Portsmouth, 01-1920. Hulk sold as scrap, 10-11-1925.
A 3	Vickers, Barrow	06-11-1902	09-05-1903	Rammed and sunk by submarine tender *Hazard* off Sandown Bay, Isle of Wight, 02-02-1912. Crew lost. Raised, sunk as target, Portland Bay, 04-1912. Wreck discovered, 02-1994.
A 4	Vickers, Barrow	19-02-1902	17-07-1904	Sunk, during signals exercise, off Spithead, Portsmouth, 16-10-1905. No casualties. Salved and returned to service. Scrapped 16-01-1920.
Group 2				
A 5	Vickers, Barrow	19-02-1903	16-02-1905	Damaged in explosion, Queenstown, alongside Hazard. 16-02-1905. Five crew died. Broken up, Portsmouth Dockyard, 1920.
A 6	Vickers, Barrow	19-02-1903	23-04-1905	Decommissioned, 1916. Sold 16-02-1920.
A 7	Vickers, Barrow	19-02-1903	16-01-1904	Sank in mud, Whitsand Bay, Cornwall, 16-01-1914 while on exercise with HMS *Pygmy*. Crew lost.
A 8	Vickers, Barrow	19-02-1903	08-05-1905	Sank off Plymouth, 08-06-1905, with loss of 15 crew. Raised and re-commissioned. Sold, 08-10-1920.
A 9	Vickers, Barrow	19-02-1903	08-05-1905	Sold, 1920.
A 10	Vickers, Barrow	19-02-1903	03-06-1905	Sank, 17-03-1917, moored alongside HMS *Pactolus*, Eghaton Dock, Ardrossan. Refloated. Sold, 01-04-1919.
A 11	Vickers, Barrow	19-02-1903	11-07-1905	Scrapped, Portsmouth Dockyard, 05-1920.
A 12	Vickers, Barrow	19-02-1903	23-09-1905	Sold, 16-01-1920, Isle of Wight.
A 13	Vickers, Barrow	19-02-1903	22-06-1908	Broken up, 1920.

British 'C' class coastal submarines 1905-1910

The British 'C' class was the final Royal Navy Holland design development and the last wholly to be powered by petrol engines. It saw stalwart service in World War I, with four U boats sunk by the class. *C3* was "expended" in the gallant block ship operations at Zeebrugge Mole on April 23 1918, designed to neutralise German submarine operations, earning her commander, Lieut. Richard Sandford, the Victoria Cross for outstanding bravery. Four boats operated in the Baltic where three were destroyed in April, 1918 at Helsingfors (Helsinki) to prevent capture by German forces that had landed nearby.

The boats had very limited endurance and low reserves of buoyancy - just 10% of surface displacement. The spindle-hulled boats were single compartment vessels, designed with no thought to crew comfort. Their shape made very good diving boats but with poor surface performance. *C1* was equipped with wireless telegraphy, according to an Admiralty memorandum of August 24 1914. Some Group 2 boats had bigger conning towers and were fitted with hydroplanes forward.

Most boats operated in the North Sea for coastal defence, based at Leith, Harwich, Hartlepool, Grimsby and Dover. All except *C4* (used for trials) were paid off at the end of the war.

SERVICE IN BALTIC, FAR EAST

Three (*C 36, C 37* and *C 38*) went to Hong Kong in February 1911 to operate with the Royal Navy's China Squadron. Four 'C' class were also sent to the Baltic in September 1915 to reinforce the submarine campaign to disrupt supplies of strategically vital Swedish iron ore to Germany. Because of vigilant German patrols at the Baltic's narrow entrances, the boats were towed in perilous voyages around the North Cape to Archangel and shipped by lighter to Kronstadt, via the White Sea Canal. Based at Revel (now Tallinn), the boats patrolled the Gulf of Riga, *C 32* and *C 29* sinking a merchant ship each.

Back in the North Sea, the Admiralty evolved new tactics to counter the growing U boat threat. Both 'C' and 'E' class boats were towed submerged by decoy trawlers - to lure a U boat into a trap. The British submarine could torpedo it when the tow (and its communication line) was slipped. The tactic was initially successful: *C 24*, operating with the decoy trawler *Taranaki*, sank *U 40*, 50 miles off Girdle Ness, North Sea, on June 23 1915. *C 27*, together with the trawler *Princess Louise* (ex-*Princess Marie Jose*) sank *U 23* in the Fair Isle Channel, between Orkney and Shetland, on July 20 1915.

Disaster was to follow. On August 4, *C 33* was mined off Great Yarmouth during operations with the armed trawler *Malta* and on August 29, *C 29* was lost after her towing trawler *Ariadne* strayed into a minefield in the Humber estuary. Both times, the crews were lost and the tactic was abandoned.

C 7 sank *UC 68* off the Schouwen Bank in the North Sea, on April 5 1917 and *C 15* torpedoed *UC 65* in the English Channel, on November 3 1917.

	Group 1	Group 2
Length (ft)	143.2 oa	143.2 oa
Beam (ft)	13.6 oa	13.6 oa
Displacement (tons)		
Surfaced	287	290
Submerged	316	320
Speed (kts)		
Surfaced	12.0 (service)	13.0+
Dived	7.0	8
Armament	2x18" torpedo tubes	2x18" torpedo tubes
	2 reloads	2 reloads
Engines	600 hp petrol	600 hp petrol
	200 hp electric	200 hp electric
	Single screw	Single screw
Range		
Surface	1500 nm at 7 kts	2000 nm at 7 kts
Submerged	50 nm at 4.5 kts	55 nm at 5 kts
Complement	16	16

The ten war losses included *C 16*, accidentally rammed by the British 'Medea' class destroyer *Melampus* (ex-*Chios*) off Harwich, on April 16 1917. In this accident, the boat bottomed at 60-feet and the first lieutenant, Lieut. S Anderson was fired through a torpedo tube to try this escape method. Sadly, he drowned, so the skipper tried to flood the boat and to effect escape through the fore hatch. However, a fender had jammed the hatch and

the crew was trapped. A poignant report on the escape attempts, by the commanding officer, Lieut. H Boase, was in a corked bottle, found lying near him when the hull was salvaged.

Another sunk by mines was *C 31*, off the Belgian coast, on January 4 1915. *C 34* was sunk by *UC 74* off Fair Isle in the Shetlands, on July 24 1917.

ATTACKED BY AIRCRAFT

C 25 was machine-gunned and bombed by a squadron of five German seaplanes off Harwich, 15 miles east of Orford Ness, on July 6 1918 while surfaced. Incendiary rounds killed the commanding officer and three lookouts on the bridge and the boat could not dive as the conning tower hatch was blocked by the body of an able seaman who was killed while passing up ammunition to the bridge Lewis gun. The first lieutenant, Sub-Lieut. Cobb, together with two engine room artificers, cut off a leg of one of the bodies with a hacksaw to free the upper hatch after another two crewmen died trying to close it. Holes in the pressure hole were plugged with clothes and *C 25* was taken under tow by *E 51*, when the seaplanes, having re-armed, returned to attack. The aircraft were driven off by the arrival of the heavily armed 'I' class destroyer *Lurcher*.

Below: C 3 the first 'C' Class boat to be commissioned, was deliberately sunk as a block ship at Zeebrugge in April 1918.

British 'C' class coastal submarine

Boat	Builder	Laid down	Commissioned	Fate
Group 1				
C 1	Vickers, Barrow	13-11-1905	30-10-1906	Converted to surface patrol boat, renamed *S8* for Adriatic service. Sold 04-1919.
C 2	Vickers, Barrow	13-11-1905	20-11-1906	Sold 08-10-1920.
C 3	Vickers, Barrow	25-11-1905	23-02-1906	Destroyed in Zeebrugge raid, 23-04-1918.
C 4	Vickers, Barrow	25-11-1905	13-03-1907	Sold 28-02-1922.
C 5	Vickers, Barrow	24-11-1905	15-12-1906	Sold 31-10-1919 Malta.
C 6	Vickers, Barrow	24-11-1905	21-01-1907	Sold 20-11-1919.
C 7	Vickers, Barrow	09-12-1905	23-05-1907	Sold 20-12-1919.
C 8	Vickers, Barrow	09-12-1905	23-05-1907	Sold 22-10-1920.
C 9	Vickers, Barrow	30-01-1906	18-06-1907	Sold 07-1922.
C 10	Vickers, Barrow	30-01-1906	13-07-1907	Sold 07-1922.
C 11	Vickers, Barrow	06-04-1906	03-09-1907	Sunk in collision with collier *Eddystone*, North Sea, S. of Cromer, Norfolk, 15-07-1909. Three survivors. Wreck discovered late 1990.
C 12	Vickers, Barrow	27-11-1906	19-01-1908	Sank in collision with destroyer in Humber estuary, 06-10-1918 Salved and re-commissioned. Sold 02-02-1920.
C 13	Vickers, Barrow	29-11-1906	19-02-1908	Sold 02-02-1920.
C 14	Vickers, Barrow	04-12-1906	13-03-1908	Sunk in collision with *Hopper No 27*, Plymouth Sound, 10-12-1913. No casualties. Salved and re-commissioned. Sold 05-12-1921.
C 15	Vickers, Barrow	07-12-1906	01-04-1908	Sold 28-02-1922.
C 16	Vickers, Barrow	14-12-1906	05-06-1908	Sunk in collision with *C 17*, S. of Cromer, Norfolk, 14-07-1909. One survivor. Salved and re-commissioned. Sunk after being rammed at periscope depth by the British destroyer *Melampus*, off Harwich, 16-04-1917. Crew lost. Salved and re-commissioned. Sold 12-08-1922.
C 17	HM Dockyard, Chatham	11-03-1907	13-05-1909	In collision with *C 16*, North Sea, S. of Cromer, Norfolk, 14-07-1909. Sold 20-11-1919.
C 18	HM Dockyard, Chatham	11-03-1907	23-07-1909	Sold 26-05-1921. Sunderland.
C 19	HM Dockyard, Chatham	11-03-1907	20-03-1909	Sold 02-02-1920.
C 20	HM Dockyard, Chatham	01-06-1908	31-01-1910	Sold 26-05-1921. Sunderland.
Group 2				
C 21	Vickers, Barrow	04-02-1908	18-05-1909	Sold 05-12-1921.
C 22	Vickers, Barrow	04-02-1908	05-05-1909	Sold 02-02-1920.
C 23	Vickers, Barrow	07-02-1908	05-05-1909	Sold 05-12-1921.
C 24	Vickers, Barrow	12-02-1908	05-05-1909	Sold 29-05-1921. Sunderland.
C 25	Vickers, Barrow	27-02-1908	28-05-1909	Sold 05-12-1921.
C 26	Vickers, Barrow	14-02-1908	28-05-1909	Baltic operations, 1915-1918. Scuttled at Helsingfors Bay, 1.5 miles off Grohara light, 04-04-1918 to avoid seizure by German forces. Salved, 08-1953 for breaking up in Finland.
C 27	Vickers, Barrow	04-06-1908	14-08-1909	North Sea operations 1915. Baltic operations 1915-18. Scuttled at Helsingfors 05-04-1918 to avoid seizure by German forces. Salved, 08-1953 for breaking up in Finland.
C 28	Vickers, Barrow	06-03-1908	14-08-1909	Sold 25-08-1921. Sunderland.
C 29	Vickers, Barrow	04-06-1908	17-09-1909	Sunk by mine, off Dowsing light vessel, Humber Estuary, whilst under tow, 29-08-1915. Crew lost.
C 30	Vickers, Barrow	10-06-1908	11-10-1909	Decommissioned, July, 1919. Sold 25-08-1921.
C 31	Vickers, Barrow	07-01-1909	19-11-1909	Mined off Belgian coast, whilst patrolling off Zeebrugge, 04-01-1915. No survivors.
C 32	Vickers, Barrow	12-01-1909	19-11-1909	1914-1916 North Sea operations. 1916-1917 Baltic operations. Ran ashore, blown up, Gulf of Riga, 22-10-1917.
C 33	HM Dockyard, Chatham	29-03-1909	13-08-1910	Mined, near Smith's Knoll, off Yarmouth, North Sea, 04-08-1915. Crew lost.
C 34	HM Dockyard Chatham	29-03-1909	17-09-1910	Sunk, while on surface, by German *UC 74* off Fair Isle, Shetlands, 24-07-1917. Crew lost.
C 35	Vickers, Barrow	03-03-1909	01-02-1910	Baltic operations, 1915-1918. Scuttled at Helsingfors 1.5 miles off Grohara light, 05-04-1918 to avoid seizure by German forces. Salved, 08-1953 for breaking up in Finland.
C 36	Vickers, Barrow	03-03-1909	01-02-1910	China squadron, Hong Kong, from 1911. Sold 25-06-1919, Hong Kong.
C 37	Vickers, Barrow	07-04-1909	31-03-1910	China squadron, Hong Kong, from 1911. Sold 25-06-1919, Hong Kong.
C 38	Vickers, Barrow	05-04-1909	31-03-1910	China squadron, Hong Kong, from 1911. Sold 25-06-1919, Hong Kong.

British 'D' class overseas service submarines 1909-1912

Above: D 3 was mistakenly attacked and sunk in 1918. All the crew were lost.

Royal Navy patrol submarines evolved from the 'D' class boats, designed to be propelled by diesel motors on the surface to avoid the horrific problems with petrol engines experienced by the British 'A' class. These much bigger boats were designed for foreign service with an endurance of 2,500 nm at 10 knots on the surface and much improved living conditions for a larger crew.

'D' boats also were fitted with twin screws (for greater manoeuvrability) and saddle tanks - and were the first British boats to be armed with guns, forward of the conning tower beginning with *D6*. Reserve buoyancy was increased to 20.6%. Three 18 inch torpedo tubes were included, two vertically in the bows and a third in the stern. Because of its role, it was also the first class to have radio fitted as standard: the aerial was attached to a mast on the conning tower that was lowered before diving. The boats cost between £79,910 and £89,410 each, excluding the gun.

Based at Harwich, Immingham, Blyth and Dover, their wartime role, (in support of the Grand Fleet), was to destroy German warships. Three units, *D2, D3* and *D8*, fought in the Battle of Heligoland Bight on August 28, 1914 when a British light cruiser force from Harwich lured German naval forces onto the guns of Admiral Beatty's more powerful battle cruisers.

Two U boats were sunk by the 'C' class. *D7* torpedoed *U45* on the surface with a single shot at 800 yards from the stern tube off the North coast of Ireland on September 12 1917, and *D 4* torpedoed *UB72* with two shots at 600 yards. This was after catching her on the surface on May 12 1918, in the English Channel between Guernsey and Portland Bill - when she was about to attack the US troopship SS *Olympic*, (which also rammed and sunk *U10* the same day.)

In turn *D6* was sunk by *UB73*, 73 miles N of Inishtrahull Island, off the West coast of Ireland, on June 28 1918. *D7* escaped unscathed, apart from damage to

her periscopes, from an underwater collision with a U boat in May 1918. Other war losses were the *D2*, sunk by German patrol craft off the Ems in the North Sea on November 25 1914. *D3*, accidentally bombed and sunk by a French airship off Fecamp in the English Channel on March 15 1918; and the *D5*, sunk by a British mine in the North Sea, on October 3 1914. *D7* was mistakenly depth-charged by the 'Repeat M' class destroyer HMS *Pelican* on February 10 1918, but survived. *D1* was sunk as a target on October 23 1918.

In the latter stages of World War I, the boats were used for training crews, based at Portsmouth.

Length (ft)	163.0 oa
Beam (ft)	13.6 oa
Displacement (tons)	
Surfaced	483
Submerged	595
Speed (kts)	
Surfaced	14.0
Dived	10.0 (design) 9.0 (service)
Armament	3x18" torpedo tubes (1 bow, 2 stern)
	2x12 pdr quick firing gun*
Engines	550 hp electric; 1,750hp diesel**
	Twin screws
Range	
Surface	2500 nm at 10 kts
Submerged	45 nm at 5 kts
Complement	25

* 1x12 pdr gun fitted in *D4* and *D6*.
** 1,200 hp only in *D1*.

British 'D' class overseas service submarine

Boat	Built	Laid down	Commissioned	Fate
D 1	Vickers, Barrow	14-05-1907	09-1909	Sunk as target, 23-10-1918.
D 2	Vickers, Barrow	10-07-1909	29-03-1911	Sunk by German torpedo boat, North Sea, 25-11-1914. Crew lost.
D 3	Vickers, Barrow	15-03-1910	30-08-1911	Mistakenly bombed and sunk by French airship AT-0 with 4 x 52 kg bombs off Fecamp, English Channel, 15-03-1918. Crew lost.
D 4	ickers, Barrow	24-02-1910	29-11-1911	Decommissioned 1919. Sold 19-12-1921.
D 5	Vickers, Barrow	23-02-1910	19-02-1911	Sank by British mine 2 miles S. of South Cross buoy, off Great Yarmouth, North Sea, 03-10-1914. Five survivors.
D 6	Vickers, Barrow	24-02-1910	19-04-1912	Sunk by German *UB73*, 73 miles N of Inishtrahull Island, W coast of Ireland, 28-06-1918. Two survivors.
D 7	HM Dockyard Chatham	14-02-1910	14-12-1911	Sold 19-12-1921.
D 8	HM Dockyard, Chatham	14-02-1910	23-03-1912	Sold 19-12-1921.

U 1 coastal submarine - first German U Boat, 1906

Although three 'Karp' class submarines were ordered from Germany by the Russian Navy in 1904[1], the first of a long line of German U boats (*unterseebooten*), U 1, was launched at the Germaniawerft yard in Kiel on August 4, 1906, becoming a test and evaluation boat for the Imperial German Navy on December 14, based at Eckernförde.

She was a much larger boat than her British counterparts, the 'A' class, with a more powerful electric engine providing nearly two knots more speed underwater. She was built with a double hull and twin screws.

Although the German Navy avoided the problems of petrol engine propulsion, the heavy oil motors had the disadvantage of emitting tell-tale clouds and sparks through an exhaust in the upper deck.

In September 1907, *U 1* completed arduous endurance trials, travelling 587 nautical miles from Wilhelmshaven, around Denmark, to Kiel in very bad weather, but performing well. She survived World War I, and was decommissioned on December 14, 1919. Under the 1919 Versailles peace treaty, one side of the boat was sliced off to render her unseaworthy. She was moved to the Deutsches Museum in Munich in 1921, where she remains on display.

Subsequent boats developed the design further, with ever larger displacement and higher speeds, both surfaced and dived, in the years up to 1911. Later boats also had four torpedo tubes, two in the bows and two in the stern - the latter not appearing in the Royal Navy until the 'D' class in 1909 - and a gun armament.

	U 1	U 2	U 3-4	U 5 -8
Length (ft)	139.0	149.0	168.24	188.0
Beam (ft)	12.3	N/K	N/K	18.3
Displacement (tons)				
Surface	238	341	421	506
Submerged	283	430	510	636
Speed (kts)				
Surfaced	10.8	13.2	11.8	13.4
Dived	8.7	9.0	9.4	10.2
Armament	1x17.7" bow tube.	4x17.7" tubes	4x17.7" tubes	4x17.7" tubes
	2 reloads. 1 mine.	(2 bow, 2 stern)	(2 bow, 2 stern)	(2 bow, 2 stern)
		2 reloads	2 reloads	2 reloads
			1x37 mm gun	1x37 mm gun*
Engines	400 hp Körting heavy oil	2x300 hp heavy oil	2x300 hp heavy oil	4x225 hp heavy oil
	400 hp electric	2x315 hp electric	2x515 hp electric	2x520 hp electric
Range				
Surfaced	1,500 nm at 10 kts	1,600 nm at 13 kts	1,600 nm at 13 kts	N/K
Submerged	50 nm at 5 kts	50 nm at 5 kts	50 nm at 5 kts	N/K
Complement	12, later 22.	22	22	28

* 1x4 pdr. gun added in *U 6* and *U 8* in 1915.

The class did not have a lucky war. *U 5* and *U 7* were among nine boats sent to attack the British Grand Fleet protected within Scapa Flow immediately on the outbreak of war, but the attack failed, with *U 5* having to prematurely turn back because of engine failures.

Below: The trademark plume of smoke from the heavy oil engines is clear in this photo.

1 KRUPP PLANT NUMBERS 109, 110 AND 111 FOR *KARP*, *KARAS* AND *KAMABALA*, 205 TONS DISPLACEMENT. THE LATTER WAS SENT BY RAIL IN SECTIONS TO SEVASTOPOL IN APRIL 1908, REASSEMBLED AND USED IN TRAINING IN THE BLACK SEA. SHE SANK ON MAY 29, 1909 AFTER BEING ACCIDENTALLY RAMMED BY THE BATTLESHIP *ROSTISLAV*, WITH THE LOSS OF 19 CREW. HER SALVED CONNING TOWER IS NOW PART OF A MEMORIAL TO THE SUBMARINERS IN KOMMUNHOZ CEMETERY NO 3, SEVASTOPOL. NORWAY'S FIRST SUBMARINE, *A 1* (EX-*KOBBEN*) WAS ORDERED FROM GERMANIAWERFT IN 1907 AND COMMISSIONED ON NOVEMBER 28, 1909

U 1 coastal submarine - first German U Boat, 1906

U 1 - U 8 experimental coastal submarine

Boat	Builder	Launched	Commissioned	Fate
U 1	Germaniawerft, Kiel	04-08-1906	14-12-1906	Decommissioned, 14-12-1919. Now in Deutsches Museum, Munich.
U 2	Kaiserliche Werft, Danzig	18-06-1908	18-07-1908	Broken up in Germany.
U 3	Kaiserliche Werft, Danzig	27-03-1909	29-05-1909	Surrendered after Armistice.
U 4	Kaiserliche Werft, Danzig	18-05-1909	01-07-1909	Destroyed during evacuation of Pola base, Adriatic, 11-1918.
U 5	Germaniawerft, Kiel	08-01-1910	02-07-1910	Mined off Zeebrugge, 18-12-1914.
U 6	Germaniawerft, Kiel	18-05-1910	12-08-1910	Sunk by British submarine E 16 off Karmöy Island, NW of Stavanger, Norway, 15-09-1915.
U 7	Germaniawerft, Kiel	28-07-1910	18-07-1911	Torpedoed in error by U 22 off Dutch coast, 21-01-1915.
U 8	Germaniawerft, Kiel	14-03-1911	18-06-1911	Sunk by explosive sweep by British destroyers Maori and Ghurka at Dover barrage, 04-03-1915.

U5 was later mined off Zeebrugge on December 18, 1914 and *U7* was torpedoed in error by *U22* off the Dutch coast on January 21, 1915. *U6* was sunk by the British *E16* off the Norwegian coast on September 15, 1915 and *U8* was sunk by an explosive sweep by the British 'F' class destroyers *Maori* and *Ghurka*, at the Dover barrage, near the Verne light vessel, on March 4, 1915. Finally, *U4* was destroyed by her own side during the evacuation of the Pola base in the Adriatic, in November, 1918.

Below: U 1, or what was left after 1919, remains on display in Munich, Germany.

U 19 - the ocean hunter, 1912-16

The four-strong *U19* (U21) class was the first to be engineered with diesels to provide long endurance patrols combined with high surface speed - necessary to fulfil their primary mission of attacking merchant ships in wartime. Despite the long hull and wide beam, space still limited the stowage of torpedo reloads. So the calibre of the deck gun was increased to 88 mm, and reliance placed on this as the main armament against shipping. Torpedoes were mainly reserved for high-profile naval targets. Even though gun attacks were mounted on the surface, none of the class was sunk by enemy action during World War I.

In these boats and their immediate successors, some of the guns were built to fold sideways to disappear into the casing to improve dived speeds. *U19* was the first to be fitted with net-cutters as well as jumping wires to penetrate net and boom defences protecting naval anchorages.

To improve damage control, four watertight bulkheads were included in the hull. The main rudder was positioned abaft the propellers.

One of the class, *U20*, torpedoed the Cunard liner, RMS *Lusitania*, 30,000 tons, south of Ireland on May 7 1915 – this was done with one shot. The vessel sank following a second explosion, caused by the ignition of coal dust, with the loss of nearly 1,200 lives, including 128 neutral US citizens.

U 21 fired the first ever torpedo in anger when it attacked the British light cruiser *Pathfinder*, 3,000 tons, off the Firth of Forth on September 5, 1914. The submarine was later despatched to the Dardanelles to aid Turkish forces, and sank the battleship *Triumph* (11,800 tons), off Gallipoli on May 25 1915, following up this success two days later, with the sinking of the elderly *Majestic* (14,900 tons), in the same area. *U 21*'s commander, Kapitan Otto Hersing, became one of the leading U boat aces, sinking 36 ships on 21 patrols over three years.

Both *U19* and *U22* survived hostilities to surrender at the end of the First World War. *U20* was blown up by her crew on November 5 1916, after becoming stranded at Harbooere, on the west coast of Jutland. *U21* was also sunk by her crew in the North Sea, while sailing from Germany to England to surrender at Scapa Flow, on February 22 1919.

Length (ft)	210.5
Beam (ft)	20.5
Displacement (tons)	
Surface	650
Submerged	837
Speed (kts)	
Surfaced	16.5 (17, *U 20-22*)
Dived	9.5
Armament	4x20" (2 bow, 2 stern) (two reloads)
	1 x 88 mm gun
Engines	2x850 hp diesel
	2x600 hp electric (2 shafts)
Range	
Surface	7,600 nm at 8 kts
Submerged	80.0 nm at 5 kts.
Maximum diving depth (ft)	152.0
Complement	35

U19 (U21) class patrol submarine

Boat	Builder	Launched	Commissioned	Fate
U 19	Kaiserliche Werft, Danzig	10-10-1912	06-07-1913	Surrendered after Armistice.
U 20	Kaiserliche Werft, Danzig	18-12-1912	05-08-1913	Stranded at Harbooere, W coast of Jutland. Scuttled by crew, 05-11-1916.
U 21	Kaiserliche Werft, Danzig	05-02-1913	22-10-1913	Sunk, North Sea, en route to surrender, 22-02-1919.
U 22	Kaiserliche Werft, Danzig	06-03-1913	25-11-1913	Surrendered after Armistice.

US 'E' and 'F' class coastal submarines 1911-12

	'E' class	'F' class
Length (ft)	135.25	142.6
Beam (ft)	14.6+-	15.4
Displacement (tons)		
Surfaced	247	290
Submerged	287	330
Speed (kts)		
Surfaced	14	14
Dived	9	9
Armament	4x18" tubes	4x18" tubes
Engines	N/K: Diesel	N/K: Niesco & Craig Diesel refitted
	N/K: Electric	N/K: Electric
Range		
Surface	2100 nm at 11 kts	2300 nm at 11 kts
Submerged	100 nm at 5 kts	100 nm at 5 kts
Complement	20	22

Above and left: In front line service for only a short time, these boats provided valuable development experience in several new submarine technology fields.

engine room, and she went down in just 10 seconds, taking 19 crew with her. *F-4* (*Skate*) sank 1.5 nm off Honolulu Harbour on March 25 1916, after losing control while dived. All the crew were lost and the inquiry found that corrosion to the lead lining of the battery tank had allowed sea water to enter the battery compartment.

Primary roles for US submarines up to World War I, were coastal and harbour defence. Therefore endurance and heavy weapon fits were thought unnecessary. Both classes were used to evaluate tactics and new equipment throughout their short careers, and were overtaken by requirements for longer-range, ocean-going boats. After hostilities, they took on a training role.

For both classes, the US Navy deliberately copied the French submarine *Aigrette* by fitting diesel propulsion. The first US boat to run on diesels, *E-1* (ex-*Skipjack*), also became the first American boat to cross the Atlantic under her own power. This boat trialled the Sperry gyrocompass in 1920, tested new hydrophones and took part in underwater radio transmission experiments.

A gas explosion and fire damaged the sister boat *E-2* (ex-*Sturgeon*) while in overhaul at the New York Navy Yard, on January 15 1916. Four crewmen were killed and seven injured. The boat was then used in trials of Edison nickel storage batteries, before being re-commissioned in March 1918 for patrols off the Eastern seaboard. *E-1* was despatched to the Azores for anti-U boat patrols.

The 'F' class was also unlucky. *F-1* (ex-*Carp*) sank off Point Loma, San Diego, California, on December 17 1917, after a collision with *F-3* (ex-*Pickerel*) during exercises of the Coast Torpedo Force, based at San Pedro. The impact ripped a hole in her port side, forward of the

US 'E' and 'F' Class coastal submarine

Boat	Builder	Launched	Commissioned	Fate
'E' class				
E-1 (ex-*Skipjack*) (SS-24)	Fore River Shipyard, Quincy, Massachusetts	27-05-1911	14-02-1912	Decommissioned Philadelphia, 20-10-1921. Sold 19-04-1922.
E-2 (ex-*Sturgeon*) (SS-25)	Fore River Shipyard, Quincy, Massachusetts	16-06-1911	14-02-1912	Gas explosion, New York Navy Yard, 15-01-1916, four killed. Decommissioned Philadelphia, 20-10-1921. Sold 19-04-1922.
'F' class				
F-1 (ex-*Carp*) (SS-20)	Union Ironworks, San Francisco, California	06-09-1911	19-06-1912	Sunk in collision with *F-3* off Point Loma, San Diego, California, 17-12-1917. 19 crew lost.
F-2 (ex-*Barracuda*) (SS-21)	Union Ironworks, San Francisco, California	19-03-1912	25-06-1912	Decommissioned Mare Island, California, 16-04-1922. Sold 17-08-1922.
F-3 (ex-*Pickerel*) (SS-22)	Moran Co, Seattle, Washington	06-02-1912	05-08-1912	Decommissioned 15-04-1922. Sold 17-08-1922.
F-4 (ex-*Skate*) (SS-23)	Moran Co, Seattle, Washington	06-01-1912	03-05-1913	Foundered 1.5 nm off Honolulu Harbour, 25-03-1915. 21 crew lost. Salved, 29-08-1915 but stricken 31-08-1915. Hulk used as fill in trench off submarine base, 1940.

WORLD WAR I DESIGNS

THE WAR AT SEA BROUGHT NEW DEMANDS ON SUBMARINE DESIGNERS.
Combat experience stressed the need for more robust boats with greater endurance as well
as specialised submarine hunters and minelayers. Germany also experimented,
unsuccessfully, with transports in a vain attempt to beat the naval
blocked that was strangling her raw material supply lines.

British 'E' class overseas patrol submarines 1911-1917

The British 'E' boats, modified and increased in numbers after the outbreak of World War I, proved the most successful class during hostilities. They accounted for an impressive tally of seven U boats and sank a significant number of surface combatants, including the Turkish battleship *Hairedin Barbarossa* and the German armoured cruiser *Prinz Adalbert,* by evading enemy defences to break into both the Baltic and the Sea of Marmara. The price was heavy with nearly half the class lost on active service.

The design included the first sub-divisions in a British submarine, protected by watertight bulkheads, to provide better survivability and damage control, and the first beam torpedo tubes. Costs were £101,900 each for hulls *E 1 – 6* and *12 - 13* and £105,700 each for *E 7 - 11* and *14 - 16.*

NORTH SEA OPERATIONS

E 22 was involved in experiments to intercept Zeppelins over the North Sea on April 24, 1916 by carrying two Sopwith Schneider seaplane scouts on her casing. The boat submerged in calm water, leaving the seaplanes floating on the surface. They took off and returned to Felixstowe, on the East Coast of England. The trials were not repeated. .

The class began the war with the 8th submarine flotilla in Harwich but later, boats moved to Northeast England for North Sea patrols, Killybegs, Donegal, (now the Irish Republic) and took part in operations in the Baltic, Dardanelles, the Adriatic and Mediterranean.

The first U boat destroyed by the class was *U 6,* sunk by *E 16* four miles south west of Karmöy Island, off Stavanger, Norway, on September 15 1915. *E 54* claimed two U boats: *UC 10,* torpedoed with two hits at 400 yards, south east of the Schowen Bank light vessel in the North Sea, on July 6 1916; and *U 81,* torpedoed in the Southwest approaches to the English Channel on May 1 1917. *E 45* torpedoed *UC 62* in the North Sea on October 15, 1917 and the sister boat *UC 63* was sunk by *E 52* near the Goodwin Sands, Dover Straits, on November 1 1917. *UB 16* was sunk by *E 34* off Harwich in the North Sea, on May 10 1918. Finally, *U 154,* one of the large 1,512 ton U boat cruisers (originally designed as cargo-carrying blockade runners) was sunk by *E 35* off the island of Madeira on May 11 1918, after British naval intelligence learnt of a planned rendezvous between two U boats off Cape St. Vincent.

	Group 1	Group 2	Group 3	Australian boats
Length (ft)	178 oa	181 oa	181 oa	176 oa
Beam (ft)	15.05 oa	15.05 oa	15.05 oa	15.05 oa
Displacement (tons)				
Surfaced	665	667	662	664
Submerged	796	807	807	780
Speed (kts)				
Surfaced	15	15.25	15	15
Dived	9.5	10.25	10	10
Armament	4x18" tubes	5x18" tubes	5x18" tubes*	5x18" tubes
	(1 bow, 2 beam, 1 stern)	(2 bow, 2 beam, 1 stern)	(2 bow, 2 beam, 1 stern)	(1 bow, 2 beam, 1 stern)
		1 x 12 pdr gun	1 x 12 pdr gun	
Engines	2x1,750 hp diesel	2x1,600 hp diesel	2x1,600 diesel	2x1,750 hp diesel
	2x 600 hp electric	2x 840 hp electric	2x 840 hp electric	2x600 hp electric
	2 screws	2 screws	2 screws	2 screws
Range				
Surface	3,000 nm at 10 kts	3,000 nm at 10 kts	3,000 nm at 10 kts	3,000 nm at 10 kts
Submerged	65 nm at 5 kts	65 nm at 5 kts	65 nm at 5 kts	65 nm at 5 kts
Diving depth	150 ft	150 ft	150 ft	150 ft
Complement	30	30	30	30

* Group 3 boats *E 24, E 34, E 41, E 45, E 46* and *E 51* built as minelayers, not equipped with beam tubes. Warload of 20 mines in 20 vertical tubes in saddle tanks, amidships. *E 41* was converted into a minelayer in early 1916.

E 23 torpedoed the German dreadnought *Westfalen,* 18,900 tons, holing her, off Terschelling, on August 19 1916 and on the same day, *E 1* torpedoed and damaged the battle cruiser *Moltke,* 23,000 tons, in the Gulf of Riga.

The 'E' class suffered 27 casualties, including the first loss of a submarine in war caused by hostile submarine attack: *E 3,* sunk by *U 27* on October 21 1914, off the Ems estuary in the North Sea, after being cut off in a bay by German destroyers. Four (*E 1, E 8, E 9,* and *E 19*) were scuttled by their crews in Helsingfors Bay (now Helsinki), on April 3/4 1918 to avoid seizure by advancing German forces who had landed nearby. *E 50* was damaged in a collision, when dived, with the submerged *UC 62* on March 19 1917, off the North Hinder light vessel. She was later mined in January 1918.

The Baltic operations, designed to disrupt supplies of Swedish iron ore to Germany, and to assist Russian naval forces, was an audacious strategy, as the entrances to the sea were closely guarded by German patrol forces. Seven of the class - together with a number of 'C' class boats -

were despatched in 1915. *E 11* failed to penetrate the defences and, because of compass failure, *E 13* ran aground near Saltholm Island, between Malmo and Copenhagen. She came under fire on August 18 1915, from two German destroyers that killed 15 crew. Only the arrival of the Danish torpedo boat, *Sölöven,* prevented her destruction. The boat was interned by the Danes and later broken up for scrap.

BALTIC AND TURKISH CAMPAIGNS

The 'E' class boats began their Baltic campaign with *E 19* sinking four German cargo ships (*Walter Leonhardt,* 2,100 tons, *Gutrune,* 5,000 tons, *Nicomedia,* 6,300 tons, *Direktor Reppenhagen,* 1,560 tons) and ran another (*Germania* 1,956 tons*)* aground in just one day - October 10 1915. In each case, to conserve torpedo stocks, the

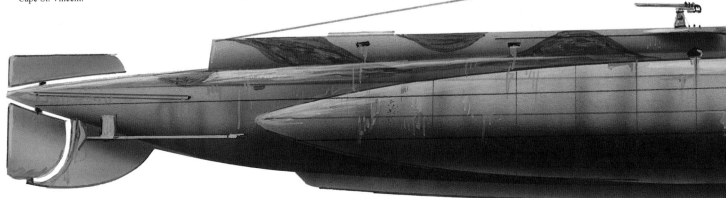

ships were either sunk by explosive charges after boarding by the submarine's crew, or by opening sea-cocks. The *Nicomedia*'s German crew gave *E 19*'s boarding party a barrel of beer before the ship was sunk. *E 19* alone sank ships carrying iron ore valued at £300,000 - more than £7 million at today's prices.

E 19 went on to sink the German cruiser *Undine* on November 7 1915, with one shot from a bow tube, south of Zealand, and *E 8* sank the three-funnelled, 9,050 armoured cruiser *Prinz Adalbert*, 20 miles West of Libau 16 days later. The German Navy withdrew heavy units from the Baltic as a result.

The only casualty through enemy action in the Baltic was the loss of *E 18* to the German decoy ship *SMS K* on May 24, 1916.

Four boats, together with the Australian *AE 2*, mounted a campaign against Turkish naval targets in the Sea of Marmara in 1915. *E 15* ran aground at Kephez Point in the Dardanelles and was shelled by Turkish shore artillery, badly damaging the boat and killing seven of her crew on April 17 1915. The next day the submarine was torpedoed by British picket boats, to prevent the Turks salving her. Sister boat *E 14* dived beneath minefields and broke into the Sea of Marmara on April 27, sinking the Turkish gunboat *Nurel Bahr*, 200 tons, on May 1, and damaging the minelayer *Peik-I-Shevket*, 1,014 tons, in a torpedo attack. Her commander, Lieut Cmdr. Courtney Boyle received the Victoria Cross.

The Australian submarine *AE 2*, which had also broken into the Sea of Marmara, was scuttled after being damaged by gunfire from the Turkish torpedo boat *Sultan Hisar*. Her 30-man crew were taken prisoner. *E 20* however, was torpedoed by the German submarine *UB 14*

on November 6 1915, following the capture from the stricken French submarine *Turquoise* of confidential books.[1] *E 12* luckily escaped when she became trapped in anti-submarine nets in the Dardanelles, her forward hydroplanes entangled, which forced her into an uncontrolled dive, levelling out at 245 feet - the greatest depth achieved by any British submarine at that time. She surfaced, only to come under shore battery fire, but managed to avoid further calamity. *E 2* also became trapped by nets while traversing the narrows, but also forced her way through.

122 TARGETS SUNK

The stunning success of the Sea of Marmara campaign was the *E 11*, which sank 122 ships including attacks mounted inside Constantinople harbour. Turkish casualties included the battleship *Hairedin Barbarossa* (ex-*Kurfürst Frederich Wilhelm*), 9,901 tons, (8 August 1915), the destroyer *Yar Hisar* 290 tons, (December 3) and the torpedo boats *Berk-i-Satvet* (1,014 tons) and *Sevket Numa*. On May 22, *E 11* spotted the torpedo gunboat *Pelenç-i-Deria*, 880 tons, anchored off Constantinople. She attacked, her torpedo hitting amidships and as the gunboat sank, she opened accurate fire on the submarine with her six pounder gun, the first

Above: E 3 had the dubious distinction of being the first submarine to be destroyed in action by an enemy submersible.

round hitting the foremost periscope. *E 11*'s commander, Lieut Cmdr M Nasmith received the Victoria Cross.

A further Victoria Cross was awarded posthumously to Lieut. Cmdr. G S White, while in command of *E 14*, again operating in the Dardanelles. On January 28 1918, she attacked a merchant ship, but the torpedo exploded prematurely, damaging the submarine. Flooding, she was forced to the surface and came under coastal battery fire off Kum Kale, and was attempting to beach safely when White was killed by shellfire. *E 14* sank, but nine of the crew survived and were taken prisoner.

One of the strangest encounters involved *E 31*, which was operating with the seaplane carrier *Engadine* in the North Sea as an air raid was mounted on the Zeppelin sheds at Tondern, on May 4 1916. The submarine, surfaced, spotted the Zeppelin *L7* approaching and dived to avoid attack. At periscope depth, it was seen that the airship was losing altitude (it had been hit by shells fired from the light cruisers *Galatea* and *Phaeton*) and *E 31* surfaced to shoot the Zeppelin down, rescuing seven survivors.

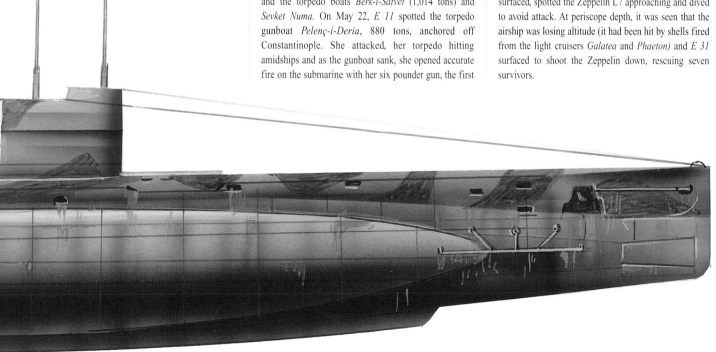

1 *Turquoise* was sunk by naval gunfire on October 31, 1915 but salved by the Turks three days later and commissioned as *Mustedieh Ombashi*. She was due to rendezvous with *E 20*.

British 'E' class overseas service submarine

Boat	Builder	Laid down	Commissioned	Fate
Group 1				
E 1 (ex-D 9)	HM Dockyard, Chatham	14-02-1911	06-05-1913	Scuttled, Helsingfors Bay, 1.5 nm off Grohara Light, Gulf of Finland, to avoid seizure by German forces, 03-04-1918.
E 2 (ex-D 10)	HM Dockyard, Chatham	14-02-1911	09-07-1913	Sold 07-03-1921, Malta.
E 3	Vickers, Barrow	27-04-1911	29-05-1914	Torpedoed by U 27 off Ems estuary, North Sea, 21-10-1914 Wreck discovered 03-11-1994.
E 4	Vickers, Barrow	16-05-1911	28-01-1913	Sunk in collision with E 41, off Harwich, 15-08-1916. Crew lost. Salved and re-commissioned. Sold 21-02-1922.
E 5	Vickers, Barrow	09-06-1911	28-06-1913	Engine room explosion, 08-06-1913, killed 13 crew. Mined, N. of Juist Island, North Sea, while rescuing survivors from patrol trawler Resono, previously mined, 07-03-1916.
E 6	Vickers, Barrow	12-11-1911	17-10-1913	Mined, off Harwich, North Sea, 26-12-1915.
E 7	HM Dockyard, Chatham	30-03-1912	16-03-1914	Scuttled after trapped in enemy nets, off Nagara, Dardanelles, 04-09-1915.
E 8	HM Dockyard, Chatham	30-03-1912	18-06-1914	Scuttled, Helsingfors Bay, 1.5 nm off Grohara light, Gulf of Finland, to avoid seizure by German forces, 04-04-1918. Salved 08-1953 for breaking in Finland.
Group 2				
E 9	Vickers, Barrow	01-06-1912	18-06-1914	Scuttled, Helsingfors Bay, 1.5 nm off Grohara light, Gulf of Finland, to avoid seizure by German forces, 03-04-1918. Salved, 08-1953 for breaking in Finland.
E 10	Vickers, Barrow	10-07-1912	10-03-1914	Lost, North Sea, 18-01-1915.
E 11	Vickers, Barrow	13-07-1912	15-09-1914	Sold, 07-03-1921, Malta.
E 12	HM Dockyard, Chatham	16-12-1912	14-10-1914	Sold 07-03-1921, Malta.
E 13	HM Dockyard, Chatham	16-12-1912	09-12-1914	Damaged by German destroyer gunfire while aground off Saltholm Island, Denmark, 18-08-1915. 15 crew died. Remainder interned, Copenhagen, 03-09-1915. Sold to Danish shipbreakers, 14-12-1921.
E 14	Vickers, Barrow	14-12-1912	18-11-1914	Sunk by Turkish coastal battery fire, off Kum Kale, Dardanelles, 28-01-1918. Nine crew rescued, made prisoners.
E 15	Vickers, Barrow	13-10-1912	13-10-1914	Stranded on Kephez Point while entering Sea of Marmara. Damaged by Turkish shore batteries and later torpedoed by picket boats from British battleships Triumph and Majestic to prevent enemy salving her, 18-04-1915.
E 16	Vickers, Barrow	15-05-1913	27-02-1915	Sunk by mine, Heligoland Bight, 24-03-1916. Crew lost.
E 17	Vickers, Barrow	16-02-1915	07-04-1915	Wrecked off Texel, North Sea, 06-01-1916. Crew rescued by Dutch cruiser Noord Brabant and interned.
E 18	Vickers, Barrow	04-03-1915	06-06-1915	Sunk by German decoy ship, SMS K off Bornholm, in Baltic, 24-05-1916. Crew lost.
E 19	Vickers, Barrow	13-05-1914	12-07-1915	Scuttled Helsingfors Bay, 1.5 nm off Grohara light, Gulf of Finland, to avoid seizure by German forces, 03-04-1918. Salved, 08-1953 for breaking up in Finland.
E 20	Vickers, Barrow	25-11-1914	30-08-1915	Torpedoed by German UB 14, Sea of Marmara, 06-11-1915. Crew lost.
Group 3				
E 21	Vickers, Barrow	29-07-1915	01-10-1915	Sold 14-12-1921.
E 22	Vickers, Barrow	27-08-1914	08-11-1915	Torpedoed by German submarine UB 18 off Great Yarmouth, North Sea, 25-04-1916. Crew lost.
E 23	Vickers, Barrow	28-09-1914	06-12-1915	Sold 06-09-1922, Sunderland.
E 24	Vickers, Barrow	09-12-1915	09-01-1916	Mined, Heligoland Bight, 24-03-1916. Attempted salvage, in error for U boat, 1973.
E 25	William Beardmore, Dalmuir	23-08-1915	04-10-1915	Sold 14-12-1921.
E 26	William Beardmore, Dalmuir	11-11-1915	03-10-1915	Originally ordered for Turkish Navy. Lost, North Sea, 06-07-1916. Crew lost.
E 27	Yarrow, Scotstoun	09-06-1917	08-1917	Sold 06-09-1922, Newport.
E 28	Yarrow, Scotstoun - - Cancelled, 20-04-1915			
E 29	Armstrong Whitworth, Newcastle-upon-Tyne	01-06-1915	10-1915	Explosion in battery compartment, 09-01-1916. 4 killed. Sold, 21-02-1922.
E 30	Armstrong Whitworth, Newcastle-upon-Tyne	29-06-1914	11-1915	Mined, off Orfordness, Suffolk, North Sea, 22-12-1916. Crew lost.
E 31	Scotts, Greenock	12-1914	08-01-1916	Sold 06-09-1922.
E 32	John White, Cowes, Isle of Wight	16-08-1916	10-1916	Sold 06-09-1922, Sunderland.
E 33	John Thornycroft, Woolston, Southampton	18-04-1916	11-1917	Sold, 06-09-1922. Newport.
E 34	John Thornycroft, Woolston, Southampton	21-01-1917	03-1917	Mined, Heligoland Bight, 20-07-1918. Crew lost.
E 35	John Brown, Clydebank	20-05-1916	14-07-1917	Sold 06-09-1922, Newcastle.
E 36	John Brown, Clydebank	07-01-1915	16-11-1916	Sunk after collision with E 43 off Harwich, North Sea, 19-01-1917. Crew lost.
E 37	Fairfield, Govan, Clyde	25-09-1915	17-03-1916	Lost, North Sea, 01-12-1916. Crew lost.
E 38	Fairfield, Govan, Clyde	13-06-1016	10-07-1916	Sold 06-09-1922. Newcastle.
E 39	Palmer, Jarrow (launched 1916) completed by Armstrong Whitworth, Newcastle-upon-Tyne	18-05-1916	10-1916	Sold 13-10-1921 but foundered, 09-1922, under tow to shipbreakers.
E 40	Palmer, Jarrow (launched 1916) completed by Armstrong Whitworth, Newcastle-upon-Tyne	09-11-1916	05-1917	Sold 14-12-1921.
E 41	Cammell Laird, Birkenhead	26-07-1915	02-1916	In collision on surface with E 4 during exercises off Harwich, 15-08-1916. 16 lost; 15 escaped, including 7 from bottom. Raised 09-1917 and re-commissioned. Sold 06-09-1922, Newcastle.
E 42	Cammell Laird, Birkenhead	23-10-1915	07-1916	Sold 06-09-1922, Poole.
E 43	Swan Hunter, Wallsend	22-12-1914	20-02-1916	Sold 03-01-1921. Stranded, under tow, W. of St. Agnes Head, Cornwall, 25-11-1921.
E 44	Swan Hunter, Wallsend	08-01-1916	18-07-1916	Sold, 13-10-1921, South Wales.
E 45	Cammell Laird, Birkenhead	29-01-1916	08-1916	Sold, 06-09-1922, South Wales.
E 46	Cammell Laird, Birkenhead	04-04-1916	10-1916	Sold, 06-09-1922. South Wales.
E 47	Launched by Fairfield, Govan. Completed, William Beardmore, Dalmuir	29-05-1916	10-1916	Lost, North Sea, 20-08-1917. Crew lost.
E 48	Launched by Fairfield, Govan, 1916. Completed, William Beardmore, Dalmuir	02-08-1916	02-1917	Used as target, 1921. Scrapped 07-1928, Newport.
E 49	Swan Hunter, Wallsend	15-02-1915	14-12-1916	Mined off Shetland Islands, (laid by UC 76 on 10-03-1917) 12-03-1917. Crew lost. Lies in 16 fathoms with bows blown off.
E 50	John Brown, Clydebank	14-11-1916	23-01-1917	Mined off South Dogger light vessel, North Sea, 31-01-1918.
E 51	Ordered from Yarrow, Scotstoun, but transferred, 03-03-1915 to Scotts, Greenock	30-11-1916	27-01-1917	Sold, 13-10-1921.
E 52	Ordered from Yarrow, Scotstoun, but transferred, 03-03-1915 to William Denny, Dumbarton	25-01-1917	N/K	Sold, 03-01-1921, Brixham.
E 53	William Beardmore, Dalmuir	N/K	03-1916	Sold, 06-09-1922.
E 54	William Beardmore, Dalmuir	N/K	05-1916	Sold, 14-12-1921.
E 55	William Denny, Dumbarton	05-02-1916	03-1916	Sold, 06-09-1922, Newcastle.
E 56	William Denny, Dumbarton	19-06-1916	N/K	Sold, 09-06-1923, Granton.
Australian 'E'				
AE 1	Vickers, Barrow	03-11-1911	28-02-1914	Foundered off Bismarck Archipelago, New Britain, Pacific, 14-09-1914.
AE 2	Vickers, Barrow	10-02-1912	28-02-1914	Scuttled after being damaged from fire from 37 mm gun of Turkish torpedo boat Sultan Hisar, Sea of Marmara, 30-04-1915. Crew prisoners.

US 'L' class ocean-going submarines, 1914-1917

	Group One	Group Two
Length (ft)	167.4	165.0
Beam (ft)	17.5	14.75
Displacement (tons)		
Surface	450	456
Submerged	542	548
Speed (kts)		
Surfaced	14	14
Dived	10.5	10.5
Armament	1x3" tube, 4x18" tubes	1x3" tube, 4x18" tubes
	3 reloads	3 reloads
	1x3" AA gun	1x3" AA gun
Engines	2x650 hp Niseco	2x600 hp Busch Sulzer
	Diesel ?600 hp electric	Diesel ?600 hp electric
Range		
Surface	4,500 nm at 7 kts	4,500 nm at 7 kts
Submerged	150 nm at 5 kts	150 nm at 5 kts
Maximum diving depth (ft)	150	150
Complement	28	28

Left: Arriving late in the war, this class failed to make a significant impact on German U-boat operations.

The 11-strong 'L' class was the US Navy's first attempt at designing and building ocean-going submarines - a yawning gap in capability compared with other major navies. Although the first hulls were laid down six months before the outbreak of European hostilities, the first boats were not commissioned until two years later, following inordinately long fitting-out periods.

Even so, after service in the Atlantic Flotilla by Group One boats, most required extensive refits at Philadelphia after the USA's entry into the First World War, reflecting the US Navy's then limited experience in ocean operations. They were despatched in November, 1917 either to Bantry Bay (now the Irish Republic) or to the Azores, on anti-U boat patrols. Following the horrendous Allied merchant ship losses in 1917, a convoy system was put in place and the American boats joined protective patrols shadowing the convoys. No U boats were sunk by the class, although *L 2* unsuccessfully attacked German boats on May 26 and July 10, 1918. Group Two boats came too late to hostilities: *L 6* and *L 7* arrived in the Azores just a week before the Armistice was signed on November 11 1917, and *L 8* was ordered back after arriving in Bermuda two days later.

The class was generally under-powered but enjoyed good endurance for patrols in the North Atlantic and in British waters.

HYDROPHONE TRIALS

After the war, the 'L' class boats were involved in trials of new torpedoes and hydrophone equipment on both the East and West coasts before decommissioning in 1922-23. Those hulls not scrapped immediately thereafter, were used for the US scrapping quota in 1933 under the London Treaty limiting naval armament.

US 'L' Class sea going submarine

Boat	Builder	Laid Down	Commissioned	Fate
Group One				
L-1 (SS-40)	Fore River Shipbuilding, Quincy, Massachusetts	13-04-1914	11-04-1916	Decommissioned, Hampton Roads, Virginia, 07-04-1922. Sold 31-07-1922.
L-2 (SS-41)	Fore River Shipbuilding, Quincy, Massachusetts	19-03-1914	29-09-1916	Decommissioned, Hampton Roads, Virginia, 04-05-1923. Scrapped under terms of London Naval Treaty, 28-11-1933.
L-3 (SS-42)	Fore River Shipbuilding, Quincy, Massachusetts	18-04-1914	22-04-1916	Decommissioned, Hampton Roads, Virginia, 11-06-1923. Scrapped under terms of London Naval Treaty, 28-11-1933.
L-4 (SS-43)	Fore River Shipbuilding, Quincy, Massachusetts	23-03-1914	04-05-1916	Decommissioned, Philadelphia, 14-04-1922. Sold 31-07-1922.
L-9 (SS-49)	Fore River Shipbuilding, Quincy, Massachusetts	02-11-1914	04-08-1916	Decommissioned, Hampton Roads, Virginia, 04-05-1923. Scrapped 28-11-1923.
L-10 (SS-50)	Fore River Shipbuilding, Quincy, Massachusetts	17-02-1915	02-08-1916	Decommissioned, Philadelphia, 05-05-1922. Sold 31-07-1922 for scrapping
L-11 (SS-51)	Fore River Shipbuilding, Quincy, Massachusetts	17-02-1915	15-08-1916	Decommissioned, Hampton Roads, Virginia, 28-11-1923. Scrapped 28-11-1933.
Group Two				
L-5 (SS-44)	Lake Torpedo Boat Co., Bridgeport, Connecticut.	14-05-1914	17-02-1918	Decommissioned, Hampton Roads, Virginia, 05-12-1922. Sold 21-12-1925 for scrapping.
L-6 (SS-45)	Originally ordered from Lake Torpedo Boat Co, but built by Craig Shipbuilding Co., Long Beach, California.	27-05-1914	07-12-1917	Decommissioned, Hampton Roads, Virginia, 25-11-1922. Sold 21-12-1925 for scrapping.
L-7 (SS-46)	Originally ordered from Lake Torpedo Boat Co, but built by Craig Shipbuilding Co., Long Beach, California.	02-06-1914	07-12-1917	Decommissioned, Hampton Roads, Virginia, 15-11-1922. Sold 21-12-1925.
L-8 (SS-48)	Portsmouth Navy Yard, Portsmouth, New Hampshire	24-02-1915	30-08-1917	Decommissioned, Hampton Roads, Virginia, 15-11-1922. Sold 21-12-1925.

British 'H' class coastal defence submarines 1915-1919

The 'H' class proved relatively successful in operations during World War I and became popular in the Royal Navy submarine service, despite their single hull, low buoyancy reserves and lack of gun. Because of insufficient building capacity in the UK, the first 10 boats were assembled by Canadian Vickers in Montreal. *H1*, *H2*, *H3* and *H4* crossed the Atlantic after commissioning in May-June 1915 from St John's, Newfoundland to Gibraltar, escorted by the armed merchant cruiser *Calgarian*.

A second batch, *H11 - H20*, were built in the USA in 1915 at Fore River, Quincy, Massachusetts, but eight were interned by Washington and only released on the USA's entry into the war. The Royal Navy did not commission them, instead ceding *H13* and *H16-20* to the Chilean Navy as some recompense for the inconvenience of purchasing two of its 28,000 ton dreadnoughts, (*Almirante Latorre* and *Almirante Cochrane*) being built at the outbreak of war. Two further boats, *H14* and *H15* were presented to the Royal Canadian Navy.

In the interim, an improved design, the *H21*, was produced with larger displacement and the new 21" torpedo tubes replacing the old 18". *H32*, commissioned on May 14, 1919, as a tender to the submarine depot ship, HMS *Maidstone*, was the first Royal Navy boat fitted with the ASDIC (Anti-Submarine Detector Investigation Committee) underwater sensor system.[1]

SUCCESSES AND LOSSES

An early success was the torpedoing of *U51* by *H5* off the Weser estuary on July 14, 1916. But the only other U boat victory was *H4*'s sinking of *UB52* in the Adriatic on May 23, 1918. *H5* was rammed and sunk by the steamship *Rutherglen* on the surface in the Irish Sea on March 6, 1918. There were no survivors. *H6* ran aground on the mud flats off Schiermonnikoog but was refloated and interned by the Dutch Navy which bought the hull and commissioned it as *0-8* on January 18, 1916. (This boat's curious history continued into the next World War. When German forces overran the Netherlands, the Dutch Navy scuttled her in May 1940, but she was raised and re-commissioned in the Kriegsmarine as *UD1*. She, in turn, was scuttled at Kiel on May 3, 1945 and was later broken up.)

Other First War losses were *H3*, mined in the Gulf of Cattaro, Adriatic, on July 15, 1916 and *H10*, lost in the North Sea on January 19, 1918. *H1* mistakenly sank the Italian coastal submarine *H5* off Cattaro on April 15, 1918.

Most of the class was sold in the late 1920s and 1930s but some venerable boats saw active service in World War II. *H31* took part in the operation to bottle up the German battle cruiser *Scharnhorst* in Brest in November, 1941 before the "Channel Dash" to German home ports in company with *Gneisenau* and *Prinz Eugen* in February, 1942. She was lost, probably by mine, during a patrol in the Bay of Biscay on December 24, 1941. *H49* was lost after being depth-charged by German patrol craft off Texel, Holland, on October 18, 1940. Seven boats, *H28, H32, H33, H34, H43, H44* and *H50* were all sold for scrap in 1944 and 1945.

	Group 1	Group 2	Group 3 (H 21)
Length (ft)	150.25 oa	150.25 oa	171.0 oa
Beam (ft)	15.3 oa	15.3 oa	15.3 oa
Displacement (tons)			
Surfaced	364	364	423
Submerged	434	434	510
Speed (kts)			
Surfaced	13	13	11.5
Dived	10	10	9.0
Armament	4x18" bow tubes	4x18" bow tubes	4x21" bow tubes
	8 reloads	8 reloads	6/8 reloads
Engines	480 hp diesel	480 hp diesel	480 hp diesel
	2x620 hp electric	2x620 hp electric	2x620 hp electric
Range			
Surface	1,600 nm at 10 kts	1,600 nm at 10 kts	2,985 nm at 7.5 kts
Submerged	130 nm at 2 kts	130 nm at 2 kts	130 nm at 2 kts
Diving depth	150 ft	150 ft	150 ft
Complement	22	22	22

Below: Commissioned in the closing months of the First World War, H 30 was sold in 1936 before the outbreak of war. Several of this class did see further active service during the early part of the Second World War.

British 'H' class coastal defence submarine

Boat	Builder	Laid down	Commissioned	Fate
Group 1				
H 1	Canadian Vickers Co, Montreal	11-01-1915	26-05-1915	Sold 07-03-1921, Malta.
H 2	Canadian Vickers Co, Montreal	11-01-1915	04-06-1915	Sold 07-03-1921, Malta.
H 3	Canadian Vickers Co, Montreal	11-01-1915	03-06-1915	Mined, Gulf of Cattaro, Adriatic, 15-07-1916.
H 4	Canadian Vickers Co, Montreal	11-01-1915	05-06-1915	Sold 30-11-1921, Malta.
H 5	Canadian Vickers Co, Montreal	11-01-1915	10-06-1915	Rammed and sunk by SS *Rutherglen*, Irish Sea, 06-03-1918 as steamer's bows crossed at speed on surface. Crew lost.
H 6	Canadian Vickers Co, Montreal	14-01-1915	09-06-1915	Ran aground on Schiermonnikoog. Refloated, interned. Bought by Dutch Navy to become *O-8*, 18-01-1916.
				Scuttled, 05-1940 but raised by German Navy and re-commissioned as *UD 1*. Scuttled, Kiel, 03-05-1945, broken up.
H 7	Canadian Vickers Co, Montreal	19-05-1915	06-1915	Sold 1921.
H 8	Canadian Vickers Co, Montreal	19-05-1915	06-1915	Sold 29-11-1921, Arbroath.
H 9	Canadian Vickers Co, Montreal	N/K	06-1915	Sold 30-11-1921, Malta.
H 10	Canadian Vickers Co, Montreal	N/K	06-1915	Lost, North Sea, 19-01-1918.
Group 2				
H 11	Fore River Yard, Quincy, Massachusetts	N/K	1915	Sold 20-10-1920, Dover.
H 12	Fore River Yard, Quincy, Massachusetts	N/K	1915	Sold 04-1920, Dover.
H 13	Fore River Yard, Quincy, Massachusetts	N/K	1918	Ceded, Chilean Navy as *Gualcolda* (*H 1*) Scrapped ?late 1940s.
H 14	Fore River Yard, Quincy, Massachusetts	N/K	06-1919	Given to Canadian Navy as *CH 14*. Scrapped 1925.
H 15	Fore River Yard, Quincy, Massachusetts	N/K	14-09-1918	Given to Canadian Navy as *CH 15*. Scrapped 1925.
H 16	Fore River Yard, Quincy, Massachusetts	N/K	N/K	Ceded, Chilean Navy as *Tegualda* (*H 2*). Scrapped c.1948.
H 17	Fore River Yard, Quincy, Massachusetts	N/K	N/K	Ceded, Chilean Navy as *Rucumilla* (*H 3*). Scrapped c.1945.
H 18	Fore River Yard, Quincy, Massachusetts	N/K	N/K	Ceded, Chilean Navy as *Guale* (*H 4*). Scrapped by 1953.
H 19	Fore River Yard, Quincy, Massachusetts	N/K	N/K	Ceded, Chilean Navy as *Quidora* (*H 5*). Scrapped by 1953.
H 20	Fore River Yard, Quincy, Massachusetts	N/K	N/K	Ceded, Chilean Navy as *Fresia* (*H 6*). Scrapped by 1953.
Group 3				
H 21	Vickers, Barrow	20-10-1917	28-01-1918	Sold 13-07-1926, Newport.
H 22	Vickers, Barrow	07-09-1918	06-11-1918	Sold 19-02-1929. Broken up, Charlestown.
H 23	Vickers, Barrow	03-03-1918	25-05-1918	Sold 04-05-1934, Sunderland.
H 24	Vickers , Barrow	13-11-1917	30-04-1918	Rammed by HMS *Vancouver* 07-1922, badly damaging conning tower. Sold 04-05-1934, Sunderland.
H 25	Vickers, Barrow	27-04-1918	16-07-1918	Sold 19-02-1929. Broken up, Charlestown.
H 26	Vickers, Barrow	15-11-1917	29-12-1918	Sold 30-08-1935, Newport.
H 28	Vickers, Barrow	18-03-1917	29-06-1918	In collision with steamer in Bruges Canal, 05-1929. Scrapped, 18-08-1944. Broken up, Troon.
H 29	Vickers, Barrow	19-03-1917	14-09-1918	Sank during trials, Devonport Dockyard following refit, 09-08-1926. Five civilians and one crewman died. Raised.
				Sold 07-10-1927, Pembroke Dock.
H 30	Vickers, Barrow	18-03-1917	19-10-1918	Sold 30-08-1935, Newport.
H 31	Vickers, Barrow	19-04-1917	21-02-1919	Lost, Bay of Biscay, 26-12-1941. Probably mined.
H 32	Vickers, Barrow	20-04-1917	14-05-1919	Sold 18-10-1944, Troon.
H 33	Cammell Laird, Birkenhead	20-11-1917	17-05-1919	Scrapped 19-05-1944. Troon.
H 34	Cammell Laird, Birkenhead	20-11-1917	10-09-1919	Sold 07-1945, scrapped, Troon.
H 35 – H40	-	-	-	Cancelled.
H 41	Armstrong Whitworth, Newcastle-upon-Tyne	17-09-1917	11-1918	Sank after collision with depot ship HMS *Vulcan*. Propeller holed pressure hull, Blyth, 18-10-1919. Raised.
				Sold 12-03-1920, Sunderland.
H 42	Armstrong Whitworth, Newcastle-upon-Tyne	09-1917	01-05-1919	Sank after being rammed by destroyer HMS *Versatile* off Gibraltar, 23-03-1922. Crew lost.
H 43	Armstrong Whitworth, Newcastle-upon-Tyne	04-10-1917	25-11-1919	Sold 11-1944. Scrapped 1945 at Troon.
H 44	Armstrong Whitworth, Newcastle-upon-Tyne	10-10-1917	15-04-1920	Sold 1944. Broken up, Troon.
H 45 – H 46	-	-	-	Cancelled.
H 47	William Beardmore, Dalmuir	20-11-1917	25-02-1919	Sank after collision with British submarine *L 12* off Milford Haven, Wales, 09-07-1929. 21 crew lost, three survivors.
H 48	William Beardmore, Dalmuir	30-11-1917	23-06-1919	Sold 30-08-1935, Llanelly.
H 49	William Beardmore, Dalmuir	15-07-1919	25-10-1919	Sank after depth-charging by German patrol craft, off Texel, Holland, 18-10-1940. One survivor.
H 50	William Beardmore, Dalmuir	23-01-1918	03-02-1920	Sold for scrapping 07-1945, Troon.
H 51	HM Dockyard, Pembroke Dock	N/K	01-09-1919	Sold 06-06-1924. Resold, 17-07-1924 to ship-breakers.
H 52	HM Dockyard, Pembroke Dock	N/K/	16-12-1919	Sold 09-11-1927.
H 53 – H 54	-	-	-	Cancelled.

German UB II class coastal submarines

The *UB II* class, Project 39, approved in April 1915, was designed as an improvement on the earlier *UB I* class which, with its 60 hp diesel engine and single screw, proved slow and difficult to manoeuvre. Even so, the new class remained under-powered and its successor, the *UB III* was fitted with two 550 hp diesels and two 394 hp electric motors.

Twenty-inch torpedoes were fitted, fired from two bow tubes mounted one above the other. Forward hydroplanes were fitted, as was a second periscope and a two masted wireless aerial. Pre-fabricated sections helped the two yards involved in their construction to complete the fitting out of some boats under two weeks from launch dates.

Apart from its design limitations, the *UB II*s proved useful boats during war service, operating out of the Flanders Flotilla's bases at Bruges and Zeebrugge (ranging as far as the Irish Sea,) and also in the Mediterranean and Black Sea.

The extent of their deployment may be judged by their casualty list. Out of the 30 boats built, only seven survived to surrender after the Armistice, including *UB 28*, which was used for training.

This number excludes two, *UB 43* and *UB 47*, transferred to the Austro-Hungarian Navy for operations

	UB 18	UB 20	UB 24	UB 30	UB 42
Length (ft)	118.5	118.5	118.5	121.0	121.0
Beam (ft)	14.3	14.3	14.3	14.3	14.3
Displacement (tons)					
Surface	263	263	265	274	272
Submerged	292	292	295	305	303
Speed (kts)					
Surfaced	9.2	9.2	8.9	9.0	8.8
Dived	5.8	5.8	5.7	5.7	6.2
Armament					
	2x20" bow tubes throughout				
	2 reloads throughout				
	1x5 cm gun	1x5 cm gun	1x5 cm gun	1x8.8 cm gun	1x8.8 cm gun
Engines					
	2x142 hp diesel	2x142 hp diesel	2x135 hp diesel	2x135 hp diesel	2x142 hp diesel
	2x140 hp electric	2x140 hp electric	2x140 hp electric	2x140 hp electric	2x140 hp electric
	twin shafts	twin shafts	twin shafts	twin shafts	twin shafts
Range					
Surfaced	6,500 nm at 5 kts throughout				
Submerged	45 nm at 4 kts throughout				
Diving depth (ft)	150 throughout				
Complement	23 throughout				

in the Adriatic and *UB 23* which was interned in Spain after limping to Corunna following a crippling attack by the British patrol boat *PC 60* off The Lizard, Cornwall, in July 1917. *UB 40* was also blown up during the evacuation of the Flanders submarine base on October 2 1918 in the face of advancing Allied troops.

DEPTH CHARGE CASUALTY

UB 29 has the dubious distinction of being the first submarine sunk by a depth charge in an action in the western English Channel in December, 1916.

The boats' slow speeds was a major contribution to their losses: two, *UB 20* and *UB 32,* were caught on the surface by aircraft within two months of each other in 1917, and bombed.

One of the class caused a diplomatic row in March, 1916, when *UB 29* torpedoed the French cross-Channel 1,350 ton steamer *Sussex*, believing it to be a minelayer. Among the steamer's 80 casualties were 25 US citizens which renewed American protests about the U boat war.

Below: UB IIs operated in most naval theatres during World War I and suffered considerable losses throughout the war.

German UB II class coastal submarine

Boat	Builder	Launched	Commissioned	Fate
UB 18 class				
UB 18	Blohm & Voss, Hamburg	21-08-1915	11-12-1915	Rammed and sunk by British armed trawler *Ben Lawer*, English Channel, 09-12-1917
UB 19	Blohm & Voss, Hamburg	02-09-1915	17-12-1915	Sunk by gunfire from British 'Q' ship *Penhurst* (Q7), 18 miles NW Casquets Lighthouse, English Channel, 30-11-1916. 16 survivors.
UB 20	Blohm & Voss, Hamburg	26-09-1915	10-02-1916	Sunk by British Curtis H.12 flying boats 8676 and 8862 off Zeebrugge, North Sea, 29-07-1917.
UB 21	Blohm & Voss, Hamburg	26-09-1915	29-02-1916	Surrendered after Armistice.
UB 22	Blohm & Voss, Hamburg	09-10-1915	02-03-1916	Mined, North Sea, 19-01-1918
UB 23	Blohm & Voss, Hamburg	09-10-1915	13-03-1916	Interned at Corunna, Spain, 29-07-1917 after being badly damaged by British patrol boat *PC 60* off The Lizard, Cornwall, 26-07-1917. Surrendered to French Navy after Armistice.
UB 24 class				
UB 24	A G Weser AG, Bremen	18-10-1915	18-11-1915	Surrendered to French Navy after Armistice.
UB 25	A G Weser AG, Bremen	22-11-1915	11-12-1915	Surrendered after Armistice
UB 26	A G Weser AG, Bremen	14-12-1915	07-01-1916	Caught in nets laid by British Le Havre drifter flotilla, depth-charged by French 'Normand' class torpedo boat, *Le Trombe*, surrendered off Le Havre but later sank off Cap de la Hève, 05-04-1916. Crew captured. Subsequently salved by French Navy and recommissioned as *Roland Moullet*
UB 27	A G Weser AG, Bremen	10-02-1916	23-02-1916	Sank after depth charging and ramming by elderly British gunboat *Halcyon* 26 miles off Great Yarmouth, North Sea, 29-07-1917.
UB 28	A G Weser AG, Bremen	20-12-1915	27-12-1915	Surrendered after Armistice.
UB 29	A G Weser AG, Bremen	31-12-1915	18-01-1916	Sunk by British destroyer *Landrail* Western English Channel, 13-12-1916. First sinking by depth charge.
UB 30 class				
UB 30	Blohm & Voss, Hamburg	16-11-1915	18-03-1916	Sank after depth-charging by British armed trawlers *John Gillman, John Brooker, Florio, Miranda II* and *Viola* off Whitby, North Sea, 13-08-1918.
UB 31	Blohm & Voss, Hamburg	16-11-1915	25-03-1916	Mined, Dover Straits, 02-05-1918.
UB 32	Blohm & Voss, Hamburg	04-12-1915	11-04-1916	Sunk by bombs dropped by British seaplane 8695, 27 miles N. Cap Barfleur, 18-08-1917.
UB 33	Blohm & Voss, Hamburg	04-12-1915	22-04-1916	Mined, Dover Barrage, SW of Varne light vessel, 11-04-1918.
UB 34	Blohm & Voss, Hamburg	28-12-1915	10-06-1916	Surrendered after Armistice.
UB 35	Blohm & Voss, Hamburg	28-12-1915	22-06-1916	Sank after depth charging by British destroyer *Leven*, N. of Calais, English Channel, 26-01-1918.
UB 36	Blohm & Voss, Hamburg	15-01-1916	22-05-1916	Lost, circumstances unknown, 06-1917.
UB 37	Blohm & Voss, Hamburg	28-12-1915	17-05-1916	Sunk by British 'Q' ship, *Penhurst* (Q7) 20 nm off Cherbourg, English Channel 14-01-1917.
UB 38	Blohm & Voss, Hamburg	01-04-1916	19-07-1916	Mined, Dover Barrage 08-02-1918.
UB 39	Blohm & Voss, Hamburg	29-02-1916	29-04-1916	Mined, E of Dover, 15-05-1917. Other reports suggest it was sunk by *Glen* in English Channel, 17-05-1917.
UB 40	Blohm & Voss, Hamburg	25-04-1916	17-08-1916	Destroyed in evacuation of Flanders base, 02-10-1918.
UB 41	Blohm & Voss, Hamburg	06-05-1916	25-08-1916	Sunk in German minefield, off Scarborough, North Sea, 05-10-1917.
UB 42 class				
UB 42	A G Weser AG, Bremen	04-03-1916	23-03-1916	Surrendered after Armistice.
UB 43	A G Weser AG, Bremen	08-04-1916	24-04-1916	Transferred to Austro-Hungarian Navy.
UB 44	A G Weser AG, Bremen	20-04-1916	11-05-1916	Sunk, Mediterranean, 30-07-1916.
UB 45	A G Weser AG, Bremen	12-05-1916	26-05-1916	Sank in Russian minefield off Varna, Black Sea, 06-11-1916. 5 survivors.
UB 46	A G Weser AG, Bremen	31-05-1916	12-06-1916	Mined, Dardanelles, 16-12-1916.
UB 47	A G Weser AG, Bremen	17-06-1916	04-07-1916	Transferred to Austro-Hungarian Navy.

German UC II coastal minelaying submarines

Like the *UB II* coastal submarines, the *UC II* coastal minelayers replaced predecessors that were grossly under-powered and poor sea-keepers. Approval for construction was given on July 15 1915, with the Navy demanding as many hulls as possible delivered before the end of the following September.

As this large class progressed through pre-fabricated section assembly at five yards, small improvements were made in speed and manoeuvrability, culminating in the much larger *UC III* class with more powerful engines.

However, these came too late for any service and the end of hostilities saw eight surrendered incomplete and three scrapped while fitting out. Thus, the *UC II* boats became the backbone of the German mining campaign in British waters and in the Mediterranean.

Inevitably, the boats became casualties of their own weapon system.

UC 32 was sunk by one of her own mines off Sunderland in February 1917, and *UC 42* and *UC 44* were lost in German minefields off the southern coast of Ireland in August and September, 1917. *UC 41* was sunk by armed trawlers after being damaged in an explosion of one of her mines off the Tay Estuary in August 1917. *UC 55* was scuttled after becoming uncontrollable while laying mines off Lewick in September 1917 and *UC 76* was damaged in an explosion whilst embarking mines at Heligoland in May 1917. At least a further five boats were casualties of mines.

Four were blown up at the Pola submarine base in the Adriatic in November 1918.

	UC16	UC 25	UC 34	UC 40	UC 46	UC 49	UC 55	UC 61	UC 65	UC 74
Length (ft)	161.9	162.2	165.2	162.2	170.1	172.8	165.7	170.1	165.2	165.5
Beam (ft)	17	17	17	17	17	17	17	17	17	17
Displacement (tons)										
Surface	417	400	427	400	420	434	415	422	427	410
Submerged	493	480	529	480	520	532	498	525	529	490
Speed (kts)										
Surfaced	11.6	11.9	11.7	11.7	11.7	11.8	11.6	11.9	12.0	11.8
Dived	7	6.7	6.7	6.7	7	7.2	7.3	7.4	7.4	7.4
Armament										
	3 x 20" G6 torpedo tubes, (2 bow, 1 stern) with four reloads, throughout									
	18 UC/200 mines in six vertical tubes throughout									
	1 x 8.8 cm gun throughout									
Engines										
	2 x 250 hp diesel in *UC 16-33* and *UC 40-45*					2 x 300 hp diesel in *UC 34-39* and *UC 46 - 79*				
	2 x 230 hp electric *UC 16 - 48*					2 x 310 hp electric *UC 49 - 79*				
Range										
Surfaced	6,430 nm at 7 kts throughout									
Submerged	55 nm at 4 kts throughout									
Diving depth (ft)	150 throughout									
Complement	26 throughout									

Below: A number of UC/200 mines are clearly visible aboard this captured example. Note the ramming damage to the hull at the top of the photograph which necessitated its surrender.

German UC II coastal minelaying submarines

Boat	Builder	Launched	Commissioned	Fate
UC 16 class				
UC 16	Blohm & Voss, Hamburg	01-02-1916	26-06-1916	Sunk by British destroyer *Melampus* (ex-*Chios*) off Selsey Bill, English Channel, 23-10-1917.
UC 17	Blohm & Voss, Hamburg	19-02-1916	23-07-1916	Surrendered after Armistice.
UC 18	Blohm & Voss, Hamburg	04-03-1916	15-08-1916	Sunk by gunfire from British 'Q' ship *Lady Olive* (Q18) 12 nm W of Jersey, English Channel, 19-02-1917.
UC 19	Blohm & Voss, Hamburg	15-03-1916	22-08-1916	Sunk by explosive sweep towed by British destroyer *Llewellyn*, Dover Straits, 04-12-1916.
UC 20	Blohm & Voss, Hamburg	01-04-1916	08-09-1916	Surrendered after Armistice.
UC 21	Blohm & Voss, Hamburg	01-04-1916	15-09-1916	Mined, off Zeebrugge, North Sea, 27-09-1917.
UC 22	Blohm & Voss, Hamburg	01-02-1916	01-07-1916	Surrendered after Armistice.
UC 23	Blohm & Voss, Hamburg	19-02-1916	28-07-1916	Surrendered after Armistice.
UC 24	Blohm & Voss, Hamburg	04-03-1916	17-08-1916	Torpedoed by French submarine *Circe* (Q87) off Cattaro, Adriatic, 24-05-1917. Two crew survived.
UC 25 class				
UC 25	A G Vulkan, Hamburg	10-06-1916	28-06-1916	Blown up at Pola Base, Adriatic, 11-1918.
UC 26	A G Vulkan, Hamburg	22-06-1916	18-07-1916	Rammed by British destroyer *Milne*, Thames estuary, 09-05-1917. Two survivors.
UC 27	A G Vulkan, Hamburg	28-06-1916	25-07-1916	Surrendered after Armistice.
UC 28	A G Vulkan, Hamburg	08-07-1916	06-08-1916	Training boat. Surrendered after Armistice.
UC 29	A G Vulkan, Hamburg	15-07-1916	15-08-1916	Sunk by gunfire from British 'Q' ship *Pargust* off SW Ireland, 07-06-1917.
UC 30	A G Vulkan, Hamburg	27-07-1916	22-08-1916	Mined, Hiorns Reef, North Sea, 21-04-1917.
UC 31	A G Vulkan, Hamburg	07-08-1916	02-09-1916	Surrendered after Armistice.
UC 32	A G Vulkan, Hamburg	12-08-1916	13-09-1916	Sunk off Sunderland, North Sea, by own mines, 23-02-1917. Three survivors.
UC 33	A G Vulkan, Hamburg	26-08-1916	25-09-1916	Rammed by British patrol boat *P 61*, SW Approaches, 26-09-1917.

Below: A rare photograph of a German minelayer under British colours after its capture.

German UC II coastal minelaying submarines

German UC II coastal minelaying submarines (continued)

Boat	Builder	Launched	Commissioned	Fate
UC 34 class				
UC 34	Blohm & Voss, Hamburg	06-05-1916	26-09-1916	Blown up at Pola Base, Adriatic, 11-1918.
UC 35	Blohm & Voss, Hamburg	06-05-1916	04-10-1916	Sunk by gunfire from French patrol vessel Ailly, W of Sardinia, 16-05-1918. Five survivors.
UC 36	Blohm & Voss, Hamburg	25-06-1916	03-11-1916	Sunk by British seaplane 8663, 20 nm ENE of Noord Hinder Lightship, 20-05-1917.
UC 37	Blohm & Voss, Hamburg	05-06-1916	13-10-1916	Surrendered after Armistice.
UC 38	Blohm & Voss, Hamburg	05-06-1916	19-10-1916	Sank after depth charging by French destroyers Mameluck and Lansquenet, Gulf of Corinth, Mediterranean, 14-12-1917. 25 survivors.
UC 39	Blohm & Voss, Hamburg	25-06-1916	29-10-1916	Sank after depth charging by British destroyer Thrasher, 4? nm S of Flamborough Head, North Sea, 08-02-1917. 17 crew and two British prisoners survived.
UC 40 class				
UC 40	A G Vulkan, Hamburg	05-09-1916	01-10-1916	Foundered on passage to surrender, North Sea, 21-02-1919.
UC 41	A G Vulkan, Hamburg	13-09-1916	11-10-1916	Sunk by British armed trawlers Jacinth, Thomas Young and Chikara after being damaged by own mine off Tay estuary, North Sea, 21-08-1917.
UC 42	A G Vulkan, Hamburg	21-09-1916	18-11-1916	Mined in German minefield, off Cork, S coast of Ireland, 10-09-1917.
UC 43	A G Vulkan, Hamburg	05-10-1916	25-10-1916	Torpedoed by British submarine G 13, 9 nm NW of Muckle Flugga Lighthouse, Shetlands, 10-03-1917.
UC 44	A G Vulkan, Hamburg	10-10-1916	04-11-1916	Mined in German minefield off Waterford, S coast of Ireland, 04-08-1917. One survivor.
UC 45	A G Vulkan, Hamburg	20-10-1916	18-11-1916	Surrendered after Armistice.
UC 46 class				
UC 46	A.G.Weser, Bremen	15-07-1916	15-09-1916	Rammed by British destroyer Liberty in Dover Straits, 08-02-1917.
UC 47	A.G.Weser, Bremen	30-08-1916	13-10-1916	Rammed by British patrol boat P 57, E of Flamborough Head, North Sea, 18-11-1917.
UC 48	A.G.Weser, Bremen	27-09-1916	06-11-1916	Interned at Ferrol, Spain, 23-03-1918.
UC 49 class				
UC 49	Germaniawerft, Kiel	07-11-1916	12-12-1916	Sunk, North Sea, 08-08-1918.
UC 50	Germaniawerft, Kiel	23-11-1916	12-12-1916	Sank after depth charging by British destroyer Zubian off Essex coast, North Sea, 04-02-1918.[1]
UC 51	Germaniawerft, Kiel	05-12-1916	06-01-1917	Sunk by British destroyer Firedrake off Start Point, English Channel, 13-11-1917.
UC 52	Germaniawerft, Kiel	23-01-1917	15-03-1917	Surrendered after Armistice.
UC 53	Germaniawerft, Kiel	27-02-1917	05-04-1917	Blown up at Pola base, Adriatic, 11-1918.
UC 54	Germaniawerft, Kiel	02-03-1917	10-05-1917	Blown up at Pola base, Adriatic, 11-1918.
UC 55 class				
UC 55	Kaiserliche, Danzig	02-08-1916	15-11-1916	Scuttled off Lerwick, after going out of control while laying mines, North Sea, 29-09-1917. Crew captured.
UC 56	Kaiserliche, Danzig	26-08-1916	18-12-1916	Interned at Santander, Spain, 24-05-1918 and surrendered to French after Armistice.
UC 57	Kaiserliche, Danzig	07-09-1916	22-01-1917	Mined, Gulf of Finland, 19-11-1917.
UC 58	Kaiserliche, Danzig	21-10-1916	12-03-1917	Surrendered after Armistice.
UC 59	Kaiserliche, Danzig	28-09-1916	12-05-1917	Surrendered after Armistice.
UC 60	Kaiserliche, Danzig	08-11-1916	25-06-1917	Training boat. Surrendered after Armistice.
UC 61 class				
UC 61	A.G.Weser, Bremen	11-11-1916	13-12-1916	Stranded off Gris Nez, English Channel, and scuttled by crew who were captured, 26-07-1917
UC 62	A.G.Weser, Bremen	09-12-1916	08-01-1917	Torpedoed by British submarine E 45, North Sea, 15-10-1917.
UC 63	A.G.Weser, Bremen	06-01-1917	30-01-1917	Torpedoed by British submarine E 52, near Dover Straits, 01-11-1917.
UC 64	A.G.Weser, Bremen	27-01-1917	22-02-1917	Mined, Dover Straits, 20-06-1918.
UC 65 class				
UC 65	Blohm & Voss, Hamburg	08-07-1916	10-11-1916	Torpedoed by British submarine C 15, English Channel, 03-11-1917. Five survivors.
UC 66	Blohm & Voss, Hamburg	15-07-1916	18-11-1916	Sank, after depth charging by British armed trawler, Sea King off The Lizard, Cornwall, 12-06-1917.
UC 67	Blohm & Voss, Hamburg	06-08-1916	10-12-1916	Surrendered after Armistice.
UC 68	Blohm & Voss, Hamburg	12-08-1916	17-12-1916	Sunk by British submarine C 7 off Schouwen Bank, North Sea, 05-04-1917.
UC 69	Blohm & Voss, Hamburg	07-08-1916	23-12-1916	Sank following collision with U 96 off Cap Barfleur, English Channel, 06-12-1917. 18 survivors.
UC 70	Blohm & Voss, Hamburg	08-08-1916	22-11-1916	Sunk by British aircraft B.K. 9983 and British destroyer Ouse off Whitby, North Sea, 28-08-1918.
UC 71	Blohm & Voss, Hamburg	12-08-1916	28-11-1916	Sank off Heligoland en route to surrender, 20-02-1919.
UC 72	Blohm & Voss, Hamburg	12-08-1916	05-12-1916	Sunk by gunfire from British 'Q' ship Acton (Q34), Bay of Biscay, 20-08-1917.
UC 73	Blohm & Voss, Hamburg	26-08-1916	24-12-1916	Surrendered after Armistice.
UC 74 class				
UC 74	A G Vulkan, Hamburg	19-10-1916	26-11-1916	Interned at Barcelona, Spain, 21-11-1918 and surrendered to French Navy.
UC 75	A G Vulkan, Hamburg	06-11-1916	06-12-1916	Rammed by British destroyer Fairy (later sank) off Flamborough Head, North Sea, 31-05-1918.
UC 76	A G Vulkan, Hamburg	25-11-1916	17-12-1916	Blew up while loading mines, Heligoland, 10-05-1917. Salvaged, surrendered after Armistice.
UC 77	A G Vulkan, Hamburg	02-12-1916	29-12-1916	Sank in Dover Straits, probably mined, 10-07-1918.
UC 78	A G Vulkan, Hamburg	08-12-1916	01-01-1917	Mined, Dover area, English Channel, 02-05-1918.
UC 79	A G Vulkan, Hamburg	19-12-1916	22-01-1917	Lost, cause, unknown, 04-1918.

1 ZUBIAN WAS BUILT FROM THE UNDAMAGED PORTIONS OF THE DESTROYERS NUBIAN, TORPEDOED OFF FOLKESTONE ON 27-10-1916 AND ZULU, MINED OFF DOVER THE SAME DAY.

German U151 class cargo-carriers/ocean cruisers, 1917

With the British naval blockade strangling German trade, the *U151* class was conceived in 1915 as submerged cargo carriers to penetrate the embargo. *Deutschland*, later *U155,* made two successful voyages to Baltimore and New London in the USA[1] but it soon became clear that even these giant submarines could not transport enough raw material to make much difference to the industrial war effort.[2]

Oldenburg, later *U151*, was the first to be modified for "unrestricted warfare" against allied shipping. *U152-U154* and *U156-U157* were all built for naval service, the remarkably short time between launch and commissioning, a huge tribute to German production techniques. The speed of production also demonstrated the pressing strategic need for submarine hulls in the water, as the land war continued in bloody stalemate.

Despite the requirement for maximum numbers of U boats for 1917's nearly successful all-out campaign against merchant shipping, this class must have been brutal boats to take out on patrol.

With the greatest beam of any of the German designs, they rolled uncomfortably in the water and were difficult to manoeuvre. The slow underwater speed - slowest of all U boat designs - and minimal torpedo armament dictating mainly surface attack, must have made their long endurance patrols nerve-wracking experiences. The presence of a prize crew numbering an extra 21, also made living conditions cramped and suffocating.

U155 staged the first naval war patrol of the class, departing in May, 1917. The 15-week cruise saw the sinking of 19 allied ships and the shelling of shore targets in the Azores. *U151* completed a 13-week patrol, steaming more than 9,700 nm, stationed off the USA's east coast, the boat laying mines and additionally accounting for 23 ships, totalling 61,000 tons displacement.

Despite the design and performance handicaps, only two were lost during hostilities. *U154* was ambushed *en route* from West Africa and torpedoed on the surface by the British submarine *E 35* off Madeira on May 11, 1918 after British naval intelligence learnt of a planned rendezvous between her and another U boat off Cape St. Vincent. *U156* was mined in the allied Northern barrage in the North Sea on September 25, 1918. The remainder surrendered after the Armistice, no doubt to the relief of their long-suffering crews.

1 She carried 348 tons of rubber, 341 tons of nickel and 93 tons of tin on her first voyage.

2 *Bremen* was lost after foundering in heavy seas off Norway on her maiden voyage in September, 1916 with the loss of 30 crew.

German U 151 class cargo-carriers/ocean cruiser submarines

Boat	Builder*	Launched	Commissioned	Fate
U 151 (ex-Oldenburg)	Germaniawerft, Kiel	04-04-1917	21-07-1917	Surrendered after Armistice. Expended as target off Cherbourg, 1921.
U 152	Germaniawerft, Kiel	20-05-1917	20-10-1917	Surrendered after Armistice
U 153	Germaniawerft, Kiel	19-07-1917	17-11-1917	Surrendered after Armistice
U 154	Germaniawerft, Kiel	10-09-1917	12-12-1917	Torpedoed by British submarine E 35 off Madeira, 11-05-1918.
U 155 (ex-Deutschland)	Germaniawerft, Kiel	28-03-1916	10-02-1917	Surrendered after Armistice. Scrapped, Morecombe UK, 1922.
U 156	Germaniawerft, Kiel	14-04-1917	28-08-1917	Mined, in Northern Barrage, North Sea, 25-09-1918.
U 157	Germaniawerft, Kiel	23-05-1917	22-09-1917	Interned 11-11-1918 and subsequently surrendered.

* Some hulls built at Flensburg, Hamburg and Bremen.

Length (ft)	213.3
Beam (ft)	29.3
Displacement (tons)	
Surface	1,512
Submerged	1,875
Speed (kts)	
Surfaced	12.4
Dived	5.2
Armament	2x20" bow tubes
	(16 reloads)
	2x15 cm gun or 2 x 10.5 cm gun
Engines	2x400 hp diesel
	2x400 hp electric
	twin shafts
Range	
Surfaced	25,000 nm at 5.5 kts
Submerged	65 nm at 3 kts
Diving depth (ft)	195
Complement	56 plus 21 prize crew

Below: Seen here undergoing modification, U 151 was the first of this class requiring modification for an attack role.

German U151 class cargo-carriers/ocean cruisers, 1917

1 Cargo space
2 Passage
3 Outercasing
4 Engineers' area
5 Crew sleeping area
6 Galley
7 Wardroom
8 Batteries
9 Walkway
10 Extra cargo carried in waterproof packing

11 Store
12 Captain's cabin
13 Radio room
14 Conning tower
15 Upper command post
16 Main command centre
17 Compensating flooding tank
18 Diving tanks
19 Fuel
20 Pressure hull

21 Engine room
22 Main frame
23 Electric motors
24 Engine controls
25 Propellor guard
26 Propellor
27 Elevators
28 Keel
29 Rudder
30 Bypass flooding pipes

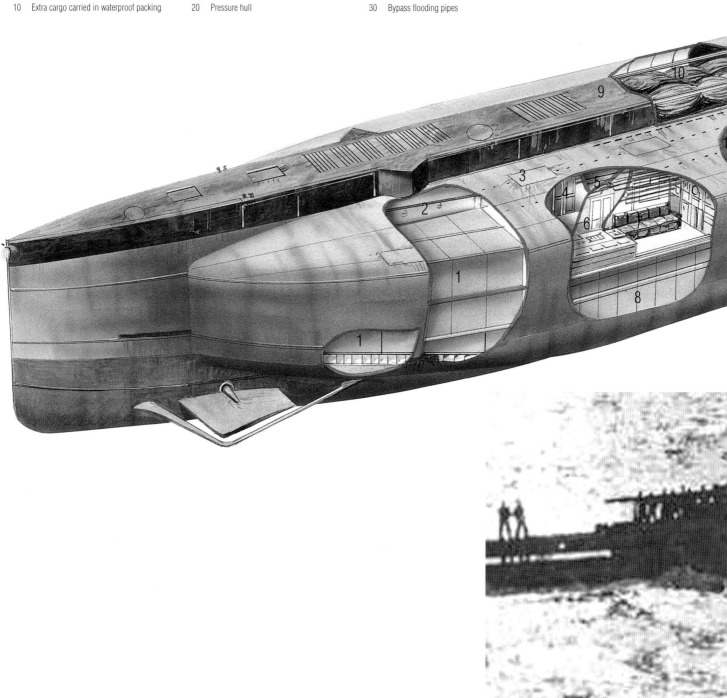

Right: The German submarine U-151, as seen from the Isabel de Bourbon. *US Navy photo.*

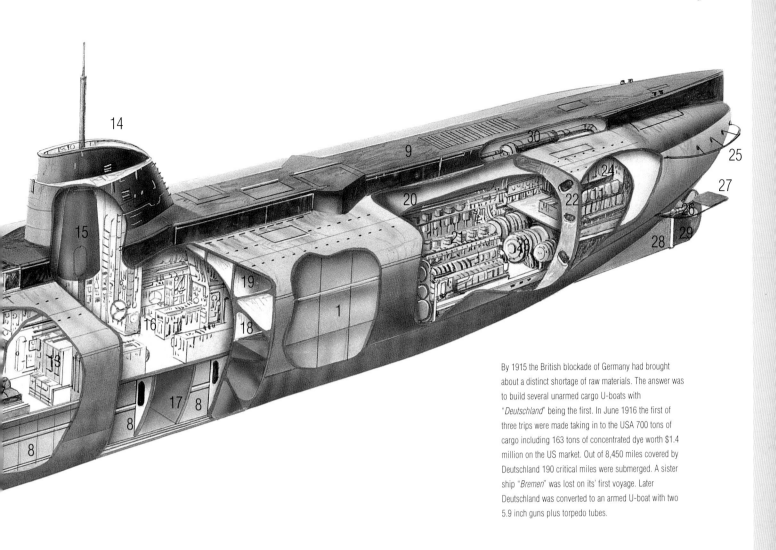

14

9

30

25

27

15

20

24

22

26

19

21

28 29

16

1

18

13

17 8

8

8

By 1915 the British blockade of Germany had brought about a distinct shortage of raw materials. The answer was to build several unarmed cargo U-boats with "*Deutschland*" being the first. In June 1916 the first of three trips were made taking in to the USA 700 tons of cargo including 163 tons of concentrated dye worth $1.4 million on the US market. Out of 8,450 miles covered by Deutschland 190 critical miles were submerged. A sister ship "*Bremen*" was lost on its' first voyage. Later Deutschland was converted to an armed U-boat with two 5.9 inch guns plus torpedo tubes.

British 'L' class overseas patrol submarines 1916-1919

While originally planned under the Emergency War Programme as an improved version of the 'E' class, the scale of change allowed the 'L' boats a separate class designation. Armament was increased with the 21" inch torpedo introduced. Group Three boats had two four inch guns mounted fore and aft on a considerably lengthened conning tower. Some of the 76 tons of fuel oil was carried in external wing tanks for the first time.

A number of Group One boats were configured as minelayers, including *L 11* and *L 12*. Within Group Two, *L 14*, *L 17* and *L 24 - L 27* were built as minelayers, carrying 16 mines, but without the normal two beam torpedo tubes.

The 'L' came late to hostilities, although *L 12* torpedoed the German *UB 90*, (with four shots, one of which hit,) west of Stavanger, Norway, on October 16 1918 and *L 10* torpedoed the 750-ton German destroyer *S 33* in the Heligoland Bight on October 4 1918, before her victim's gunfire sank her with all hands. *L 55*'s loss came after the end of the war with Germany. Based at Tallinn, Estonia, she attacked two 1,260 ton Bolshevik minelaying destroyers, *Gavril* and her sister ship *Azard* on the surface in Caporsky Bay, in the Gulf of Finland on June 9 1919. She missed her targets and was forced into a minefield before being sunk by gunfire from the destroyers' main armament, so becoming the only British submarine to be sunk by hostile Soviet vessels. The hull was salved and re-commissioned as a Soviet boat with her original number on August 7 1931 and used for training up to the beginning of World War II.

L 2 survived a fierce accidental attack by three US destroyers on February 24 1918. Her skipper, Lieut. Cmdr. Anworth reported that at a depth of 200 ft -

"the first heavy depth charge exploded and at the same time the after hydroplanes jammed hard up. We now took a tremendous inclination to stern, our tail touching bottom at 300 ft. Four more very heavy explosions shook the boat and bright flashes were seen ... The boat was at an angle of about 45° and we were unable to correct this trim with the forward hydroplane, so I gave the order to blow No 5 and No 6 [ballast tanks]. The boat slowly commenced to rise ... on breaking surface, three destroyers opened a hot fire at us [from] about 1,500 yards, one shot striking the pressure hull just abaft the conning tower. Rifle grenades were fired and White Ensigns were waved and the destroyers ceased fire. Under very trying conditions, the crew behaved in an exemplary manner..."

	Group 1	Group 2	Group 3
Length (ft)	231 oa	238.5 oa	235 oa
Beam (ft)	23.8	23.5	23.5
Displacement (tons)			
Surface	891	895	960
Submerged	1,074	1,089	1,150
Speed (kts)			
Surfaced	17.3	17.0	17.5
Dived	10.5	10.5	10.5
Maximum diving depth (ft)	150*	150	150
Armament	6x18" tubes	4x21" bow tubes	6x21" bow tubes
	(4 bow, 2 beam)	2x18" beam tubes	6 reloads
		Minelayers: 16 mines	
	1x3" AA gun, replaced by 4" gun	1x4" gun**	2x4" gun on bridge†
Engines	2x12 cylinder solid injection 2,400 hp diesels	2x12 cylinder solid injection 2,400 hp diesels	2x1,920 hp diesel
	2 x 1,600 hp electric motors	2 x 1,600 hp electric motors	2x1,150 hp electric
	1 x 20 hp auxiliary motor for slow running	1 x 20 hp auxiliary motor for slow running	twin screws
	twin screws	twin screws	
Range			
Surface	2,800 nm at 10 kts	2,800 nm at 10 kts	2,800 nm at 10 kts
Submerged			
Diving depth	150 ft*	150 ft	150 ft
Complement	35	38	44

* L 2 reached 300 ft during an uncontrolled dive.

** L 11 had no deck gun.

L 17 carried 14 mines of a more efficient type.

† Afr 4" gun removed in 1925-6 and replaced with Type UBC Asdic dome.

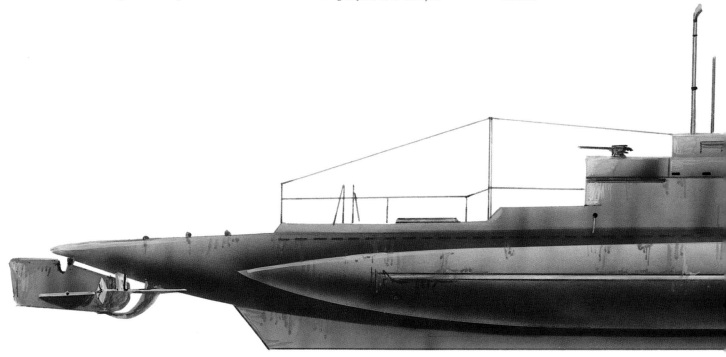

These sturdy, well built boats carried on through the 1920s, some placed in reserve at home and in Hong Kong. *L 4* rescued the SS *Irene* and her crew from pirate attack, after opening fire with her deck gun, off Hong Kong, in 1927. Two of the uncompleted 'L' class were built by Armstrong Whitworth for the Yugoslav navy as *Harabi* and *Nebojsa* in 1927.

Most British 'L' boats were sold for scrap during the 1930s, but three mounted operational patrols in 1940 before leaving the frontline for the training role. In February, 1940, *L 23* was depth charged by two German destroyers but escaped through a "lucky escape of oil," which fooled the German ships into believing she was destroyed. By 1944, at least two were in Canada for anti-

Above: Group Two *L20* was commissioned too late to take part in hostilities and saw service in the Far East.

submarine warfare training for convoy escorts. The last of the class, *L 23* and *L 26* were scrapped in 1946 after long and distinguished service.

Below: Group 3 'L class' with two 4" guns on bridge before fitting of Type U3C Asdic dome in aft position in 1925-6.

British 'L' class overseas patrol submarine

Boat	Builder	Laid down	Commissioned	Fate
Group 1				
L 1 (ex-E 57)	Vickers, Barrow	18-05-1916	10-11-1917	1919, sailed Hong Kong. 1923, Reserve Flotilla, Hong Kong. Sold 03-1930. Scrapped Newport.
L 2 (ex-E 58)	Vickers, Barrow	18-05-1916	18-12-1917	1919, sailed Hong Kong. 1923 Reserve Flotilla, Hong Kong. Sold 03-1930.
L 3	Vickers, Barrow	21-06-1916	31-01-1918	1923, Reserve Flotilla, Hong Kong. Sold 02-1931. Broken up, Charlestown.
L 4	Vickers, Barrow	21-06-1916	26-12-1918	Rescued SS *Irene* from pirates off Hong Kong, 20-10-1927. Sold 24-02-1934. Broken up, Charlestown.
L 5	Swan Hunter, Wallsend	23-08-1916	15-05-1918	Sold 1931. Broken up: Charlestown.
L 6	William Beardmore, Dalmuir	10-1916	03-07-1918	Sold 01-1935, Newport.
L 7	Cammell Laird, Birkenhead	05-1916	12-1917	Sold 26-02-1930, Blyth.
L 8	Cammell Laird, Birkenhead	28-05-1916	12-03-1918	1919, sailed Hong Kong. 1923, Reserve Flotilla, Hong Kong. Sold 07-10-1930. Scrapped Newport.
Group 2				
L 9	William Denny, Dumbarton	10-1916	27-05-1918	Sank, Hong Kong harbour, in typhoon, 18-08-1923. Salved, 06-09-1923, re-commissioned. Sold 30-06-1927, Hong Kong.
L 10	William Denny, Dumbarton	26-02-1917	04-06-1918	Sunk by gunfire from German destroyer *S 33* which had been torpedoed by *L 10*, 04-10-1918. No survivors.
L 11	Vickers, Barrow	17-01-1917	27-06-1918	Sold 02-1932.
L 12	Vickers, Barrow	22-01-1917	30-06-1918	In collision with *H 47* off Milford Haven, Wales, 09-07-1929. Boat resurfaced and returned to Milford Haven. Three crew died. Sold 16-02-1932, Newport.
L 13	-	-	-	Not ordered.
L 14	Vickers, Barrow	19-01-1917	N/K	Sold 05-1934, Newport.
L 15	Fairfield, Govan, Clyde	16-11-1916	N/K	Sold 02-1932, Newport.
L 16	Fairfield, Govan, Clyde	21-11-1916	N/K	Sold 02-1934, Granton.
L 17	Vickers, Barrow	24-01-1917	N/K	Sold 02-1934, Pembroke Dock.
L 18	Vickers, Barrow	22-06-1917	N/K	Sold 10-1936, Pembroke Dock.
L 19	Vickers, Barrow	18-07-1917	N/K	Sold 12-04-1937, Pembroke Dock.
L 20	Vickers, Barrow	26-07-1917	28-01-1919	1919, sailed Hong Kong. 1923, Reserve Flotilla, Hong Kong. Sold 07-01-1935, Newport.
L 21	Vickers, Barrow	15-09-1917	N/K	Sold 02-1939. Stranded on way to breakers.
L 22	Vickers, Barrow	28-11-1917	N/K	Sold 30-08-1935, Newport.
L 23	Vickers, Barrow. Completed by HM Dockyard, Chatham	29-08-1917	N/K	1919 Sank *en route* to shipbreakers in Nova Scotia, 05-1946.
L 24	Vickers, Barrow	13-02-1919	N/K	Sank following collision with battleship HMS *Resolution*, off Portland Bill, English Channel, 10-01-1924. Crew lost.
L 25	Vickers, Barrow	25-02-1918	N/K	Sold 1935, Newport.
L 26	Vickers, Barrow. Completed by HM Dockyard, Portsmouth	31-01-1917	N/K	1919 Damaged, Mediterranean, 03-1929 but repaired at Gibraltar. Training submarine, 1940-42. Anti-submarine training, Canada, 1944. Scrapped, Canada, 1946.
L 27	Vickers, Barrow. Completed by HM Dockyard, Sheerness.	30-01-1918	N/K	Training boat, Portsmouth, end World War II. Broken up, Canada, 1944.
L 28	-	-	-	Cancelled.
L 29	-	-	-	Cancelled.
L 30	-	-	-	Cancelled.
L 31	-	-	-	Cancelled.
L 32	Vickers, Barrow	-	-	Incomplete hull sold for scrap, 01-03-1920.
L 33	Swan Hunter, Wallsend	26-09-1917	N/K	Sold 02-1932, Sunderland.
L 34	-	-	-	Cancelled.
L 35	HM Dockyard, Pembroke Dock	-	-	Cancelled.
L 36	-	-	-	Cancelled.
L 37 - L 49	-	-	-	Not ordered.
L 50	Cammell Laird, Birkenhead	-	-	Cancelled.
L 51	Cammell Laird, Birkenhead	-	-	Cancelled.
Group 3				
L 52	Armstrong Whitworth, Newcastle-upon-Tyne.	16-5-1917	N/K	Sold for scrap 09-1935. Wrecked off Barry, South Wales.
L 53	ArmstrongWhitworth, Newcastle-upon-Tyne. Completed HM Dockyard, Chatham	19-06-1917	N/K	Sold 23-01-1939.
L 54	William Denny, Dumbarton. Completed at HM Dockyard, Devonport	14-5-1917	N/K	Sold 02-02-1939, Pembroke Dock.
L 55	Fairfield, Govan, Clyde	21-09-1917	19-12-1918	Sank by gunfire from Bolshevik destroyers *Gavril* and *Azard*, Caporsky Bay, Gulf of Finland, 09-06-1919. Salved, 1928, and re-commissioned as Soviet boat, 07-08-1931, used for training up to World War II.
L 56	Fairfield, Govan, Clyde	16-10-1917	14-08-1918	Sold 25-03-1938.
L 57	Fairfield, Govan, Clyde	-	-	Cancelled.
L 58	Fairfield, Govan, Clyde	-	-	Cancelled.
L 59	William Beardmore, Dalmuir	-	-	Cancelled.
L 60	Cammell Laird, Birkenhead	-	-	Cancelled.
L 61	Cammell Laird, Birkenhead	-	-	Cancelled.
L 62	Fairfield, Govan, Clyde	-	-	Cancelled.
L 63	Scotts, Greenock	-	-	Cancelled.
L 64	Scotts, Greenock	-	-	Cancelled.
L 65	Swan Hunter, Wallsend	-	-	Cancelled.
L 66	Swan Hunter, Wallsend	-	-	Cancelled.
L 67	Armstrong Whitworth, Newcastle-upon-Tyne	N/K	N/K	Completed as *Harabi* for Yugoslavia, 1927.* Captured by Italian forces in World War II. Fate unknown.
L 68	Armstrong Whitworth, Newcastle-upon-Tyne	N/K	N/K	Completed as *Nebojsa* for Yugoslavia, 1927.* Captured by Italian forces in World War II. Fate unknown.
L 69	William Beardmore, Dalmuir. Completed at HM Dockyard, Rosyth	07-07-1917	N/K	Sold 02-1939.
L 70	William Beardmore, Dalmuir	-	-	Cancelled.
L 71	Scotts, Greenock	29-08-1917	23-12-1919	Sold 25-03-1938. Milford Haven.
L 72	Scotts, Greenock	-	-	Cancelled.
L 73	William Denny, Dumbarton	-	-	Cancelled.
L 74	William Denny, Dumbarton	-	-	Cancelled.
L 75	William Denny, Dumbarton	-	-	Cancelled.

* NAMES MEAN 'GALLANT' AND 'DREADNOUGHT' *HARABI* CARRIED A SECOND GUN ON CONNING TOWER.

US 'O' class ocean-going submarines 1917-1918

Drawing on lessons from the earlier US 'L' class, the US Navy's 'O' class were more robust boats, with greater power and endurance for ocean patrols. Although enjoying much quicker building rates, the entire class was commissioned in 1918, Group Two boats just before or after the end of the First World War. Eight of the first group were recommissioned for service in the training role in 1941 and served up to the end of the Second World War.

The earlier boats operated off the USA's East coast on anti-U boat patrols after commissioning. *O4* and *O6* came under fire from a British merchantman in the Atlantic on July 24, 1918, the steamer scoring six hits on *O4's* conning tower and pressure hull before her identity was discovered. Fortunately the boat did not sustain substantial damage, as most was caused by shell splinters. *O3* to *O10* were part of a 20-strong US submarine force that left Newport, Rhode Island on November 2 1918, for the Azores but were recalled after the Armistice was signed, nine days later.

The second group ran into problems, particularly concerning electrical circuits, immediately after commissioning: *O11* went into Philadelphia Navy Yard for a five month overhaul only a few months after entering service. Even before commissioning, *O13* rammed and sunk the patrol boat Mary Alice during submerged trials off Long Island. *O15* also underwent a refit and then went straight into reserve, before service at Coco Solo, in the Panama Canal Zone, which also involved a further overhaul. *O16* also went into dry dock fifteen months after commissioning, later suffering a major fire in the conning tower in December 1919. It is hardly surprising that the Group Two boats all decommissioned in June 1924 and were scrapped (save *O12*), in July 1930, under the terms of the London Naval Treaty. *O12* was demilitarised and used by Sir Hubert Wilkins' Arctic expedition, renamed Nautilus. After being returned to the US Navy, she was sunk in November 1931 in a Norwegian fjord.

Above: Serving mainly during the inter-war years many vessels were brought back into service for training purposes in the 1930s.

The first group rendered more satisfactory service although *O5* was rammed by a cargo ship near the Panama Canal in October 23, sinking almost immediately with the loss of three crew. The remainder were recommissioned in the first four months of 1941 for training submarine crews, based at New London, Connecticut. Unfortunately, in June 1941, *O9* sank in more than 400 feet of water, 15 miles off Portsmouth, New England, during deep submergence trials. Thirty-three crew were lost.

	Group One	Group Two
Length (ft)	172.33	175
Beam (ft)	18.0	16.6
Displacement (tons)		
Surface	520.6	491
Submerged	625	565
Speed (kts)		
Surfaced	14	14
Dived	10	11
Armament	4x18" tubes	4x18" tubes
	4 reloads	4 reloads
	1x3" AA gun	1x3" AA gun
Engines	2x850hp	2x800hp
	Niesco diesel	Busch Sulzer diesel
	2x?600 hp electric	2x?600 hp electric
Range		
Surface	5,000 nm at 11 kts	5,000 nm at 11 kts
Submerged	250 nm at 5 kts	250 nm at 5 kts
Maximum diving depth(ft)	150	150
Complement	29	29

US 'O' class ocean-going submarines

Boat	Builder	Laid down	Commissioned	Fate
Group One				
O-1 (SS-62)	Portsmouth Navy Yard, Portsmouth, New Hampshire	26-03-1917	05-11-1918	Decommissioned, New London, Connecticut, 11-06-1931. Stricken 18-05-1938. Scrapped.
O-2 (SS-63)	Puget Sound Navy Yard, Washington	27-07-1917	19-10-1918	Decommissioned, New London, Connecticut 26-07-1945. Sold 16-11-1945
O-3 (SS-64)	Fore River Shipbuilding, Quincy, Massachusetts	02-12-1916	13-06-1918	Decommissioned, Portsmouth, New Hampshire, 11-09-1945. Sold 04-09-1946
O-4 (SS-65)	Fore River Shipbuilding, Quincy, Massachusetts	04-12-1916	29-05-1918	Decommissioned, Portsmouth, New Hampshire, 20-09-1945. Scrapped 02-1946
O-5 (SS-66)	Fore River Shipbuilding, Quincy, Massachusetts	08-12-1916	08-06-1918	Sank after being rammed by steamer *Abangarez* off Panama, 28-10-1923. Three crew lost. Raised, sold for scrap 12-12-1924.
O-6 (SS-67)	Fore River Shipbuilding, Quincy, Massachusetts	06-12-1916	12-06-1918	Decommissioned at Portsmouth, New Hampshire, 11-09-1946. Scrapped, 1946.
O-7 (SS-68)	Fore River Shipbuilding, Quincy, Massachusetts	14-02-1917	04-07-1918	Decommissioned, New London, Connecticut, 02-07-1945. Sold 01-1946.
O-8 (SS-69)	Fore River Shipbuilding, Quincy, Massachusetts	27-02-1917	11-07-1918	Decommissioned, Portsmouth, New Hampshire, 11-09-1945. Sold 04-09-1946.
O-9 (SS-70)	Fore River Shipbuilding, Quincy, Massachusetts	15-02-1917	27-07-1918	Sank during deep-submergence trials, 15 miles off Portsmouth, New Hampshire, 20-06-1941. Crew lost.
O-10 (SS-71)	Fore River Shipbuilding, Quincy, Massachusetts	27-02-1917	17-08-1918	Decommissioned, Portsmouth, New Hampshire, 10-09-1945. Sold 21-08-1946.
Group Two				
O-11 (SS-72)	Lake Torpedo Boat Co., Bridgeport, Connecticut.	06-03-1916	19-10-1918	Decommissioned, Philadelphia, 21-06-1924. Sold 30-07-1930.
O-12 (SS-73)	Lake Torpedo Boat Co., Bridgeport, Connecticut.	06-03-1916	18-10-1918	Stricken 29-07-1930. As *Nautilus* deployed on Arctic expedition. Scuttled in Norwegian fjord 20-11-1931.
O-13 (SS-74)	Lake Torpedo Boat Co., Bridgeport, Connecticut.	06-03-1916	27-11-1918	Decommissioned, Philadelphia, 11-06-1924. Sold 30-07-1930.
O-14 (SS-75)	California Shipbuilding, Long Beach, California	06-07-1916	01-10-1918	Decommissioned, Philadelphia, 17-06-1924. Scrapped 30-07-1930
O-15 (SS-76)	California Shipbuilding, Long Beach, California	21-09-1916	27-08-1918	Decommissioned, Philadelphia, 11-06-1924. Scrapped 30-07-1930
O-16 (SS-77)	California Shipbuilding, Long Beach, California	07-10-1916	01-08-1918	Decommissioned, Philadelphia, 21-06-1924. Scrapped 30-07-1930

British 'R' class - U Boat hunter/killers, 1917-1919

Mainly due to the crisis caused by merchant ship losses to U Boats in 1917, this class was conceived as anti-submarine boats and nicknamed "the Little Arthurs." With small engines for surface propulsion, but with two large electric motors, the spindled-hull class was designed to have higher speeds when dived than on the surface - for submerged pursuit of targets. With their main emphasis on underwater performance, the 'R' class were the ancestors of today's nuclear hunter-killer submarines.

The streamlined hull, for the 15 kt designed dived speed, and internal ballast tanks, to assist quick diving, only allowed space for one propeller shaft. Large rudder and hydroplane areas were also aids to quick diving, once

an enemy submarine had been spotted. The class had 23.5% reserve buoyancy - a considerable improvement on the 16.6% of the 'H' class. Some were equipped with five powerful hydrophones for tracking hostile boats. One report commented: "They could approach an enemy and obtain her position without using the periscope."

But the small diesel engine was inadequate to charge the boats' batteries. This had to be done alongside in harbour - taking a full day. On the surface, the class also proved difficult to manoeuvre, rolling badly in beam seas. Additions to the casing of the only boat to continue into the early 1930s - R 4 - produced slight sea-keeping improvements but reduced dived speeds to 13 kts.

The 'R' class came too late in the First World War to

influence the war against the U boats. Six were in service by the close of hostilities, based at Blyth, in Northeast England, and Killybegs, Donegal, now the Irish Republic. Only R 7 is recorded as making an attack, in which it fired a salvo of six torpedoes from its bow tubes - and every one missed. The target U boat disappeared after a merchant ship approached. R 4 continued with the 6th Submarine Flotilla at Portland, Dorset, where, because of her poor surface steering, she was nicknamed 'the slug.'

Length (ft)	163.75 oa
Beam (ft)	15.54 oa
Displacement (tons)	
Surfaced	420
Submerged	503
Speed (kts)	
Surfaced	9.5
Dived	15 (design) 14.25 (service)
Armament	6x18" tubes (bow) 6 reloads
Engines	2x240 hp diesel
	2 x 1,200 hp electric
	25 hp auxiliary
	1 screw
Range	
Surface	2,000 nm at 9 kts
Submerged	15 nm at 15 kts
Diving depth	150 ft
Complement	22

British 'R' class anti-U Boat submarine

Boat	Builder	Laid down	Commissioned	Fate
R 1	HM Dockyard, Chatham	04-02-1917	14-10-1918	Sold 20-01-1923.
R 2	HM Dockyard, Chatham	04-02-1917	20-12-1918	Sold 21-02-1923.
R 3	HM Dockyard, Chatham	04-02-1917	17-03-1919	Paid off 09-1919. Sold 21-02-1923.
R 4	HM Dockyard, Chatham	04-02-1917	23-08-1919	Sold 26-05-1934, Sunderland.
R 5	HM Dockyard, Pembroke Dock	03-1918	-	Cancelled 28-08-1919.
R 6	HM Dockyard, Pembroke Dock	03-1918	-	Cancelled 28-08-1919.
R 7	Vickers, Barrow	11-1917	29-06-1918	Sold 21-02-1923.
R 8	Vickers, Barrow	11-1917	26-07-1918	Sold 21-02-1923.
R 9	Armstrong Whitworth, Newcastle-upon-Tyne .	12-1917	14-10-1918	Sold 21-02-1923
R 10	Armstrong Whitworth, Newcastle-upon-Tyne	07-12-1917	12-04-1918	Sold 19-02-1929, Newport.
R 11	Cammell Laird, Birkenhead	12-1917	08-08-1918	Sold 21-02-1023.
R 12	Cammell Laird, Birkenhead	12-1917	29-10-1918	Sold 21-02-1923.

Below: The 'R' class came too late to have an impact on the war against U Boats and suffered from poor sea keeping.

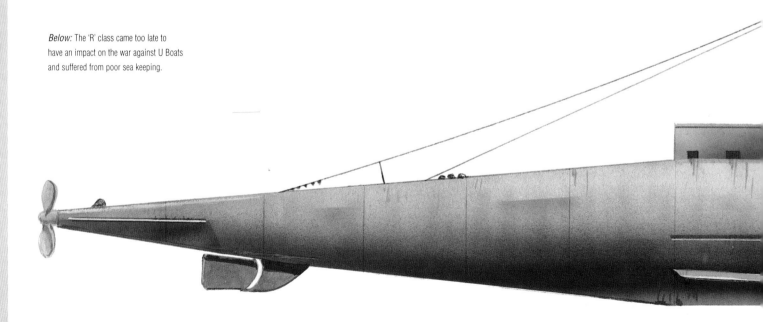

Above: The 'R' class with clean lines and tall conning tower, were designed for submerged persuit of U Boats.

The 'Kalamity Ks' and the 'Battle of May Island'

The disastrous British 'K' class was born out of the Admiralty dream of a submarine fast enough to accompany the main battle fleet on operations. Following the loss of the battleship *Formidable*, torpedoed by *U24* off Portland on January 1 1915, the Director of Naval Construction was ordered to design a submarine capable of at least 20 kts surface speed - fast enough to keep pace with heavy armoured units.

After much design work, steam power was fatefully chosen to fulfil the requirement even though the only British experiment in this area, *Swordfish* (S1) had proved a disappointment. The class was to prove successful at high speeds: *K13* achieved 23.5 kts during sea trials in January 1917 - but the design proved costly in men and submarines. It took an average five minutes to shut down the boilers, evacuate the boiler room and shut down the ventilators before a boat could dive: the fastest was 3 minutes and 25 seconds recorded by *K8*. Several times, seas shipped down the funnels, putting out the boilers, and left boats temporarily helpless.

Approval was given to build the first eight 'K' class later in January 1915 at a cost of £300,000 per boat with a further 10 ordered in May. The design was doomed from the start: with 12 hatches and hundreds of valves, its

	Group One	Group Two
Length (ft)	338 oa	351.5 oa
Beam (ft)	26.7	28
Displacement (tons)		
Surfaced	1,980	2,140
Submerged	2,566	2,770
Speed (kts)		
Surfaced	24	23.5
Dived	9	9
Armament	8x18" tubes, (4 bow, 4 beam)	4x21" tubes bow, 4x18" tubes beam
	1 or 2 4" gun 1 x3" AA gun*	3x4" gun
	1 depth charge thrower in some	
Engines	2x5,250 hp geared steam turbines	2x5,250 hp geared steam turbines
	800 hp auxiliary diesel	800 hp auxiliary diesel
	4x,350 hp electric motor	4x,350 hp electric motor
	twin shafts	twin shafts
Range		
Surfaced	800 nm at full power. 12,500 nm at 10 kts.	800 nm at full power. 12,500 nm at 10 kts.
Submerged	30 nm at 4 kts	30 nm at 4 kts
Complement	59	65

* Two guns forward, below and abaft conning tower were removed after bows modified. *K 17* had a 5.5-inch gun at the time of her loss. Two torpedo tubes in the superstructure were also removed and the number of torpedoes carried reduced to 16. Removed guns used to fit British 'Q' ships.

1	Improved bow for better seakeeping	11	main control centre	21	Boilers
2	Torpedo room	12	Batteries	22	Fuel
3	Spare torpedoes	13	Compensating tank	23	Pressure hull
4	Crew space	14	Keel	24	Turbine
5	Telescopic wireless aerials	15	Outer Hull	25	Gearbox
6	Crane	16	4 inch gun	26	Main motors
7	Main tanks	17	Mount	27	Diesel
8	Bridge	18	Telescopic funnel	28	Stores
9	Upper control centre	19	Upper valves to close over funnel openings	29	Rudder
10	Wireless room	20	Valves to close over funnel openings to hull	30	Propellors

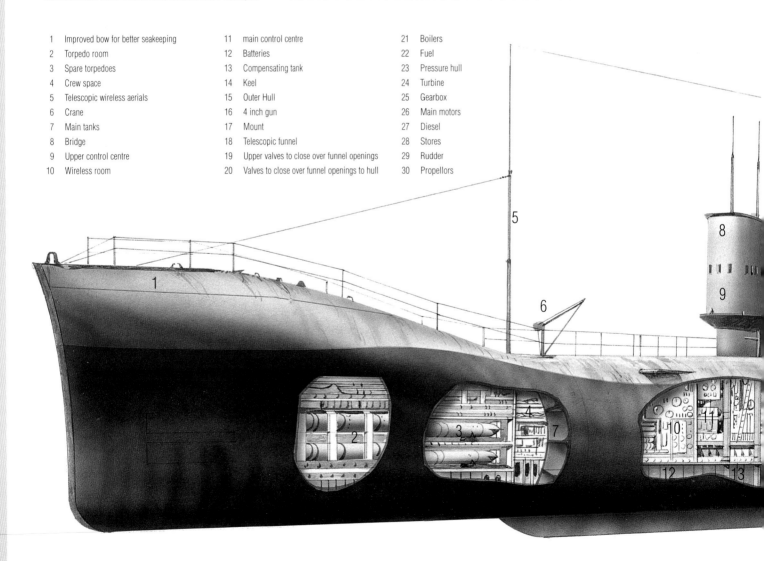

Above: K26 was one of the class to
have three 4" guns fitted.

watertight integrity was always in question. The hull, with
flush level bows, encouraged 'K' boats to trim by the
head and dive "on their own." Therefore, the bows were
raised by converting them into a bulbous swan shape - the
first modified being *K6*. This was none too soon: first of
class *K3* went into an uncontrollable dive with the future
King George VI on board as a guest, plunging to 150 ft
with the stern and propellers racing raised above the
waves. It took an anxious 20 minutes to free the
submarine bows from the sea-bed mud and surface
successfully. *K13* behaved in a similar manner during

final diving trials in the Gareloch, and became trapped on
the bottom. It took more than 48 hours to cut holes in her
hull to free the 67 trapped within, 31 already having
drowned. The boat was salved and a superstitious
Admiralty commissioned her as *K22*.

It always was an unlucky class but it was in fulfilment
of the design role that the worst was to occur. A taste of
what was to come befell *K1* of the 12th Submarine
Flotilla, operating with the light cruiser *Blonde* off the
Danish coast in November 1917. *Blonde* was forced to
turn sharply to port to avoid three units from the 4th Light

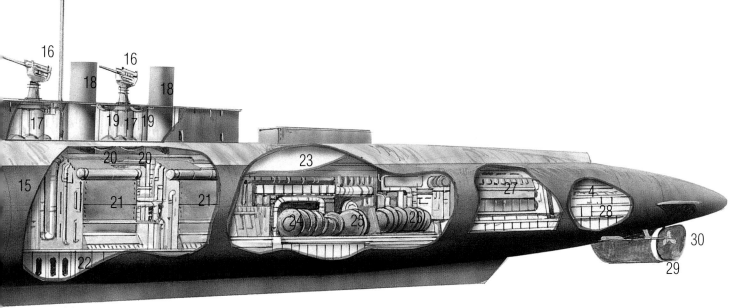

The 'Kalamity Ks' and the 'Battle of May Island'

British 'K' class ocean-going submarine

Boat	Builder	Laid Down	Commissioned	Fate
Group One				
K 1	HM Dockyard, Portsmouth	13-11-1915	05-1917	Sunk by 4" gunfire by British light cruiser *Blonde* after collision with *K 4*, off Danish coast, 18-11-1917. Crew rescued.
K 2	HM Dockyard, Portsmouth	13-11-1915	02-1917	Explosion and fire during first diving trials at Portsmouth, 01-1917. In collision with *K 12* while leaving Portland for fleet exercises, 11-01-1924. Collided with *H 29* during exercises, 07-11-1924. Sold 13-07-1926, Newport.
K 3	Vickers, Barrow	21-05-1915	04-08-1916	12-1916: Suddenly dived in 150 ft of water, Stokes Bay, Gosport, burying bows in sea-bed mud. Surfaced successfully. 09-01-1917: Shipped a sea down both funnels, flooding boiler-room, North Sea. Uncontrolled dive to 266 ft, crushing parts of hull. 02-05-1918. Sold 26-10-1921, London.
K 4	Vickers, Barrow	28-06-1915	01-01-1917	17-11-1917: Collided with *K 1* off Danish coast. 31-01-1918: *K 6* collided with *K 4*, almost slicing her in half, off May Island, Firth of Forth. Sank with no survivors.
K 5	HM Dockyard, Portsmouth	13-11-1915	19-05-1917	06-1920: Uncontrolled dive in Firth of Forth, with bows buried in mud. Surfaced successfully. 07-1920: in collision with obsolete destroyer under tow. Sank during exercise dive, Tor Bay, off Torquay. 20-01-1921. All crew lost.
K 6	HM Dockyard, Devonport	08-11-1915	05-1917	1917: Refused to surface during submerged trial in North Dockyard, Devonport. 31-01-1918: In collision with *K 4*, sinking her, off May Island, Firth of Forth. Sold, 13-07-1926, Newport.
K 7	HM Dockyard, Devonport	08-11-1915	07-1917	Sold 09-09-1921, Sunderland.
K 8	Vickers, Barrow	28-06-1915	06-03-1917	Sold, 11-10-1923.
K 9	Vickers, Barrow	28-06-1915	09-05-1917	1921: Placed in reserve. Sold, 23-07-1926. Charlestown.
K 10	Vickers, Barrow	28-06-1915	26-06-1917	Sold, 04-11-1921. Foundered in tow, 10-01-1922.
K 11	Armstrong Whitworth, Newcastle-upon-Tyne	10-1915	02-1917	1917: Fire, forcing boat to surface during North Sea patrol. Destroyer took her under tow. Sold, 04-11-1921.
K 12	Armstrong Whitworth, Newcastle-upon-Tyne	10-1915	08-1917	11-01-1924: In collision with *K 2* while leaving Portland; hole in forward casing. Scrapped 1926, Charlestown.
K 13	Fairfield, Govan, Clyde	21-05-1915		During final dive trial in Gareloch, 29-01-1917, boiler room flooded and boat would not surface. After more than 48 hours, 67 were rescued by cutting hole through hull. 31 died. Salved 15-03-1917, and recommissioned as *K 22*.
K 14	Fairfield, Govan, Clyde	11-1915	22-05-1917	In collision with *K 22*, off May Island, Firth of Forth, damaging bows. Two men lost. 31-01-1918. Sold 16-02-1926, Granton.
K 15	Scotts, Greenock.	19-04-1916	30-04-1918	Sank alongside light cruiser *Canterbury*, Portsmouth Harbour, 25-06-1921. Salved 07-1921 Sold 08-1924, Upnor.
K 16	William Beardmore, Dalmuir	06-1916	13-04-1918	Sudden dive in Garloch after failure of hydroplanes. Successfully surfaced. Paid off, 12-12-1920. Sold 22-08-1924. Resold, 09-1924, Charlestown.
K 17	Vickers, Barrow	05-1916	20-09-1917	Sank in collision with light cruiser *Fearless*, off May Island, Firth of Firth. 48 crew lost. 31-01-1918
K 18	Vickers, Barrow	13-07-1916	-	Became submarine monitor *M 1*
K-19	Vickers, Barrow	13-07-1916	-	Became submarine monitor *M 2*
K 20	Armstrong Whitworth, Newcastle-upon-Tyne	04-12-1916	-	Became submarine monitor *M 3*
K 21	Armstrong Whitworth, Newcastle-upon-Tyne	N/K Laid down as *M 4*.		Cancelled. Sold as incomplete hull, 30-11-1921.
K 22 (ex-K 13)	Fairfield, Govan, Clyde, refitted as *K 22*	21-05-1915	18-10-1917	Rammed by battle cruiser *Inflexible* off May Island, 31-01-1918. Returned safely to Rosyth. Sold 16-12-1926, Sunderland. Scrapped 1926
K 23	Armstrong Whitworth, Newcastle-upon-Tyne	-	-	Cancelled
K 24	Armstrong Whitworth, Newcastle-upon-Tyne	-	-	Cancelled
K 25	Armstrong Whitworth, Newcastle-upon-Tyne	-	-	Cancelled
Group Two				
K 26	Vickers, Barrow and HM Dockyard, Chatham	06-1918	28-06-1923	Scrapped 03-1931, Malta.*
K 27	Vickers, Barrow	-	-	Cancelled
K 28	Vickers, Barrow	-	-	Cancelled.

* Her Asdic Type 118 was fitted in *L 26* in 11-1931.

Right: K7, with the bulbous swan bows, retrofitted in an attempt to avoid unexpected and unwelcome dives by the boats.

Below: K22 started service as *K13* but 31 died after she failed to surface in a diving trial. Raised and recommissioned as *K22* she was rammed by the battlecruiser *Inflexible* in the 'Battle of May Island'.

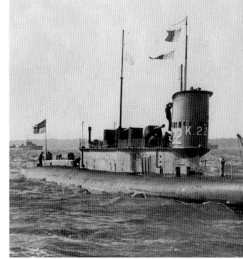

Cruiser Squadron crossing her bows. Astern, were *K1, K3, K4, and K7* and in the confusion that followed the change of course, *K4* rammed *K1* by the conning tower. *K1* was beginning to founder and after her crew was rescued, she was sunk by gunfire from *Blonde.*

The so-called 'Battle of May Island' was to demonstrate the idiocy of steam-powered submarines operating with the battle fleet. On January 31 1918, OPERATION EC1 was mounted, an exercise involving the main fleet's battle squadrons from Scapa Flow and Rosyth. The 13th Submarine Flotillla, led by the light cruiser *Ithuriel*, comprised *K11, K17, K14, K12* and *K22*.

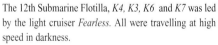

The 12th Submarine Flotilla, *K4, K3, K6* and *K7* was led by the light cruiser *Fearless*. All were travelling at high speed in darkness.

First into trouble, off May Island in the Firth of Forth, was the 13th Submarine Flotilla which unexpectedly met some minesweeping trawlers. *K14*'s steering jammed and *K11* and *K17* took avoiding action. *K22*, following astern, rammed *K14* behind the forward torpedo compartment. Two men were lost. Twenty-seven minutes later, the 20,000 ton battle cruiser *Inflexible*, last in line of the battle squadron, sliced into *K22*'s bows while she was still dead in the water. Fortunately, she remained afloat.

The 12th Submarine Flotilla, with *Fearless* were still steaming at full speed, met the survivors of the 13th flotilla crossing their course, seeking men in the water from the earlier collisions. *Fearless* rammed the third in line, *K17*, forward of the conning tower, badly damaging her bows. The boat sank in just eight minutes, killing 48 crew. Astern of *Fearless, K4* heard her warning siren, stopped engines and narrowly avoided a collision with *K3. K6* hit *K4,* practically cutting her in half and badly damaging herself. *K7*'s bows ran over the sinking *K4* whose crew were all lost.

The result of just 75 minutes of exercises with the main

Above: K22 demonstrates folding her funnels, necessary before diving.

battle fleet, was two submarines lost, three badly damaged and the loss of 105 men.

The perils of exercising with heavy units were again learnt in 1924, when *K2* collided with *K12* as they departed Portland Harbour in the early hours for operations with the Atlantic Fleet. *K2* smashed a hole in the forward casing of her sister boat and buckled her bows for about six feet.

'Q' Ships and Sea Lions: the Battle for Sea Control in the First World War

Above: The crew of HM Submarine H24 pose in German uniforms during the filming of a feature film about Q Ships in 1927.

The German High Seas Fleet had 20 operational U Boats in the North Sea, spread out along a thin defensive line, as war was declared between Britain and Germany on August 4 1914. Britain's more numerous submarine force was concentrated for local defence of the English Channel and East coast ports[1] with seven 'C' class at Dover, six each at Sheerness and on the Humber and 12 'Cs' at Leith. Ten 'E' class were at Harwich, together with four 'D' class. Ageing and obsolete 'A' and 'B' class boats were at Adrossan, Devonport and Malta. By the time hostilities were over, on November 11 1918, both services were to suffer appalling casualties.

The submarine would also have been firmly established as a potent and formidable weapon of war. Its strategic value would be demonstrated by the U boat war against shipping and by the British submarine campaigns in the Baltic and the Dardanelles.

Britain was to be brought almost to her knees, strangled by the U-boat onslaught of 1917 which saw 3,660,000 tons of her shipping sunk in that single year, out of total merchant shipping losses of more than six million tons. More than 6,500 lives, out of a total of 14,721 British merchant navy killed, were lost in 1917 alone.

Of the 12,618,283 tons of merchant shipping lost in the First World War, some 11,135,460 were sunk by U boat, 88% of the total.[2] The most successful U Boat skipper (indeed, the most successful of all time) was Kapitan Lothar von Arnauld de la Periere (1886-1941) who sank 194 ships, totalling 454,000 tons, using his 88 mm deck gun and just four torpedoes. Important tactical lessons were learnt that were to be used effectively by the German Navy in the Second World War.

The Allies lost 39 large surface combatants (destroyer and above) to submarine action, including nine battleships (UK five, France three and Italy one) and seven cruisers (six UK, one Italian).

First victory was to the Royal Navy when the 'Chatham' class cruiser *Birmingham,* 5,440 tons, rammed and sank *U15* with all hands off Fair Isle, between the Orkney and Shetland Islands, on August 9. First blood for the German boats came on September 5 1914, with *U21*'s torpedoing of the 3,000 ton British light cruiser *Pathfinder,* on September 5, near St. Abb's Head, off the Firth of Forth. Eighteen days later, the elderly 12,000 ton cruisers *Aboukir, Hogue and Cressy* were torpedoed and sunk by *U9* in just 75 minutes off the Hook of Holland, with the loss of 1,460 British sailors. Under a month later, on October 20, *U17* sank the first merchant ship in wartime, with the British *Glitra,* 866 tons, sent to the bottom with her crew in lifeboats, off southern Norway.

On February 4 1915, the German Navy declared the waters around the British Isles a war zone, warning that from February 18 "every enemy merchant ship found within… will be destroyed without it always being possible to avoid danger to the crews and passengers."

Neutral shipping was also warned and was the first to suffer. The Norwegian ship *Belridge* was torpedoed without warning, on February 19, by *U16* in the English Channel. The neutral Dutch *Medea* was sunk on March 25, after being stopped and searched and on May 1, the American *Gulf-Light* was torpedoed without warning by *U30* off the Scilly Isles. Six days later came the loss of the *Lusitania,* 30,000 tons, with one shot from *U20.* The death toll was 1,198.

In the 12 months up to and including December 1915, nearly 900,000 tons of British shipping had been destroyed, including 94 ships lost to mines laid by German 'UC' class boats of the Flanders Flotilla, based at the captured Belgian ports of Bruges and Zeebrugge.

For the Royal Navy, the signs and portents were grim. Although the tally of sunk U Boats was rising, the efficient German war machine was building them at an ever-increasing rate: 52 were built in 1915 alone with 19 U boats sunk; in 1916, 108 were built against 22 sunk. The Admiralty was losing the numbers game.

It resorted to new tactics to lure U boat into traps. Submerged 'C' and 'E' class boats were towed by decoy trawlers and when a German submarine launched a surface attack on the vessel, the tow was slipped and the British boat would torpedo it. The tactic was initially successful: *C24* sank *U40,* on June 23, 1915 and *C 27, U23* less than a month later.

Disaster was to follow. On August 4, *C33* was mined during operations with the armed trawler *Malta* and on August 29, *C29* was lost when her trawler strayed into a minefield. The tactic was abandoned. New techniques and equipment had to be evolved.

The 'Q' ship, or "Special Service Ship," was born. These were elderly surface vessels with guns hidden within dummy deckhouses, which would lure a U Boat into close range attack, and then open fire. A total of 193 old tramp steamers and innocent-looking schooners were pressed into service: only *Hyderabad,* launched August 27 1917, was designed and built as a 'Q' ship.

The first success came on July 24 1915, when *Prince Charles,* a 270 ton collier, sank *U36,* 10 nm WNW of North Rona in the Hebrides. Then the armed smack *Inverlyon,* 93 tons, sank *UB4,* off Great Yarmouth, in the North Sea, on August 11 1915. Fourteen U Boats were to be sunk by Q ships before the end of the war, and 60 damaged.

Four 'Q' ships sank two U boats each. *Farnborough* (Q5) sank *U68,* off the coast of Kerry, Ireland on March 22 1916, and *U83,* 67 miles W of the Fastnet on February 17 1917.

Privet (Q 19) sank *U85* 25 miles S by of Start Point on March 12 1917 (she sank after the action but was salvaged the following day) and, with *ML155, U34,* in the Gibraltar Straits on November 9 1918. *Baralong* accounted for *U27* off the Scilly Islands, on August 19

World War I submarine losses by cause

Cause	Australia	Austria	Britain	France	Germany	Italy	Russia	USA
Depth-charge	-	-	-	-	22	-	-	-
Gunfire	-	-	4	3	23	1	2	-
Ramming	-	1	-	1	20	-	-	-
Enemy mines	-	3	11	1	38	1	-	-
Own mines	-	-	2	-	10	-	-	-
Aircraft	-	-	1	1	6	-	-	-
Enemy submarine	-	1	5	3	19	2	-	-
Own torpedo	-	-	-	-	2	-	-	-
Scuttled	1	1	9	2	17	-	12	-
Interned	-	-	1	-	9	-	-	-
Wrecked	1	-	4	-	8	-	-	-
Accident	-	-	9	2	2	-	2	2
Other	-	2	3	-	8	2	-	-
Unknown	-	1	7	1	25	1	4	-
Surrendered	-	-	-	-	175	-	-	-
Captured	-	-	-	-	1	1	8	-
TOTAL	**2**	**9**	**56**	**14**	**385**	**8**	**28**	**2**

NOTE 'Other' column includes 'friendly fire' incidents. These are:-

Germany - 1; **Britain** - 3; **Italy** - 2

(*H 5,* mistakenly sunk by British submarine *H 1* off Cattaro, Adriatic, 15-04-1918 and *Alberto Guglielmotti,* sunk in error by a British destroyer off Sardinia, 03-1917)

| WORLD WAR I - TOTAL MERCHANT SHIPPING LOSSES | | | | | | | (Gross registered tonnage totals) |
| | ALLIED | | | | NEUTRAL | | |
	Britain/British Empire	USA*	Other Allied**	Total Allied	USA*	Other neutral	Total Neutral	TOTAL
1914	252,738	-	18,548	271,286	-	48,480	48,480	319,766
1915	885,471	-	213,067	1,098,538	16,154	197,424	213,578	1,312,116
1916	1,231,867	-	468,819	1,700,686	14,720	590,163	604,883	2,305,569
1917	3,660,054	148,424	986,419	4,794,897	17,538	1,265,687	1,283,225	6,078,122
1918	1,632,228	142,230	475,258	2,249,716	-	352,994	352,994	2,602,710
TOTAL	7,662,358	290,654	2,162,111	10,115,123	48,412	2,454,748	2,503,160	12,618,283

*The USA entered the war against Germany on April 6, 1917. Shipping losses are included in neutral columns before this date, and separately listed under Allied thereafter. Total US merchant shipping losses were 339,066 tons.

**Treaty of Brest-Litovsk on March 3, 1918 ended Russian participation in the war. Russian shipping losses thereafter are included in neutral losses.

1915, and *U41,* 90 miles W of Ushant on September 24 1915. Finally, *Penhurst* (Q7),[3] 1,191 tons, sank *UB19* 18 miles NW of the Casquets Lighthouse, on November 30 1916, and *UB37,* 20 miles off Cherbourg on January 14 1917. In turn, more than 20 were sunk by U boats.[4]

Some technical means had to be found to counter the U Boat threat. In July 1915, the Board of Invention and Research was set up by the Admiralty which investigated a host of different technologies and tactics. Seagulls were suggested as track detectors as were sea-lions - a forerunner of US and Russian methodologies to come in the 1970s with dolphins. Two unsuccessful experiments with sea lions were held in the Gareloch in Scotland on January 7 and May 17, 1917.

But in 1916, Asdic emerged as a powerful potential weapon for submarine detection. The system - the acronym stands for Anti-Submarine Detector Investigation Committee - was the forerunner of sonar. First experiments used passive hydrophones towed behind a ship to pick up submarine noise. The Asdic system was evolved using a sound wave or "ping" transmitted through the water that emitted an echo if it bounced off an underwater object. The echo's direction and the time it took to return indicated range, depth and bearing. First trials began with Asdic at Harwich, on June 5 1917 - too late to have any impact in the submarine war.[5] Hydrophones, however, detected the brave but unsuccessful attack, on October 28 1918 on the British Grand Fleet's base at Scapa Flow by *UB116*. The boat was mined.

Mines themselves were powerful anti-submarine weapons, accounting for 38 U Boats (See table). A new mine barrage at the eastern end of the English Channel, laid in the winter of 1917, barred this area to German submarines operating out of the Belgian ports and sunk 14 boats in 1917-18.

With bloody stalemate continuing on land, in February 1917, the German High Command decided on a policy of unrestricted submarine warfare, aimed at knocking Britain out of the war. New ocean-going U Boat cruisers, together with the converted cargo carriers, became operational in the Atlantic, particularly near the US eastern seaboard. With 100 U boats at sea, total merchant ships sinking rocketed to 540,000 tons that month, 593,840 in March and a peak of 881,000 in April 1917. In the latter month, 423 British ships were lost and on April 19 alone, 11 British merchant ships and eight fishing vessels were sunk. The Admiralty estimated that this scale of losses could not be sustained for more than five months without crippling Britain. The German policy was working.

Although the convoy system of protection had been used successfully by the Royal Navy in Napoleonic times, the lessons had been forgotten. With losses still mounting, the Admiralty tried the system as an experiment, with the first convoy departing Gibraltar for the UK on May 10 1917, with two 'Q' ships, *Mavis* and *Rule* as escorts. A week later, an Admiralty convoy committee was set up. On May 24, another experimental convoy sailed from Newport News in the USA under the protection of the old 10,850 ton cruiser *Roxburgh*.[6]

On June 17, the Admiralty approved plans for convoy protection, scraping together escorts from hard-pressed destroyer flotillas until a new class of sloop, the 39-strong 'Flower', 1,290 tons, hurriedly built between August 1917 and June 1918, eased the pressure.[7] The first purpose-built surface anti-submarine ships had arrived, equipped with two four-inch guns, or two 12 pounder AA guns and four depth charge throwers. The first regular protected convoy of merchant ships left Hampton Roads, Virginia on July 2 1917.

Thereafter, losses declined with 1918's total just 44%

of 1917's carnage. In 1917, 57 U boats were lost by enemy action, 65 in 1918. (Three, *UB20, UB32* and *UC36,* sank after bombing on the surface by British aircraft). The U Boat gamble had failed.

The last attack, albeit unsuccessful, mounted on a merchant ship was on *Sarpedon* on November 7. The Royal Navy's last ship to be sunk, the minesweeper, *Ascot,* 810 tons, was torpedoed by *UB67* off the Farne Islands on November 10.

At the end of the war, 210 U Boats had been lost in action, with nearly 5,000 crew killed. Still operational were 175 boats[8] and a further 224 were under construction. The operational boats surrendered, beginning at Harwich on November 19 1918, with five foundering *en route.* Under the Peace Treaty, Germany was forbidden to build or maintain merchant or naval submarines. The Allies had learnt a hard lesson.

1 THE MAIN FRENCH SUBMARINE FORCE WAS ALSO CONCENTRATED FOR LOCAL DEFENCE AT CHERBOURG.

2 THIS COMPARED WITH 8% SUNK BY MINE AND 4% SUNK BY SURFACE WARSHIP.

3 SUNK BY *U110* IN APPROACHES TO BRISTOL CHANNEL ON DECEMBER 24, 1917.

4 THE BRITISH SUBMARINE *J 6* WAS ACCIDENTALLY SUNK BY THE BARQUENTINE Q SHIP *CYMRIC* OFF BLYTH, OCTOBER 15, 1918. A TOTAL OF 38 Q SHIPS WERE LOST.

5 ANALYSIS OF THE SECOND ASDIC SEA TRIAL WAS IN JULY 1921.

6 *ROXBURGH* RAMMED AND SANK *U 89* OFF MALIN HEAD, N COAST OF IRELAND, FEBRUARY 12, 1918.

7 20 OF THIS CLASS WERE LOST DURING THE WAR, 12 SUNK BY U BOAT TORPEDO.

8 65UB COASTALS, 42 UC COASTAL MINELAYERS, EIGHT OCEAN CRUISERS, 60 OCEAN-GOING.

Below: Britain's XI, armed with two twin 5.2 inch guns, was designed to destroy all armed merchant ships.

INTER WAR SUBMARINE DESIGN

AFTER THE FIRST WORLD WAR SUBMARINE DESIGNERS PRODUCED BOATS

with greater endurance for long-range patrols, notably the German Type VIIB

and the British 'T' class which was to see service into the 1960s.

The major naval powers also toyed with 'big gun' commerce

raiding submarines, culminating in France's ill-fated *Surcouf*.

Russia's 'Dekabrist' class ocean going submarine

Length (ft)	251.2 oa
Beam (ft)	20.9 oa
Displacement (tons)	
Surfaced	940
Submerged	1,240
Speed (kts)	
Surfaced	15.3
Dived	8.7
Armament	6x21" bow tubes, 2x21" stern tube
	5 reloads
	1x4-inch B-2 deck gun. 120 rounds
	1x45 mm 21K AA gun 500 rounds
Engines	MAN 1100 hp diesel (in *D-1, D-2*)
	Russian 42B6 1100 hp diesel in remainder
	525 hp electric
Range	
Surfaced	8,950 nm at 8.9 kts
Submerged	158 nm at 2.9 kts
Diving depth	295 ft max. 246 ft operating
Complement	53

Russian 'Dekabrist' patrol submarine

Boat	Builder	Laid down	Commissioned	Fate
Dekabrist (D-1)	Plant 189, Leningrad Shipyard	05-03-1927	18-11-1930	Sank after negative buoyancy tank accidentally flooded during Baltic exercises, 11-40.
Narodovoletz (D-2)	Plant 189, Leningrad Shipyard	05-03-1927	11-10-1931	Badly damaged in German air raid, 11-08-1941. Removed from frontline service, 08-1956. Training role as *UTS-6*. Decommissioned 05-03-1987. Now on display, Central Navy Museum, St. Petersburg
Krasnogvardeyetz (D-3)	Plant 189, Leningrad Shipyard	05-03-1927	11-11-1931	Sank during Baltic exercises, 1935. Salved and recommissioned. Lost off Norway, 06-1942, probably mined.
Revoltusioner (D-4)	Marti Yard, Nikolayev, Black Sea	14-04-1927	05-01-1931	Sunk by German surface ships, 04-12-1943.
Spartakovetz (D-5)	Marti Yard, Nikolayev, Black Sea	14-04-1927	17-05-1931	Scrapped 1957.
Yakobinetz (D-6)	Marti Yard, Nikolayev, Black Sea	14-04-1927	12-06-1931	Destroyed by bombs in German air raid on Sevastopol, 12-11-1941.

Based on First World I operational experience, the Soviet Union's first attempt at domestic submarine construction came with the *Dekabrist* class in 1927. The design bureau was headed by engineer Boris Malinin, who built the *Bars* class in 1916-17, although there are persistent reports of Italian technical assistance. These were the first Russian boats with watertight bulkheads and were designed for long-range attacks on enemy communications.

The first three boats were laid down in March, 1927. All had riveted hulls of high-strength steel (realistically, if not prudently, designers stipulated pre-Bolshevik era production) and generous 45% reserve buoyancy. Originally, it was planned that the class should have two four-inch deck guns fore and aft of the conning tower, but later, the aft gun was replaced by a 45mm AA gun.

The *Dekabrist* class proved good sea boats, manoeuvrable and quick-diving, marred only by poor maintenance and constant repair. *Dekabrist* proved unstable in handling during her trials in June, 1930 and displayed a distressing tendency for the quick dive tank to unexpectedly open while operating at depth.

The class was 10 years behind its Western counterparts in technology and were modernised in 1938-41 for war service in the Baltic and Black Seas. In June 1944, *Narodovoletz* was fitted with a British Asdic-129 sonar and a new torpedo launching system.

But domestic submarine construction was now firmly established, leading onto the *Leninetz* class of six minelaying boats laid down in 1928 and 1930, based on the same hull and retaining the same or poorer performance. In this class, which entered service in 1933, the two stern torpedo tubes were discarded in favour of tubes for 20 ground mines.

Left, above and below: The lines of this class betray their First World War design basics but with a well proven pedigree they proved to have excellent sea-keeping abilities.

British 'O' class - built for Far East operations

The British 'O' class, designed for long endurance operations in the Far East, were the first class to be named rather than being identified by class initial and hull number. Longer range than the earlier 'L' class was achieved by fitting external fuel saddle tanks, with almost 200 tons capacity. Unfortunately, these riveted tanks suffered from frequent seepage that caused revealing slicks of fuel on the surface when boats were submerged.

The class had strengthened pressure hulls, ram bows, and the gun mounted on a platform immediately forward of a tall conning tower.

Two boats, of slightly different design, OA1 and OA2 were built by Vickers for the Royal Australian Navy. Both

British 'O' class overseas patrol submarine, 1924-1928

Boat	Builder	Laid down	Commissioned	Fate
Group One				
Oberon (ex-O 1)	HM Dockyard, Chatham	22-04-1924	24-08-1927	Sold, 14-08-1945
Group Two				
Oxley (ex-AO 1)	Vickers, Barrow	24-08-1925	22-07-1927	Departed for Australia, 02-1928. Reserve, 05-1930. Recommissioned RN, Sydney, 04-1931. Accidentally sunk by British submarine Triton, off Obrestad, Norway, 10-09-1939.
Otway (ex-AO 2)	Vickers, Barrow	24-08-1925	09-09-1927	Departed for Australia, 02-1928. Into reserve, 05-1930. Recommissioned, RN, Sydney, 04-1931. Sold and scrapped 14-08-1945
Almirante Simpson	Vickers, Barrow	15-11-1927	14-09-1929	Built for Chilean Navy. Scrapped, 1958.
Capitan O'Brien	Vickers, Barrow	15-11-1927	19-06-1929	Built for Chilean Navy. Scrapped 1958.
Capitan Thomson	Vickers, Barrow	15-11-1927	24-05-1929	Built for Chilean Navy. Scrapped 1959.
Group Three				
Osiris	Vickers, Barrow	12-05-1927	27-02-1929	Scrapped, South Africa, 09-1946.
Otus	Vickers, Barrow	31-05-1927	05-07-1929	Sold, South Africa, 05-1946. Scuttled off Durban 09-1949.
Oswald	Vickers, Barrow	30-05-1927	05-07-1929	Rammed and sunk by Italian destroyer Ugolino Vivaldi, 01-08-1940, off Cape Spartivento, 'toe' of Italy. 52 survivors.
Odin	HM Dockyard, Chatham	23-06-1927	21-12-1929	Sunk by Italian destroyer Strale in Gulf of Taranto, 13-06-1940.
Olympus	William Beardmore, Dalmuir	14-04-1927	14-06-1930	Adapted to stores/ personnel carrier, Malta, 1940. Mined off Malta 08-05-1942. Nine survivors.
Orpheus	William Beardmore, Dalmuir	14-04-1927	23-09-1929	Sunk by Italian destroyer Turbine N.of Tobruk, 16-06-1940.

	Group 1	Group 2
Length (ft)	275 oa*	283.5 oa
Beam (ft)	28 oa	30 oa
Displacement (tons)		
Surfaced	1,311*	1,781
Submerged	1,892	2,030
Speed (kts)		
Surfaced	15.5	17.5
Dived	9	9
Armament	6x21" bow tubes, 2x21" stern tubes	
	16 reloads	
	1x 4-inch deck gun.	
	2 Lewis machine guns	
Engines	2 x 4600 hp diesel	
	2 x 1350 hp electric	
	twin screws	
Range		
Surfaced	8,400 nm at 10 kts	
Submerged	70 nm at 4 kts	
Diving depth	300 ft	
Complement	54	

* The two ex-Australian boats, Oxley and Otway displaced 1,349 tons surfaced and 1,872 submerged. Length of these boats was 278.5-feet oa. Surface speed was 15 kts.

left England in February, 1928 but paid off and went into reserve in May, 1930 because of budgetary restrictions. The boats were recommissioned into the Royal Navy as Oxley and Otway at Sydney in April, 1931.

Three more were built for the Chilean Navy which served into the late 1950s.

Oxley became the first British submarine casualty of World War II, when she was mistakenly torpedoed, outside her notified patrol area, by Hms/m Triton off Obrestad, Norway, on September 10, 1939. There were only two survivors.

Odin, Olympus, Orpheus, and Otus served in the Far

East, based either at Singapore or Hong Kong in 1930-39. Shortly after the outbreak of war, these were transferred to the Mediterranean, via a brief tour of duty at Colombo. In 1942, they were pulled back from frontline duties and were involved in training.

The class suffered five war losses (Oxley, Oswald, Odin, Olympus, Orpheus), three of which were sunk by Italian destroyers.

The follow-on six-boat Parthian class was an improved version of the later Oberons, and six-feet longer. Four served on the China Station pre-war and like the Oberons, the class returned for war service in the Mediterranean

Royal Navy 'S' class - biggest class ever built in Britain

Britain's 'S' class was built to meet the need for a modern long range patrol submarine and became the Royal Navy's largest class of boat, building in three groups over 13 years from 1930. Unlike the leaky 'O' class boats with external riveted fuel tanks, Admiralty designers positioned the 'S' class tanks internally.

Spearfish became the first British naval unit to be attacked in World War II, when at 11.04 on September 3 1939 - four minutes after the declaration of war became effective - she came under torpedo attack by a German submarine but escaped undamaged. *Sturgeon* claimed the first British submarine success when she sank the German anti-submarine trawler *Gauleiter Telshow,* on November 20 1939.

On September 14, in a repeat episode of *Triton's* unfortunate attack on *Oxley, Sturgeon* fired a fan of three torpedoes at her sister boat *Swordfish* off the coast of Norway. Happily, this time they all missed. After this second friendly fire incident in four days, the Admiralty increased the operating distance between British submarines off Norway from four to 16 miles.

The class accounted for six U Boats and two Italian submarines and *Salmon* torpedoed the cruisers *Nurnberg* and *Leipzig* during German mining operations off the

	Group 1	Group 2	Group 3
Length (ft)	202.4	208.6	216.8
Beam (ft)	23.9	23.9	23.6
Displacement (tons)			
Surfaced	730	768	865
Submerged	927	960	990
Speed (kts)			
Surfaced	13.5	13.5	14.5
Dived	10	10	9
Armament	6x21" bow tubes, 6 reloads	6x21" bow tubes, 6 reloads	7x21" (6 bow, 1 stern) tubes
	or 12 M2 mines	or 12 M2 mines	1x4 in deck gun
	1x3 in deck gun*	1x3 in deck gun*	Extra 20 mm cannon in some
Engines	2 diesel, 1,550 hp	2 diesel, 1,550 hp	2 diesel 1,900 hp
	2 electric 1,300 hp	2 electric 1,300 hp	2 electric 1,440 hp
	twin screws	twin screws	twin screws
Range			
Surfaced	3,700 nm at 10 kts	3,800 nm at 10 kts	6,000 nm at 10 kts
Submerged	N/K	N/K	N/K
Diving depth	300 ft	300 ft	300 ft
Complement	38	40	49

* 1 x 20 mm Oerlikon AA gun added during refits in 1944 to some hulls.

Above: The classic 'Jolly Roger' flown here denotes a 'kill' by this 'S' class boat returning to port in the early part of the Second World War.

Left: An early 'S' boat after commissioning. These vessels took part in some of the earliest naval actions of the war.

Royal Navy 'S' class - biggest class ever built in Britain

Tyne on December 13, 1939, damaging them both, and putting them into repair for five months and a year respectively. *Spearfish* torpedoed and damaged the pocket battleship *Lützow* north of the Skaw, just after midnight on April 11, 1940, knocking her out of the war for a year. Both her propellers were blown off and her rudder jammed.

The class was involved in a number of X-craft midget submarine attacks on German capital ships and naval facilities. *Stubborn* was among several 'S' and 'T' class boats which supported X-craft in an audacious attack on *Tirpitz* and *Scharnhorst* in Altenfjord, Norway, on September 22 1943. They towed *X-7* which successfully placed explosive charges under *Tirpitz* and put her out of action until April 1944. Sceptre towed *X 24* in OPERATION HECKLE, in September 1944, in a successful attack on the 8,000 ton floating dock at Bergen, Norway.

Stubborn recorded the then deepest dive at 540-feet in February 1944, following an attack on German convoys off Trondheim, Norway, in which two enemy ships were sunk. The subsequent depth-charge attack jammed her after hydroplanes and rudder and she plunged to 400 ft before surfacing and making an immediate further uncontrolled dive, this time hitting the seabed. After several hours on the bottom, under depth charge attack, the crew blew the main ballast tanks with the last remaining compressed air and broke surface at a bows-up angle of 70°. She reached harbour safely eight days later.

Seraph was the submarine that took part in the elaborate disinformation campaign, later dramatised in the film *The Man Who Never Was*. This involved dumping the body of a fictitious Royal Marine 'Major Martin' on the Spanish coast, on April 30 1943, with fake classified documents to distract the German High Command from the Allied landings in Sicily.[1]

Sanguine was fitted with a dummy snort mast simulating a U Boat for anti-submarine exercises off the Isle of Man, in October 1945.

Statesman fired the last torpedo of World War II, three days after Japan's surrender, at a derelict vessel that had to be destroyed.

After the war, *Stoic* was involved in crush trials. Her hull was submerged 18 miles north of Kyle, West Scotland, until she crushed at 600 ft. *Scotsman* was also sunk deliberately in Kames Bay, Isle of Bute, to exercise Clyde salvage vessels in 1964.

Sea Scout was one of the longest serving 'S' boats, first commissioned in May 1944, and remaining in service until 1963.

1 Her role was played by *Scythian* in the film.

HMS Swordfish

1	Rudder	17	Bilge pump	29	Main frame
2	Screw	18	Exhaust	30	Torpedoe tubes
3	Auxillary tank	19	Wireless mast	31	Air bottle storage
4	Steering position	20	Patrol periscope	32	Torpedoe tubes
5	Engineers' position	21	Attack periscope	33	Crew area/galley
6	Shaft	22	Bridge	34	Petty officers mess
7	Electric motors	23	Conning tower	35	Wardroom
8	Control panels	24	3 inch gun	36	Bow planes
9	Diesel	25	Main control centre		
10	Fuel	26	Batteries		
11	Ballast tanks	27	Compensation tanks		
12	Engine exhaust tank	28	Pressure hull		
13	Exhaust				
14	Outer hull				
15	Wireless office				
16	Sonar office				

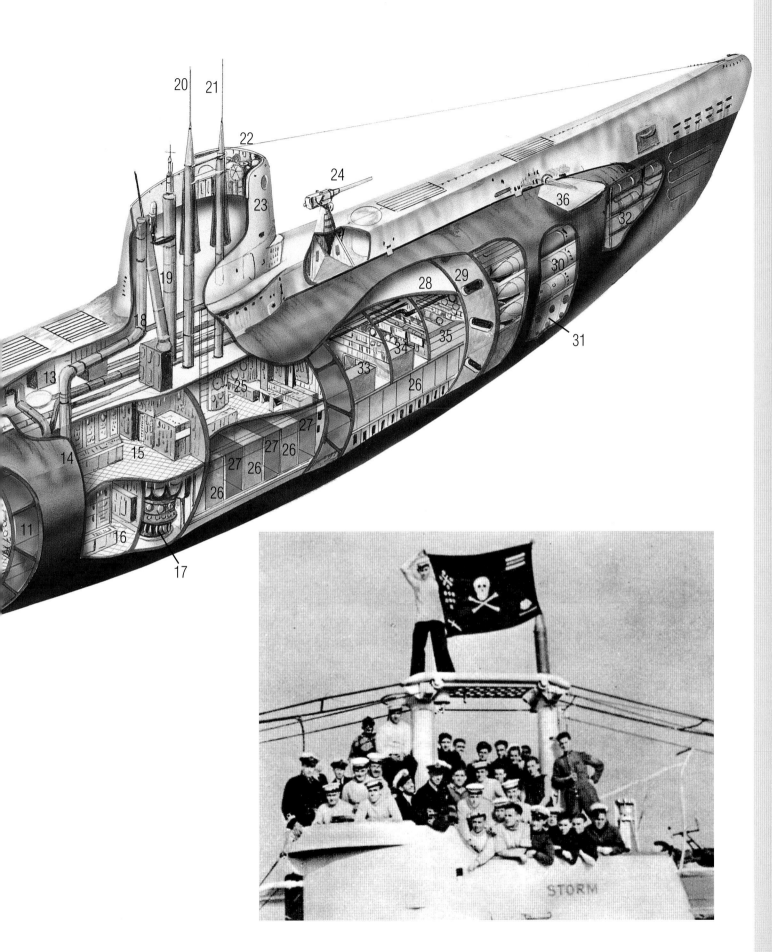

British 'S' class overseas patrol submarine

Boat	Builder	Laid down	Commissioned	Fate
Group One				
Swordfish	HM Dockyard, Chatham	01-12-1930	16-09-1932	Mined off Isle of Wight, 07-11-1940. Wreck found 1983 in two halves.
Sturgeon	HM Dockyard, Chatham	01-01-1931	15-12-1932	Lent to Dutch Navy, 11-10-1943 to 14-09-1945 as Zeehond. Returned to RN. Broken up, Granton, 01- 1946.
Seahorse	HM Dockyard, Chatham	14-09-1931	26-07-1933	Depth charged and sunk by German minesweepers, Heligoland Bight, 07-01-1940.
Starfish	HM Dockyard, Chatham	26-09-1931	03-07-1933	Depth charged and sunk by German minesweeper M 7, Heligoland Bight, 09-01-1940. Crew captured.
Group Two				
Shark	HM Dockyard, Chatham	12-06-1933	05-10-1934	Attacked by German aircraft off Skudeneshavn, Norway 05-07-1940. Sank under tow by German minesweepers, 06-07-1940. Two killed, 19 wounded.
Salmon	Cammell Laird, Birkenhead	15-06-1933	08-03-1935	Mined SW of Stavanger, Norway, 09-07-1940.
Sealion	Cammell Laird, Birkenhead	16-05-1933	21-12-1934	Expended as Asdic target, off Arran 03-03-1945.
Snapper	HM Dockyard, Chatham	18-09-1933	14-06-1935	Lost, Bay of Biscay, 11-02-1941. Probably mined.
Spearfish	Cammell Laird, Birkenhead	23-05-1935	11-12-1936	Torpedoed by U 34, SW Stavanger, Norway, 01-08-1940. One survivor.
Seawolf	Scotts, Greenock	25-05-1934	12-03-1936	Scrapped Montreal, Canada, 11-1945.
Sunfish	HM Dockyard, Chatham	22-07-1935	02-07-1937	Transferred to Soviet Navy as V 1, 30-05-1944.[1] Bombed in error and sunk by RAF Liberator aircraft, 27-07-1944 while on passage to Murmansk. Crew lost.
Sterlet	HM Dockyard, Chatham	14-07-1936	06-04-1938	Sunk by three German corvettes, UJ 125, UJ 126 and UJ 128, in Skaggerrak, 18-04-1940.
Group Three				
Safari (ex-P 61, P 211)	Cammell Laird, Birkenhead	05-06-1940	15-02-1942	Sold, Newport, 07-01-1946. Wrecked under tow to breakers, 08-01-1946
Sahib (ex-P 62, P 212)	Cammell Laird, Birkenhead	05-07-1940	30-05-1942	Depth-charged by Italian corvettes Gabbiano Euterpe torpedo boat Climene and bombed by German Ju 88, off Cape Milazzo, Sicily. Scuttled by crew, 24-04-1943.
Saracen (ex-P 63, P 213, P 247)	Cammell Laird, Birkenhead	16-07-1940	27-06-1942	Sank by Italian corvettes Minerva and Euterpe off Bastia, Corsica, 18-08-1943. Four crew lost.
Satyr (ex-P 64, P 214)	Scotts, Greenock	08-06-1940	28-09-1942	Lent to French Navy as Saphir, 02-1952 to 08-1961. Broken up, Charlestown, Fife, 06-1962.
Sceptre (ex-P 65, P 215)	Scotts, Greenock	25-07-1940	01-1943	Sold, Gateshead, 09-1949
Seadog (ex-P 66, P 216)	Cammell Laird, Birkenhead	31-12-1940	24-09-1942	Sold, 24-12-1947. Scrapped 08-1948, Troon.
Sibyl (ex-P 67, P 217)	Cammell Laird, Birkenhead	31-12-1940	16-08-1942	Scrapped, 03-1948, Troon.
Sea Rover (ex-P 68, P 218)	Scotts, Greenock. (Launched 25-02-1943). Completed by Vickers, Barrow.	14-02-1941	07-07-1943	Scrapped 10-1949, Faslane.
Seraph (ex-P 69, P 219)	Vickers, Barrow	16-08-1940	27-05-1942	Sold. Broke adrift for 24 hours after under tow to breakers, 14-12-1965. Scrapped, Swansea 12-1965.
Shakespeare (ex-P 71, P 221)	Vickers, Barrow	13-11-1940	10-07-1942	Damaged by gunfire and bombing, N of Sumatra, 03-01-1945. Towed by Stygian to Ceylon. Not repaired. Sold 14-07-1946 for scrap.
P 222	Vickers, Barrow	10-08-1940	03-11-1942	Italians claimed to have sunk boat while on patrol off Naples, 12-12-1942.
Sea Nymph (ex-P 223)	Cammell Laird, Birkenhead	06-05-1941	29-07-1942	Scrapped 06-1948, Troon.
Sickle (ex-P 74, P 224)	Cammell Laird, Birkenhead	08-05-1941	01-12-1942	Mined, Antikithera Channel, eastern Mediterranean, 18-06-1944.
Simoon (ex-P 75, P 225)	Cammell Laird, Birkenhead	14-07-1941	28-11-1942	Possibly torpedoed by U 565 off Kos, eastern Mediterranean, or mined, 15-08-1943.
Sirdar (ex-P 76, P 226)	Scotts, Greenock. (Launched, 26-03-1943.) Completed, Vickers, Barrow	24-04-1941	18-08-1943	Scrapped 31-05-1955.
Spiteful (ex-P 77, P 227)	Scotts Greenock	19-09-1941	06-10-1943	Transferred to French Navy as Sirene, 25-01-1952. Returned RN, 24-10-1958. Scrapped Faslane, 1963.
Splendid (ex-P 78, P 228)	HM Dockyard, Chatham	07-03-1941	04-08-1942	Scuttled after depth charging by German destroyer Hermes (ex-Vasilevs Georgios) W. of Corsica, 21-04-1943. 18 crew lost; remainder taken prisoner.
Sportsman (ex-P 79, P 229)	HM Dockyard, Chatham	01-07-1941	21-12-1942	Transferred to French Navy as Sibylle, 1951. Sank off Toulon, 24-09-1952. Crew lost.
Stoic (ex- P 231)	Cammell Laird, Birkenhead	18-06-1942	31-05-1943	Sunk in deep diving trial, 1948. Raised and sold for scrap, Dalmuir, 07-1950.
Stonehenge (ex-P 232)	Cammell Laird, Birkenhead	04-04-1942	15-06-1943	Lost between Sumatra and Nicobar Islands, 03-1944.
Storm (ex-P 233)	Cammell Laird, Birkenhead	23-06-1942	09-07-1943	Sold 11-49. Scrapped, Troon.
Stratagem (ex-P 234)	Cammell Laird, Birkenhead	15-04-1942	14-08-1943	Depth-charged by Japanese patrol craft No 35 off Malacca, 22-11-1943.
Strongbow (ex-P 235)	Scotts, Greenock	27-03-1942	17-11-1943	Scrapped, Preston, 04-1946.
Spark (ex-P 236)	Scotts, Greenock	10-10-1942	28-04-1944	Sold 28-10-1949. Broken up at Faslane.
Scythian (ex-P 237)	Scotts, Greenock	21-02-1943	11-07-1944	Scrapped 08-08-1960, Charlestown.
Stubborn (ex-P 88, P 238)	Cammell Laird, Birkenhead	10-09-1941	20-02-1943	Destroyed as Asdic target off Malta, 30-04-1946.
Surf (ex-P 239)	Cammell Laird, Birkenhead	02-10-1941	18-11-1943	Sold, 28-10-1948. Scrapped at Faslane.
Syrtis (ex-P 241)	Cammell Laird, Birkenhead	14-10-1941	24-03-1943	Mined off Bodo, Norway, 28-03-1944.
Scotsman	Scotts, Greenock	15-04-1943	27-10-1944	In reserve, Gareloch, 1961. Sunk in 1964 for lifting exercises. Salved 06-1964. Sold 19-11-1964, Troon. Broken up.
Shalimar	HM Dockyard, Chatham	17-04-1942	03-04-1944	Scrapped 07-1950, Isle of Bute.
Spirit (ex-P 245)	Cammell Laird, Birkenhead	27-10-1942	N/K	Sold 04-01-1950. Scrapped.
Statesman (ex-P 246)	Cammell Laird, Birkenhead	02-11-1942	13-12-1943	Transferred to French Navy as Sultane, 1952. Returned RN, 05-11-1959. Scrapped, 03-11-1961, Portsmouth.
Sturdy (ex-P 248)	Cammell Laird, Birkenhead	22-12-1942	29-11-1943	Sold, 09-1957, Malta. Scrapped 05-1958, Dunton.
Stygian (ex-P 249)	Cammell Laird, Birkenhead	06-01-1943	29-02-1944 S	Sold 28-10-1949. Scrapped at Faslane.
Subtle (ex-P 251)	Cammell Laird, Birkenhead	01-02-1943	11-03-1944	Sold, 06-1958. Scrapped, 07-1959, Charlestown.
Supreme (ex-P 252)	Cammell Laird, Birkenhead	15-02-1943	20-05-1944.	Converted for ship target trials, 17-06-1947. Pressure hull collapsed in tests. Raised and examined. Sold 12-07-1949. Scrapped at Troon.
Sea Scout	Cammell Laird, Birkenhead	01-04-1943	15-05-1944	De-equipped for sale, 12-1963. Sold, 09-12-1965. Scrapped, Swansea, 14-12-1965.
Selene	Cammell Laird, Birkenhead	16-04-1943	10-06-1944	Scrapped 06-06-1961, Gateshead.
Sea Devil	Scotts Greenock	05-05-1943	31-03-1945	Scrapped 15-12-1965
Sleuth	Cammell Laird, Birkenhead	30-06-1943	02-09-1944	Scrapped, 15-09-1958, Charlestown.
Sidon	Cammell Laird, Birkenhead	07-07-1943	24-10-1944	Sank, badly damaged in explosion of hydrogen peroxide-powered torpedo, alongside Maidstone, Portland, 16-06-1955, 13 killed. Raised 23-06 and expended as Asdic target off Portland, 14-06-1957.
Spearhead	Cammell Laird, Birkenhead	18-08-1943	21-11-1944	Sold to Portuguese Navy as Neptuno, 08-1948. Taken out of service, 01-09-1967. Scrapped, 1967.
Seneschal	Scotts, Greenock	01-09-1943	31-07-1945	Scrapped 23-08-1960, Dunton.
Solent	Cammell Laird, Birkenhead	07-09-1943	29-07-1944	Scrapped, 28-08-1961, Troon.
Sentinel	Scotts, Greenock	15-11-1943	28-11-1944	Sold 28-02-1962. Scrapped at Gillingham.
Spur	Cammell Laird, Birkenhead	01-01-1944	06-01-1945	Sold to Portuguese Navy as Narval, 30-11-1958. Scrapped in Israel.
Sanguine	Cammell Laird, Birkenhead	10-01-1944	15-02-1945	Sold to Israeli Navy as Rahav, 23-02-1959. Broken up, Haifa, 1969.
Saga	Cammell Laird, Birkenhead	05-04-1944	27-05-1945	Transferred to Portuguese Navy as Nautilo, 11-10-1948 for £129,000. Decommissioned 25-01-1969. Scrapped.
Springer	Cammell Laird, Birkenhead	08-05-1944	02-07-1945	Sold to Israeli Navy as Tanin, 21-09-1958. Scrapped in Israel, 1972.
Scorcher	Cammell Laird, Birkenhead	14-12-1944	06-02-1945	Broken up, Charlestown, Fife, 08-1962.
Sea Robin	Cammell Laird, Birkenhead	-	-	Cancelled
Sprightly	Cammell Laird, Birkenhead	-	-	Cancelled
Surface	Cammell Laird, Birkenhead	-	-	Cancelled
Surge	Cammell Laird, Birkenhead	-	-	Cancelled

1 URSULA, UNBROKEN AND UNISON WERE ALSO TRANSFERRED TO THE SOVIET NAVY.

British *Porpoise* class minelaying submarines

	Porpoise	Remainder
Length (ft)	288 oa	293 oa
Beam (ft)	29.75 oa	25.5 oa
Displacement (tons)		
Surfaced	1,500	1,520
Submerged	2,053	2,117
Speed (kts)		
Surfaced	15.5	16
Dived	9	9
Armament	6x21" bow tubes	6x21" bow tubes
	(12 reloads)	(12 reloads)
	1x4" gun, 2 machine guns	1x4" gun, 2 machine guns
	50 mines	50 mines
Engines	2x1,650 hp diesel	2x1,650 hp diesel
	2x1,630 hp electric	2x1,630 hp electric
	twin screws	twin screws
Range		
Surface	11,500 nm at 8 kts	11,500 nm at 8 kts
Submerged	N/K	N/K
Diving depth	300 ft	300 ft
Complement	55	55

British *Porpoise* class minelaying submarine

Boat	Builder	Laid down	Commissioned	Fate
Porpoise	Vickers, Barrow	22-09-1931	25-04-1933	Bombed by Japanese aircraft, Malacca Straits, 16-01-1945. Last British submarine to be lost in WW II.
Grampus	HM Dockyard, Chatham	20-08-1934	10-03-1937	Depth charged and sunk by Italian torpedo boats *Circe* and *Clio* off Syracuse, Sicily, 16-06-1940.
Narwhal	Vickers, Barrow	29-05-1934	28-02-1936	Sunk by German aircraft, off Kristensand, Norway, 30-07-1940.
Rorqual	Vickers, Barrow	01-05-1935	21-11-1936	Sold, 17-03-1946. Scrapped.
Seal	HM Dockyard, Chatham	12-09-1936	28-01-1939	Mined in Kattegat, 04-05-1940, later bombed by two Arado Ar 196 seaplanes, surrendered. Commissioned in German Navy 30-11-1940 as *UB*. Decommissioned 31-07-1941. Scuttled, 03-05-1945, Heikendorf Bay. Salved and scrapped.
Cachalot	Scotts, Greenock	12-05-1936	15-08-1938	Rammed and sunk by Italian torpedo boat *Generale Achille Papa* off Benghazi, Libya, 30-07-1941.
(*P 411*)	Scotts, Greenock	-	-	Cancelled
(*P 412*)	Scotts, Greenock	-	-	Cancelled
(*P 413*)	Scotts, Greenock	-	-	Cancelled

The *Porpoise* class was the first and only submarine minelayer purpose-built for the Royal Navy, based on lessons learnt with the converted *M 3* - fitted with a conveyor belt-like chain within a deep casing, discharging mines through stern doors. More boats were planned but were abandoned when a new type of ground mine was developed that could be laid through the 21-inch torpedo tubes. Even so, the *Porpoise* class undertook the bulk of submarine minelaying in World War II, sowing more than 3,000, of which 2,284 were laid by *Rorqual* - the only boat to survive the war.

Minelaying operations were conducted off Bay of Biscay ports in July and August 1940, and off Norway and in the Kattegat, off Denmark, in April-October of that year. Operations then switched to the Mediterranean

It was during the Kattegat minelaying that *Seal* was captured by the German Navy. The boat had left Immingham on April 29 to lay a mine barrage in the Baltic, straddling a German transit route to occupied Norway. On May 4, the boat's stern was damaged by a mine explosion and it sank in 100 ft. After 23 hours, the boat surfaced and it was decided, because of the damage, to steer for neutral Sweden and internment. With the rudder damaged and a subsequent engine failure, the submarine was helpless when two German Arado Ar 196

Below: Although only a class of six boats, the 'Porpoises' undertook the bulk of submarine minelaying in the Second World War.

British *Porpoise* class minelaying submarines

seaplanes attacked - machine-gunning and dropping two bombs. The boat surrendered and was towed to Frederikshavn and later to Kiel for repair.

It was commissioned as *UB* by the German Navy, on November 30 1940, but apart from the propaganda victory, there was little operational use for the Kriegsmarine. It was decommissioned on July 31 1941, and scuttled on May 3 1945, ahead of advancing Allied troops.

The class had a creditable record in sinking enemy submarines. *Porpoise* sank *U 1* off southern Norway, on April 16 1940. *Rorqual* sank the Italian submarine *Pier Capponi,* S of Stromboli on March 31 1941, and *Cachalot* torpedoed *U 51* in the Bay of Biscay on August 20 1941.

Porpoise was bombed and sunk by Japanese aircraft in the Malacca Straits on January 16 1945 - the 77th and last Second World War British submarine loss.

Above: This first of this class suffered the ignominity of being the last Allied submarine casualty of the War.

Japan's KD6 class - fastest boats in the 1930s

Japanese KD6 class submarine

Boat*	Builder	Launched	Completed	Fate
KD6A class				
I-168 (ex-I-68)	Kure Navy Yard	26-06-1933	31-07-1934	Blown up by US submarine *Scamp* (SS-277) that returned fire with four torpedoes 60 nm off New Ireland, Bismarck Archipelago, 27-07-1943.
I-169 (ex-I-69)	Mitsubishi Shipyard Kobe	15-02-1934	28-09-1935	Sank in accidental flooding, off Truk Island, Caroline Islands when torpedo tube door was opened. 04-04-1944.
I-170 (ex-I-70)	Sasebo Navy Yard	14-06-1934	09-11-1935	Sunk by aircraft from USS *Enterprise*, 200 nm NE of Oahu Island, Hawaii, 10-12-1941
I-171 (ex-I-71)	Kawasaki Shipyard, Kobe	25-08-1934	24-12-1935	Sunk by US destroyers, *Hudson* and *Guest*, 15 nm W of Buka Island, Solomon Islands, 01-02-1944.
I-172 (ex-I-72)	Mitsubishi Shipyard, Kobe	06-04-1935	07-07-1937	Sunk by unidentified US warship near Guadalcanal, Solomon Islands, 11-11-1942.
I-173 (ex-I-73)	Kawasaki Shipyard, Kobe	20-06-1935	07-07-1937	Torpedoed by US submarine *Gudgeon* (SS-211) 230 nm W Midway Island, 27-08-1942 when *I-173* was returning from a patrol off the W coast of USA.
KD6B class				
I-174 (ex-I-74)	Sasebo Navy Yard	28-03-1937	15-08-1938	Lost 03-04-1944.
I-175 (ex-I-75)	Mitsubishi Shipyard, Kobe	16-09-1936	18-12-1938	Sunk by US destroyer *Walker* 01-02-1944.

* Renumbered on May 20, 1942

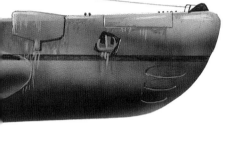

Japan's KD6 class, built in 1934-38, had the highest surface speed of any submarine of their time. Their range and formidable armament made them potent war weapons, limited only by a shallow operating depth.

The class proved successful during World War II, although *I-70* became the first major Japanese casualty when she was sunk by aircraft from USS *Enterprise* NE of Oahu, on December 10 1941 - only three days after the attack on Pearl Harbour. Of the eight built, seven were war casualties, with *I-174* additionally lost in an accident on April 3 1944, when a torpedo door was left open.

I-168 sank the damaged carrier *Yorktown* and a US destroyer on June 7 1942, later being sunk by the US submarine *Scamp* off New Ireland on July 23 1943. *I-175* sank the escort carrier *Liscombe Bay* in 1943.

Two boats of the class, *I-171* and *I-174* were converted into transport vessels carrying landing craft in 1943, to move stores to isolated Japanese garrisons in the Solomon Islands. The main gun was removed in these boats.

	KD6	KD6B
Length (ft)	343.4 oa	344.5 oa
Beam (ft)	27	27
Displacement (tons)		
Surfaced	1,785	1,805
Submerged	2,440	2,560
Speed (kts)		
Surfaced	23	
Dived	8.25	
Armament	4x21" bow tubes, 2x21" stern tube	4x21" bow tubes, 2x21" stern tube
	8 reloads	8 reloads
	1x 10 cm/65 calibre deck gun.*	1x 10 cm/65 calibre deck gun.*
	2 x 13mm AA or 2x25 mm AA guns	2 x 13mm AA or 2x25 mm AA guns
Engines	2 x diesels 9,000 hp	2 x diesels 9,000 hp
	1800 hp electric	1800 hp electric
	2 shafts	2 shafts
Range		
Surfaced	14,000 nm at 10 kts	10,000 nm at 16 kts
Submerged	65 nm at 3 kts	65 nm at 3 kts
Diving depth	245 ft	245 ft
Complement	70	70

* Gun replaced by a 12 cm/50 cal weapon in *I-171-173* together with the two KD6B boats

Below: All eight of the KD6 class were lost during the Second World War.

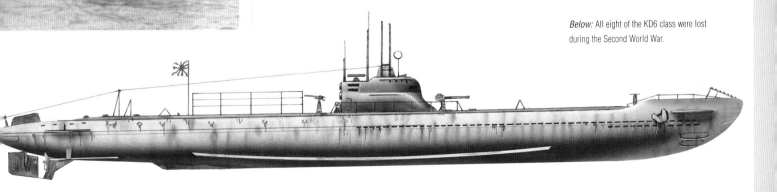

J3 Cruiser Boats - Japanese giants

Japan's two J3 boats, the largest submarines in service with the Imperial Japanese Navy before World War II, were designed as squadron flagships, based on the KD type, with double hulls and a hanger for a seaplane. *I-8* sailed to the German-held port of Brest in 1943, carrying extra personnel to crew a Type IXC/40 U Boat which was to be handed over to Japan by the Kriegsmarine. She also carried quinine as cargo on her outward voyage.

Both were patrolling off Hawaii as the Japanese surprise attack on Pearl Harbor was mounted. In 1943, *I-8* sailed for occupied France, specially fitted with a 5.5-inch gun and accompanied by the submarine *I-10*, acting as a tanker and supply ship. Off the Azores, *I-8* met a German U boat and was escorted into Brest, arriving at the French naval base on September 5 1943. Her spare crew transferred across to *U 1224*, re-named *RO 501* for service in the Imperial Japanese Navy.[1]

The following year, *I-8* was converted to carry four manned Kaiten suicide torpedoes and her main gun and aircraft hanger were removed.

Both boats did not survive hostilities.

1 SHE WAS COMMISSIONED ON FEBRUARY 15, 1944 BUT WAS SUNK ON MAY 13, 1944 OFF THE CAPE VERDE ISLANDS IN THE ATLANTIC BY THE US DESTROYER *FRANCIS M ROBINSON*.

Above: Pictured here entering the French port of Brest in 1943, *I-8* was sunk by the US Navy in March 1945.

Length (ft)	358.5 oa
Beam (ft)	29.75 oa
Displacement (tons)	
Surfaced	2,525
Submerged	3,583
Speed (kts)	
Surfaced	23
Dived	8
Armament	6x 21" bow tubes, 14 reloads
	1x 5.5-inch/50 calibre deck gun.
	5 x 13 mm machine guns*
	1 floatplane
Engines	2 x diesels 11,200 hp
	2 x electric motors, 2,800 hp
	2 shafts
Range	
Surfaced	14,500 nm at 16 kts
Submerged	60 nm at 3 kts
Diving depth	330 ft
Complement	80

* One MG replaced by twin-barrelled 25 mm AA gun in both boats in 1943.

Japanese J3 submarine

Boat	Builder	Launched	Commissioned	Fate
I-7	Kure Navy Yard	12-09-1934	31-03-1937	Damaged by US destroyer *Monaghan*, 22-06-1943 and again by US aircraft, 05-07-1943. Scuttled off Aleutian Islands 05-07-1943.
I-8	Kawasaki Shipbuilding, Kobe	20-07-1936	15-10-1938	Sunk by US destroyers *Morrison* and *Stockton*, SE of Okinawa, 31-03-1945.

US *Salmon* class - an enemy ship sunk by periscope

Length (ft)	308
Beam (ft)	26.2
Displacement (tons)	
Surfaced	1,435
Submerged	2,198
Speed (kts)	
Surfaced	21.0 design, 17 operational
Dived	9
Armament	4x21" bow tubes, 4x21" stern tubes
	12 reloads plus 4 external (later removed)
	1x3 in/50 cal. deck gun.
	2x.50 cal, 2 x.30 cal machine guns,
	2x20 mm cannon added in some
Engines	4 diesel, 5,500 shp
	2 electric motors, 3,300 hp
Range	
Surfaced	11,000 nm at 10 kts
Submerged	100 nm at 5 kts
Diving depth	260 ft
Complement	55

One of the American *Salmon* class has the distinction of sinking a Japanese freighter by holing her hull with her periscope. *Seal* was patrolling sea-lanes around Palau Island, east of the Philippines, on November 16 1942, when she attacked a two-line convoy of five enemy cargo ships escorted by a destroyer.

After firing torpedoes from her bow tubes at the lead merchantman, the boat was in collision with another ship, blinding her periscope. After surviving a depth charge attack, *Seal* safely surfaced some hours later and found her periscope had been bent back at right angles, the radar antenna was broken off and rice and vegetables were trapped beneath the wooden slats forming the deck of the bridge. Her periscope had punctured the hull of the Japanese cargo ship *Boston Maru*, 3,500 tons, sending her to the bottom.

A periscope proved useful to sister boat *Stingray* while patrolling to rescue shot-down US Navy pilots during air strikes on Guam in the Mariana Islands, in June 1944. One airman was reported splashed more than a quarter of a mile off an enemy beach and the boat made four submerged runs under fire in attempts to locate him. The last time, the pilot grabbed hold of one of *Stingray's* periscopes and was towed through shellfire to safety.

Salmon, fitted with two 20 mm cannon in 1943, made an audacious surface attack on Japanese anti-submarine vessels during an action against a damaged tanker in the Ryukyu Islands, off Japan, in October, 1944. After fierce depth-charging by four escorts had forced her to a depth of 500-feet, *Salmon* was forced to surface because of leaks in her pressure hull.

As the Japanese ships closed in for the kill, the American boat swept down the port side of one escort, pouring 20 mm fire onto the superstructure from just 60 yards. The enemy vessel was stopped dead in the water and the others, fearing further torpedo attacks, failed to press home their attack. *Salmon* escaped with further minor damage from small calibre rounds.

The class sank 33 enemy ships during their campaign in the Pacific before ending their careers in training roles and as targets.

Above: With a number of glamorous and unusual tales to tell, all six Salmon class boats survived hostilities.

US *Salmon* class - an enemy ship sunk by periscope

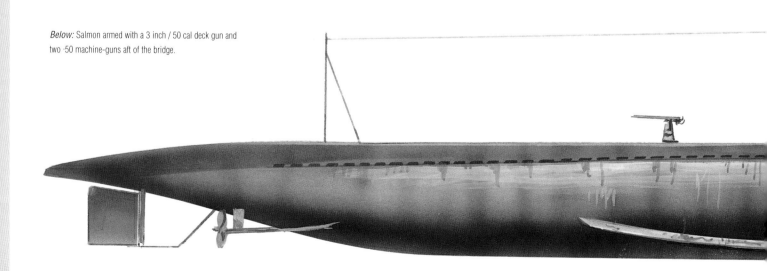

Below: Salmon armed with a 3 inch / 50 cal deck gun and two ·50 machine-guns aft of the bridge.

US *Salmon* class

Boat	Builder	Laid down	Commissioned	Fate
Salmon (SS-182)	Electric Boat, Groton, Connecticut	15-08-1936	15-03-1938	Scrapped 04-1946
Seal (SS-183)	Electric Boat, Groton, Connecticut	25-05-1936	30-04-1937	Scrapped 05-1957, New York.
Skipjack (SS-184)	Electric Boat, Groton, Connecticut	22-07-1936	30-06-1938	Used as target during second atomic bomb test, Bikini Atoll, 07-1946. Raised and sunk as target by air-launched rockets off Californian coast, 08-1948
Snapper (SS-185)	Portsmouth Navy Yard, Portsmouth, New Hampshire	23-07-1936	15-12-1937	Sold for scrap, New York, 18-05-1948.
Stingray (SS-186)	Portsmouth Navy Yard, Portsmouth, New Hampshire	01-10-1936	15-03-1938	Struck from Navy list, 03-07-1946. Scrapped 1947.
Sturgeon (SS-187)	Mare Island Navy Yard, Vallejo, California	27-10-1936	25-06-1938	Sold for scrap, New York, 12-06-1948.

Left: Stingray sank a japanese freighter after her periscope struck the enemy vessel's hull after the submarine mounted a submerged attack on a Japanese convoy.

British 'T' class, much-modified long endurance ocean patrol submarines

The Royal Navy's long-lived 'T' class - the first was laid down in 1936 and the last was paid off in August 1969 - underwent numerous modifications for war service and for patrols in the Cold War. They were designed to replace the *Oberons*, *Parthians* and second 'R' class boats but the displacement was deliberately reduced (below that of the earlier classes) to permit more hulls to be built within the London Naval Treaty national tonnage restrictions.

The first group had riveted hulls that restricted operating depth and six watertight compartments. These boats had increased torpedo armament with midships and bow tubes all facing forward. Unfortunately, the forward tubes forced the construction of high bulbous bows, which threw up a prominent bow wave and made depth-keeping difficult. *Triton* logged a surface speed of 16.29 kts during trials. Internal fuel tanks were fitted.

The class had a distinguished war record. In the first group, five enemy submarines were destroyed, four of them Italian in the Mediterranean and the Bay of Biscay.[1] The solitary U Boat was *U 644*, sunk by *Tuna* off Jan Mayen Island in the North Atlantic, on April 7 1943.

This group also sunk and damaged a number of major surface combatants. *Truant* was patrolling off Kristiansand, Norway, on April 10 1940, when she spotted the *Köln* class cruiser *Karlsruhe* escorted by three destroyers. The submarine fired a salvo of 10 torpedoes and the cruiser was badly damaged aft and was abandoned, having to be sunk by torpedoes from one of her escorts, *Greif*.

Trident torpedoed the cruiser *Prinz Eugen* off Norway, on February 23 1942, jamming her rudder and damaging her engines. *Triumph* damaged the Italian heavy cruiser *Bolzano* north of Sicily, on August 26 1941, and

	Group 1	Group 2	Group 3
Length (ft)	275.5 oa	273.5 oa	273.3 oa
Beam (ft)	26.6	26.6	26.6
Displacement (tons)			
Surface	1,325*	1,327	1,327
Submerged	1,573	1,571	1,571
Speed (kts)			
Surfaced	15.25	15.75	15.75
Dived	8.75	8.75	8.75
Armament	10x21" tubes ††	11x21" tubes	11x21" tubes
	(8 bow, 2 midships)	(8 bow, 3 stern)	(8 bow, 3 stern)
	6 reloads	6 reloads/12 Mk II mines	6 reloads/12 Mk II Mines
	1x4"/40 QF Mk XII gun	1x4"/40 QF Mk XII gun	1x4"/40 QF Mk XII gun**
	3x.303 MGs †	3x.303 MGs ‡	3x.303 MGs
			1x20 mm AA gun
Engines	2,500 bhp diesels	2,500 bhp diesels	2,500 bhp diesels
	1,450 bhp electric	1,450 bhp electric	1,450 bhp electric
	twin screws	twin screws	twin screws
Range			
Surface	8,000 nm at 10 kts §	8,000 nm at 10 kts	11,000 nm at 10 kts
Submerged	80 nm at 4 kts	80 nm at 4 kts	80 nm at 4 kts
Diving depth	300 ft	300 ft	300 ft ¶
Complement	62	61	63

* Except *Triton* which displaced 1,330 tons surfaced, 1,585 tons submerged.

** Except *Tabard*, *Talent* (3), *Tapir*, *Teredo*, *Thermopylae* which had a Mk XXII.

† Except *Thunderbolt*. 1x20 mm Oerlikon added in some in 1942.

†† One stern tube added to *Taku*, *Thunderbolt*, *Tigris*, *Torbay*, *Tribune*, *Trident*, *Truant* and *Tuna* in 1942.

‡ 20 mm Oerlikon AA gun fitted in *Thrasher* and *Trusty* from 1943.

§ *Torbay* and *Trident* had an endurance of 11,000 nm at 10 kts.

¶ Except boats with fully-welded hulls (*Tiptoe* onwards) which had a depth limit of 350-feet.

Right: The 'T' class included the ill-fated Thetis which foundered during sea trials in 1939. She was raised and re-named Thunderbolt.

Left: Many of the T-Class served for two decades, hence the multitude of modifications throughout their service life.

1 ONE OF THESE WAS BY GUNFIRE. *SALPA* WAS SUNK BY *TRIUMPH* OFF MERSA MATRUH, LIBYA, ON JUNE 27, 1941.

British 'T' class overseas patrol submarine

Boat	Builder	Laid down	Commissioned	Fate
Group One				
Triton	Vickers, Barrow	28-08-1936	09-11-1938	Sunk by Italian torpedo boat *Clio*, South Adriatic, 18-12-1940.
Thunderbolt (ex-*Thetis*)	Cammell Laird, Birkenhead	21-12-1936	04-1940	Foundered on acceptance trials, Mersey Bay, 01-06-1939. 99 lost, 4 survivors. Raised, 11-1939, recommissioned as *Thunderbolt*. Sunk by Italian corvette *Cicogna* off Cape St. Vito, Sicily, 14-03-1943.
Trident	Cammell Laird, Birkenhead	12-01-1937	01-10-1939	Sold for scrap, 17-02-1946, Newport.
Tribune	Scotts, Greenock	03-03-1937	17-10-1939	Sold for scrap, 07-1947.
Triumph	Vickers, Barrow	19-03-1937	02-05-1939	Mined, South Aegean Sea, off Milo, 14-01-1942.
Tarpon	Scotts, Greenock	05-10-1937	08-03-1940	Sunk by armed German trawler, *M 6*, North Sea, 14-04-1940.
Taku	Cammell Laird, Birkenhead	18-11-1937	03-10-1940	Sold for scrap, 11-1946, South Wales.
Thistle	Vickers, Barrow	07-12-1937	04-07-1939	Torpedoed on surface by *U 4*, off Skudenaes, NW of Stavanger, Norway, 10-04-1940.
Truant	Vickers, Barrow	24-03-1938	31-10-1938	Sold 19-12-1945. Wrecked *en route* to breakers, Normandy, 09-12-1946.
Triad	Vickers, Barrow	24-03-1938	16-09-1939	Sunk by Italian submarine *Enrico Toti*, off Libya, 15-10-1940.
Tigris	HM Dockyard, Chatham	11-05-1938	20-06-1940	Mined, Gulf of Tunis, 10-03-1943.
Tuna	Scotts, Greenock	13-06-1938	01-08-1940	Scrapped 24-06-1946
Tetrarch	Vickers, Barrow	24-08-1938	15-02-1940	Mined in Sicilian channel on passage, Malta-Gibraltar, 02-11-1941.
Talisman	Cammell Laird, Birkenhead	27-09-1938	29-06-1940	Mined, Sicilian Channel, 16-09-1942.
Torbay	HM Dockyard, Chatham	21-11-1938	14-01-1941	Sold for scrap, 19-12-1945.
Group Two				
Thrasher	Cammell Laird, Birkenhead	14-11-1939	14-05-1941	Scrapped 09-03-1947
Tempest	Cammell Laird, Birkenhead	06-01-1940	06-12-1941	Torpedoed by Italian torpedo boat *Circe*, Gulf of Taranto, 13-02-1942. Sank later under tow.
Traveller	Scotts, Greenock	17-01-1940	10-04-1942	Mined, Gulf of Taranto, 08-12-1942.
Thorn	Cammell Laird, Birkenhead	20-01-1940	26-08-1941	Depth charged by Italian torpedo boat, *Pegaso* off Crete, 14-08-1942.
Trusty	Vickers, Barrow	15-03-1940	30-07-1941	Scrapped, Milford Haven, 07-1947.
Turbulent	Vickers, Barrow	15-03-1940	02-12-1941	Probably sank after depth charging by Italian ships off Sardinia, 14-03-1943.
Trooper	Scotts, Greenock	26-03-1940	29-08-1942	Mined, Leros area of Aegean sea, 10-10-1943.
Group Three				
P 311*	Vickers, Barrow	25-04-1941	07-08-1942	Mined off Maddalena, Sardinia, 31-12-1942
Trespasser (ex- *P 92, P 312*)	Vickers, Barrow	08-09-1941	25-09-1942	Scrapped 26-09-1961
Thule (ex- *P 325*)	HM Dockyard, Devonport	20-09-1941	13-05-1944	Damaged in collision with RFA *Black Ranger*, English Channel, 18-11-1960. Scrapped 14-09-1962.
Tudor (ex- *P 326*)	HM Dockyard, Devonport	20-09-1941	16-01-1944	Scrapped 23-07-1963
Taurus (ex- *P 93, P 313, P 339*)	Vickers, Barrow	30-09-1941	03-11-1942	04-06-1948 Loaned to Royal Netherlands Navy, renamed *Dolfijn* 04-06-1948 07-12-1953. Scrapped 04-1960.
Tireless	HM Dockyard, Portsmouth	30-10-1941	18-04-1945	Modernised and streamlined. Scrapped 11-1968
Token (ex-*P 238*)	HM Dockyard, Portsmouth	06-11-1941	15-12-1945	Modernised and streamlined. Sold for scrap, Portsmouth, 03-1970.
Tactician	Vickers, Barrow	13-11-1941	29-11-1942	Sold 06-12-1963 and scrapped, Newport.
Truculent (ex-*P95, P315*)	Vickers, Barrow	04-12-1941	31-12-1942	Sank after collision with MV *Divina* in Thames Estuary, 12-01-1950. 15 killed, 58 survivors. Raised 14-03-1950. Sold for scrap, 12-05-1950.
Templar (ex-*P 96, P 316*)	Vickers, Barrow	28-12-1941	15-02-1943	Sunk as target, Loch Striven, 1950. Raised, 04-12-1958, scrapped 17-07-1959.
Tradewind (ex-*P 329*)	HM Dockyard, Chatham	11-02-1942	18-10-1943	Scrapped 14-12-1955.

Boat	Builder	Laid down	Commissioned	Fate
Tally Ho (ex-*P 97, P 317*)	Vickers, Barrow	25-03-1942	12-04-1943	Scrapped 10-02-1967
Trenchant (ex-*P98, P 318*)	HM Dockyard, Chatham	09-05-1942	26-02-1944	Scrapped 23-07-1963.
Tantalus (ex-*P 98, P 318*)	Vickers, Barrow	06-06-1942	02-06-1943	Scrapped 11-1950.
Tantivy (ex- *P99, P 319*)	Vickers, Barrow	04-07-1942	25-07-1943	Sunk as target, Cromarty Firth, 1951.
Telemachus (ex-*P 321*)	Vickers, Barrow	25-08-1942	25-10-1943	Scrapped, Charlestown, Fife, 08-1961
Talent (ex-*P322*)	Vickers, Barrow	13-10-1942	04-12-1943	Sold to Royal Netherlands Navy 23-03-1943. Commissioned as *Zwaardvisch*. 23-11-1943. Renamed *Zwaardvis*, 1950. Decommissioned, 11-12-1962. Scrapped, Antwerp, 12-07-1963.
Terrapin (ex-*P 323*)	Vickers, Barrow	19-10-1942	21-01-1944	Declared constructive total loss after being badly damaged by Japanese depth-charge attacks in Java Sea, 19-05-1945. Last RN submarine casualty of World War II. Scrapped 06-1946.
Totem	HM Dockyard, Devonport	22-10-1942	09-01-1945	Rebuilt, 1950/51. Sold to Israeli Navy, recommissioned as *Dakur*, 10-11-1967. Lost, 500 km NW of Isreali coast, 26-01-1968. Collision with merchant ship? 69 lost.
Thorough	Vickers, Barrow	26-10-1942	01-03-1944	Scrapped 29-06-1961
Truncheon	HM Dockyard, Devonport	05-11-1942	25-05-1945	Rebuilt, 1950/51. Sold to Israeli Navy, recommissioned as *Dolphin*, 09-01-1968. Decommissioned 08-1975. Used as pier, Sinai coast.
Tiptoe	Vickers, Barrow	10-11-1942	12-04-1944	Rebuilt, 1950/51. Last of 'T' class to be paid off, 29-08-1969. Scrapped, 1975.
Trump	Vickers, Barrow	13-12-1942	08-07-1944	Rebuilt, 1950/51 Scrapped 08-1971
Taciturn	Vickers, Barrow	09-03-1943	08-10-1944	Rebuilt, 1950/51. Recommissioned 12-03-1951. Scrapped, 1971.
Tapir (ex-*P 335*)	Vickers, Barrow	29-03-1943	30-12-1944	16-12-1953 Modernised, and streamlined Loaned to Royal Netherlands Navy, 18-06-1948–16-07-1953 as *Zeehond*. Scrapped 02-1966.
Thor	HM Dockyard, Portsmouth	05-04-1943	-	Cancelled, 1945
Tiara	HM Dockyard, Portsmouth	09-04-1943	-	Cancelled, 1945
Turpin	HM Dockyard, Portsmouth	24-05-1943	18-12-1944	Rebuilt, 1950/51. Sold to Israeli Navy, renamed *Leviathan*, 19-05-1967. Sunk in torpedo trials as target, 12-1973.
Tarn (ex-*P 336*)	Vickers, Barrow	12-06-1943	07-04-1945	Transferred to Royal Netherlands Navy, recommissioned as *Tijgerhaai*, 28-03-1945 Streamlined, 1961/1962. Decommissioned, 29-09-1964. Sold for scrap, 05-11-1965.
Thermopylae	HM Dockyard, Chatham	16-10-1943	05-12-1945	Rebuilt, 1950/51. Scuttled in Loch Striven, raised in training exercise. Scrapped 07-1970, Troon.
Talent (3) (ex-*Tasman, P 337*)	Vickers, Barrow	21-03-1944	27-07-1945	Modernised and streamlined. Renamed, 04-1945 as *Talent*. Paid off, 12-1966. Sold for scrap, Troon, 28-02-1970.
Teredo (ex-*P 338*)	Vickers, Barrow	17-04-1944	21-01-1944	Modernised and streamlined. Scrapped 05-06-1965
Tabard	Scotts, Greenock	06-09-1944	25-06-1946	Rebuilt 1950/51. Refitted, Sydney and recommissioned in Royal Australian Navy 27-03-1962. Returned as display boat, Gosport, 1968. Scrapped, 14-03-1974.
Typhoon	-	-	-	Not ordered
Threat	Vickers, Barrow	-	-	Cancelled, 1944
Theban	Vickers, Barrow	-	-	Cancelled, 1944
Talent (2)	Scotts, Greenock	-	-	Cancelled, 1944

* Was to be named *Tutankhamen*

British 'T' class, much-modified long endurance ocean patrol submarines

Thunderbolt's two-man chariot diver submersibles sank the Italian light cruiser *Ulpio Triano* in a daring raid inside Palermo harbour, on January 3 1943.

The second group's war record included *Trooper*'s sinking, (with one torpedo,) of the Italian minelaying submarine *Pietro Micca* in the Otranto Strait, on July 29 1943 and *Thorn*'s sinking of the submarine *Medusa*, south of Brioni Island in the Adriatic, on January 30 1942.

Part of the third group were built with all-welded hulls and these boats were stationed in the Far East with extra fuel reserves for greater endurance. All were fitted with Type 291W combined air/surface search radar but by the end of the war, this had been replaced by the Type 267W.

The Far East boats accounted for four submarines: *I-34*, in the Malacca Strait, on November 13 1943, (*Taurus*); *I-166* in the same area on July 17 1944 (*Telemachus*) *U-It 23²* off Penang, Malaya, on February 14 1944, (*Tally Ho*) and *U 859*, also off Penang, on September 23 1943, (*Trenchant*). Two German U boats were also destroyed in the North Atlantic: *U 308* by *Truculent* north of the Faeroes on June 4 1943 and *U 486* by *Tapir* North west of Bergen in Norway, on April 12 1945.

Tally Ho also sank the Japanese heavy cruiser *Kuma* off Penang in the Malacca Straits, on January 11 1944. She was carrying a very large number of troops as reinforcements for Singapore. *Trenchant*, lying inside an Allied minefield at the entrance of Bank Strait, off Palembang, Sumatra, torpedoed and sank the Japanese

Nachi class cruiser *Ashigara*, 12,700, with a spread of eight torpedoes, of which five hit - blowing off the enemy ship's bow.

Two 'T' class boats were supplied to the Royal Netherlands Navy during the war, one of which, *Zwaardvisch* sank *U 168* off the North coast of Java, on October 6 1944, with six torpedoes at 900 yards. She rescued 27 survivors, three of whom escaped at a depth of 120 ft without breathing apparatus.

After the war, a number of modifications were made to later boats of the class. Five of the riveted hull boats (*Tapir, Tireless, Talent, Teredo and Token*), were streamlined and updated with a new sonar and a fin-type conning tower. Later, in 1949-56, eight welded hull boats were completely rebuilt with a 12 to 20-foot long plug inserted in the pressure hull to lengthen it. Diesel power was increased by 300 bhp and a second pair of electric motors, with a fourth battery compartment, were installed. The external tanks were removed as was the gun. The fin was fitted with two radar masts, two snort masts and a wireless mast.

Thorough became the first submarine to circumnavigate the globe, returning to Portsmouth on December 16, 1957.

The last 'T' class to be paid off was *Tiptoe* on August 29, 1969.

A number of 'T' boats were sold or loaned to overseas navies: four to the Netherlands, three to Israel and one to Australia.

Full conversion 'T' class

	Group 'A'**	Group 'B'***
Length	285.5†	293.5
Beam	Unchanged	Unchanged
Displacement		
Surface	1,544	1,535
Submerged	1,696	1,734
Speed		
Surface	14.2 - 15. 4 kts	14.2 - 15. 4 kts
Submerged	8.75 kts	8.75 kts
Armament	6 x 21" torpedo tubes	6 x 21" torpedo tubes
	or Mk II mines	or Mk II mines
Engines	2,800 bhp diesel	2,800 bhp diesel
	2,900 bhp electric	2,900 bhp electric
Diving depth	350 ft	350 ft
Crew	68	68

* *Taciturn, Thermopylae, Totem, Turpin*

** *Tabard, Tiptoe, Trump, Truncheon*

† *Taciturn* was 287.5-feet long.

2 Ex-Italian submarine *Reginaldo Guiliani*.

Left and below: Truculent sank after a collision in 1950 with the loss of 15 souls.

US *Sargo* class - first into the Pacific war

Length (ft)	310.5
Beam (ft)	27.08 oa
Displacement (tons)	
Surfaced	1,450
Submerged	2,350
Speed (kts)	
Surfaced	20.0
Dived	8.75
Armament	4 x 21" bow tubes, 4x21" stern tubes
	12 reloads plus 4 external (later removed)
	1 x 3-ins 50 cal. (1x4-ins later on some)
	2 x.50 cal, 2 x.30 cal machine guns
Engines	4 diesel, 2,740 shp
	2 electric motors, 3,300 hp
Range	
Surfaced	11,000 nm at 10 kts
Submerged	100 nm at 5kts
Diving depth	260 ft
Complement	55

The US *Sargo* class patrol submarines were first into action after the Japanese attacks on the US naval bases in Hawaii on December 7, 1941. Seven boats of the class began their first war patrols the next day, with *Sargo* making eight attacks on enemy shipping in the South China sea. Although her Mk 14 torpedoes all failed to hit, either running erratically or too deep - a familiar and frustrating problem early in the Pacific war.

Sealion and *Seadragon* meanwhile were caught by an enemy air raid on Cavite Navy Yard in the Philippines on December 10. *Sealion* received a direct hit on the conning tower after end and a second bomb penetrated the pressure hull and exploded in the engine room. She sank immediately and was scuttled on December 25. *Seadragon* was damaged in the attack but was towed away from a burning wharf by the submarine rescue tender *Pigeon*.

The class had an active war, sinking 73 enemy ships, including the aircraft carrier *Chuyo* and a Japanese submarine despite ferocious depth charging by escorts. Poignantly, *Chuyo* was carrying 21 survivors of *Sculpin*'s crew when she was torpedoed on December 4/5 1943, 240 nm south east of Yokosuka, Japan, by the sister boat *Sailfish*. Twenty American prisoners were killed.

Sailfish had been laid down as *Squalus* and, on May 12 1939, began test dives off Portsmouth, New Hampshire. The following day, she submerged again off the Isle of Shoals but a valve failed, flooding the after engine room and she sank in 240-feet of water, releasing a distress buoy and a red smoke bomb. The newly developed McCann rescue diving bell brought 33 survivors safely to the surface - the first successful rescue by the US Navy at that depth. However, 26 died, trapped in the flooded engine room. *Squalus* was salvaged and towed back to Portsmouth Navy Yard. After repair, she was recommissioned on May 15 1940, as *Sailfish*.

In addition to *Sealion*, there were three war casualties among the class.

Sculpin was scuttled after fierce depth-charging by Japanese destroyers after her attack on a large convoy, on November 19 1944. The commander of a three-boat wolfpack, Cmdr John Cromwell, chose to go down with *Sculpin* rather than risk divulging, under interrogation, the knowledge he had of imminent assaults on the Pacific Islands.

Swordfish was lost on her 13th war patrol near Okinawa in early February 1945. *Seawolf* was probably lost in an accidental attack by aircraft from the carrier USS *Midway* and the destroyer *Richard M Rowell* on October 3 1944, in the Morotai area of the then Dutch East Indies (now Indonesia).

After the war, the class moved to the training role. *Searaven* was a target ship during an atomic weapon test on Bikini Atoll in 1946. Damage was reported "negligible" and she was later expended as a target. *Sailfish* was due to be a target in the same test series but was scrapped in 1948.

Above: These vessels were amongst the first to strike back against the Japanese after the attack on Pearl Harbour, but troubles with Torpedoes blighted their early months of operations.

Above: Seadragon was lucky to survive an air-raid within the first few days of World War Two, but continued in service throughout the war.

US *'Sargo'* class patrol submarine

Boat	Builder	Laid down	Commissioned	Fate
Sargo (SS-188)	Electric Boat Company, Groton Connecticut	12-05-1937	07-02-1939	Decommissioned 22-06-1946. Sold for scrap, 19-05-1947.
Saury (SS-189)	Electric Boat Company, Groton Connecticut	28-06-1937	03-04-1939	Decommissioned 22-06-1946. Scrapped 10-1948.
Spearfish (SS-190)	Electric Boat Company, Groton Connecticut	09-09-1937	17-07-1939	Decommissioned Mare Island, 22-06-1946. Scrapped 10-1947.
Sculpin (SS-191)	Portsmouth Navy Yard, New Hampshire	07-09-1937	16-01-1939	Scuttled after depth-charging and gunfire by Japanese destroyer 19-12-1944. 42 survivors captured.
Sailfish (ex-*Squalus*) (SS-192)	Portsmouth Navy Yard, New Hampshire	18-10-1937	01-03-1939	15-05-1940 Flooded and sank on diving trials 23-05-1939. 26 crew lost, 33 survivors. Raised and recommissioned as *Sailfish*. Decommissioned, 27-10-1945. Sold for scrap 18-06-1948.
Swordfish (SS-193)	Mare Island Navy Yard, Vallejo, California	27-10-1937	22-07-1939	Lost, near Okinawa, Japan, 02-1945.
Seadragon (SS-194)	Electric Boat Company, Groton Connecticut	18-04-1938	23-10-1939	Decommissioned 29-10-1946 and placed in Atlantic Fleet Reserve. Sold for scrap, 02-07-1948.
Sealion (SS-195)	Electric Boat Company, Groton Connecticut	20-06-1938	27-11-1939	Two direct hits in Japanese bombing raid on Cavite, Philippines, 10-12-1941. Four killed. Scuttled, 25-12-1941.
Searaven (SS-196)	Portsmouth Navy Yard, New Hampshire	09-08-1938	02-10-1939	Target ship in 1946 Bikini Atoll nuclear test. Minimal damage. Decommissioned 11-12-1946. Sunk as target 11-09-1948.
Seawolf (SS-197)	Portsmouth Navy Yard, New Hampshire	27-09-1938	01-12-1939	Probably sunk after air attack by US aircraft from escort carrier *Midway* and depth-charging by destroyer *Richard M Rowell*, Morotai Island, Indonesia, 03-10-1944.

Atlantic warrior: The German Type VIIB 1937-1940

Length (ft)	218.12 oa
Beam (ft)	20.34 oa
Displacement (tons)	
Surfaced	753
Submerged	857
Speed (kts)	
Surfaced	17.9
Dived	8.0
Armament	4 x 21" bow tubes, 1 x 21" stern tube
	9 reloads
	1 x 88 mm 45 calibre gun. 220 rounds
	26 TMA mines
Engines	3200 hp diesel
	750 hp electric
Range	
Surfaced	8,700 nm at 10 kts
Submerged	90 nm at 4 kts
Diving depth	720 ft
Complement	44

The German Type VIIB U Boat was a substantial improvement on the 10 boats of the preceding Type VIIA class built in 1935-37. More power and an additional rudder provided greater manoeuvrability but more importantly, extra fuel capacity stored in external saddle tanks offered an additional 2,500 nm at cruising speed for Atlantic patrols.

The 24-strong class, built at three yards in 1937-41, went on to sink 277 ships displacing a total 1,549,884 tons in 1939-43 and damaging a further 37 totalling 253,384 tons after which the survivors were relegated to a training role. It included the most successful U Boat of the Second World War, *U 48* which sank 52 ships in 11 patrols between September 1939 and June 1941.

U 47 attacked and sank the Royal Navy battleship *Royal Oak* within the safety of the Scapa Flow anchorage, 1.7 miles from Scapa Pier light on October 14 1939, in probably the most daring U boat exploit of World War II. It was reported missing on March 7 1942, off Rockall in the North Atlantic, probably being sunk in a minefield.

U 73 sank the British aircraft carrier *Eagle* with four torpedoes at a range of under a mile, south of Majorca, on August 11 1942, during OPERATION PEDESTAL, the re-supply of the beleaguered island of Malta.

U 100 was sunk off the Faeroe Islands on March 17 1941 after being located by radar by the British destroyer *Vanoc* - the first operational detection of a U Boat by this means.

The Type VIIC, the so-called workhorse of the U Boat fleet in World War II, was a design based on the VIIB, although slower than the earlier boats. A total of 568 were built and commissioned in 1940-45.

German Type VIIB U Boats

Boat	Builder	Laid down	Commissioned	Fate
U 45	Germaniawerft, Kiel	26-02-1937	25-06-1938	Sank after depth charging by British destroyers *Inglefield*, *Ivanhoe* and *Intrepid*, escorting convoy KJF.3, SW of Irish Republic, 14-02-1939.
U 46	Germaniawerft, Kiel	25-02-1937	02-11-1938	Scuttled off Neustadt, 04-05-1945.
U 47	Germaniawerft, Kiel	27-02-1937	17-12-1938	Missing, North Atlantic, 03-1941. Royal Navy records claim sunk by *Wolverine* with depth charges after attack on convoy OB.293, 08-03-1941.
U 48	Germaniawerft, Kiel	11-11-1936	22-04-1939	Scuttled 03-05-1945.
U 49	Germaniawerft, Kiel	15-09-1938	12-08-1939	Sank off Narvik, North Norway, after depth charging by British destroyer *Fearless*, 15-04-1940.
U 50	Germaniawerft, Kiel	03-11-1938	12-12-1939	Mined, North of Shetland Islands, 06-04-1940.
U 51	Germaniawerft, Kiel	10-02-1937	06-08-1938	Torpedoed, Bay of Biscay, by British submarine *Cachalot*, 20-08-1940.
U 52	Germaniawerft, Kiel	04-03-1937	04-02-1939	Scuttled, Kiel, 03-05-1945.
U 53	Germaniawerft, Kiel	13-03-1937	24-06-1939	Sank after depth charging by British destroyer *Gurkha*, S of Faeroe Islands, 23-02-1940.
U 54	Germaniawerft, Kiel	13-09-1937	23-09-1939	Scuttled at Kiel, 03-05-1945.
U 55	Germaniawerft, Kiel	02-11-1938	21-11-1939	Sank following depth charging by British warships *Whitshed*, *Fowey* and Sunderland aircraft Y/288, 90 miles SW of Isles of Scilly, 30-01-1940. (Convoy OA.80G).
U 73	Bremer Vulkan, Bremen	05-11-1939	30-09-1940	Sank, following depth charging by US destroyers *Woolsey* and *Trippe*, N. of Oran, Mediterranean, 16-12-1943. 34 taken prisoner.
U 74	Bremer Vulkan, Bremen	05-11-1939	31-10-1940	Sank following depth charging by British destroyers *Wishart* and *Wrestler* and Catalina aircraft C/202 S. of Cartagena, Spain, 02-05-1942. Crew lost.
U 75	Bremer Vulkan, Bremen	15-12-1939	19-12-1940	Sank following depth charging by British destroyer *Kipling*, off Mersa Matruh, Libya, 28-12-1941. 30 crew captured.
U 76	Bremer Vulkan, Bremen	28-12-1939	03-12-1940	Sank following depth charging by British destroyer *Scarborough* and sloop *Wolverine*, S of Iceland, 05-04-1941. (Convoy SC.26).
U 83	Flender-Werke, Lübeck	05-10-1939	08-02-1941	Sank following depth charging by British Hudson aircraft, V/500 SE of Cartagena, Spain, 04-03-1943.
U 84	Flender-Werke, Lübeck	09-11-1939	29-04-1941	Lost, North Atlantic, 08-1943.
U 85	Flender-Werke, Lübeck	18-12-1939	07-06-1941	Sank after being shelled by US destroyer *Roper* off Cape Hatteras, USA, 14-04-1942.
U 86	Flender-Werke, Lübeck	20-01-1940	08-07-1941	Lost, North Atlantic, 12-1943.
U 87	Flender-Werke, Lübeck	18-04-1940	19-08-1941	Sank, following depth charging by Canadian destroyer *St Croix* and corvette *Shediac*, N. Atlantic, 04-03-1943. (Convoy KMS.10).
U 99	Germaniawerft, Kiel	31-03-1939	18-04-1940	Scuttled after depth charge attack by British destroyer *Walker*, off Faeroes, 17-03-1941. (Convoy HX.112). First operational detection of U Boat by radar.
U 100	Germaniawerft, Kiel	22-05-1939	30-05-1940	Sank after ramming by British destroyers *Vanoc* and *Walker* off Faeroes, 17-03-1941.
U 101	Germaniawerft, Kiel	31-03-1939	11-03-1940	Scuttled 03-05-1945.
U 102	Germaniawerft, Kiel	22-05-1939	27-04-1940	Sank following depth charging by British destroyer *Vansittart*, SW of Iceland, 01-07-1940.

Giants of the Ocean: the ill-fated British 'M' class Monitors

The grotesque 'M' class monitors were designed to bring heavy guns to the submarine armoury. Intended as raiders against merchant shipping, the 12-inch Mark IX guns, salvaged from the sunken battleship *Formidable,* were fired with the muzzle above water, while the submarine ran submerged 12-20-feet below. A bead sight on the muzzle enabled the gun to be sighted via a periscope. Utility was strictly limited: the gun had no turntable and the boat had to surface to reload.

M 1 was commissioned on April 17 1918 and 24 hours after, in company with the destroyer *Dove* and submarines *L 2* and *L 8,* she sighted a large unidentified U Boat on the surface in the Irish Sea - but it dived before she could bring her gun to bear. In June, she was sent to the Mediterranean to bombard Constantinople but this mission was cancelled. After a period in reserve, she was recommissioned in August 1920 - for gunnery trials against surplus U boat hulls and sank two.

M 2 was used for various experiments in 1923, including deep dives and one involving a simulated poison gas attack on the surface. In 1925, work began at HM Dockyard Chatham to convert her into a seaplane

Above: Whilst complying with the terms of the Washington Naval Treaty, the 12-inch gun was later removed in favour of an aircraft hangar.

	M 1 - M 3	M 3(conversion)
Length (ft)	295.75	295.75
Beam (ft)	20.33	20.33
Displacement (tons)		
Surfaced	1,594	1,670
Submerged	1,946	2,006
Speed (kts)		
Surfaced	15	15
Dived	8.5	8.5
Armament		
	1 x 12"/35 cal Mk. IX gun (*M 1*)	100 Type B mines
	(50 rounds)	
	1 x 3" Mk 2 High Angle AA Gun	1 x 3" Mk 2 High Angle AAGun
	4 x 18" bow torpedo tubes	4 x 18" bow torpedo tubes
	(4 reloads)	(4 reloads)
	Parnall Peto seaplane (*M 2*)	
Engines	2 x 1,200 hp diesel	2 x 1,200 hp diesel
	2 x 800 hp electric	2 x 800 hp electric
	twin screws	twin screws
Range		
Surface	4,500 nm at 10 kts	4,500 nm at 10 kts
Submerged	80 nm at 2 kts	80 nm at 2 kts
Diving depth	200 ft*	200ft
Complement	64**	60

* *M 2* achieved 239 ft in an uncontrolled dive in 1923.

** *M 2* had a complement of 55 after conversion into a seaplane carrier, including two RAF officers.

British 'M' class submarine monitors

Boat	Builder	Laid Down	Commissioned	Fate
M 1 (ex-K 18)	Vickers, Barrow	13-07-1916	17-04-1918	Sunk in collision with Swedish collier *Vidar* while diving, off Start Point, Devon, 12-11-1925. Crew lost.
M 2 (ex-K 19)	Vickers, Barrow	13-07-1916	04-1920	Failed to surface after dive in West Bay, off Portland, 26-01-1932. Crew lost.
M 3 (ex-K 20)	Armstrong-Whitworth, Newcastle-upon-Tyne	04-12-1916	07-1920	Sold 16-02-1932. 04-1932, scrapped at Newport.
M 4 (ex-K 21)	Armstrong-Whitworth, Newcastle-upon-Tyne	N/K	-	Cancelled. Sold as incomplete hulk, 30-11-1921.

Below: The ill-fated *M2* complete with hangar, recovery crane and launching ramp for her seaplane. In 1923 the boat went out of control off Lerwick when water flooded through an open hatch after diving, striking the seabed at 230ft. A similar accident may have caused her later loss with all hands.

carrier at a cost of £60,000. An aircraft, the Parnall Peto, was specially designed as a scout aircraft and a hanger, ramp and derrick was added for launching and recovery operations. Her 12-inch gun was removed to comply with the 1922 Washington Naval Conference terms, which limited submarine guns to an eight-inch calibre.

M 3 had her main gun armament removed at Chatham in 1927-28 and the upper deck modified to carry a casing with a conveyor belt to carry and launch over the stern, first 80 and then 100 Type B mines.

In 1924, all the 'M' class were re-painted to test hull colours as seen from aircraft. M 1 was painted grey-green; M 2, dark grey and M 3 dark blue.

On November 12 1925, M 1 departed Plymouth in company with M 3 for exercises involving a cruiser attack on a submarine-escorted troop convoy. The boat was seen to simulate gun attacks with her Mark IX gun muzzle breaking surface. Afterwards, she disappeared. A clue to her fate came eight days later when the Swedish collier Vidar, 2,000 tons, berthed at Stockholm with damage to her stem. Her captain reported two heavy blows forward in the exercise area and had assumed they were "submarine bombs."

M 1's wreck was discovered by a salvage vessel in September 1967, and dives in July 1999 demonstrated that the collision with Vidar had ripped off the gun barrel and pushed the mounting ring through the pressure hull, flooding the shell room. The 58 tons weight of the gun mounting, together with the flooding, carried the submarine to the sea bed 240-feet down.

M 2 left Portland for exercises in West Bay, 15 nm west of Portland on January 26 1932. She too disappeared, and it is believed she sank after the hanger door failed to close correctly during a dive after launching the seaplane. M 2 today is used as a target for training sonar operators.

M 3 was used to generate electric power for the Royal Victoria and Albert and King George V Docks in London during the General Strike on May 9-15 1926. She proved a successful minelayer and experience gained was used in the design of the Royal Navy's Porpoise class minelayers.

Right: The end of the *M1* on November 12 1925. After simulating gun attacks, the collier *Vidor* strikes the *M1's* gun mounting. The submarine floods and sinks in 240ft of water.

Above: M2 flying her scout aircraft in 1928. M2 sank in January 1932, while diving after launching her Parnell Peto aircraft.

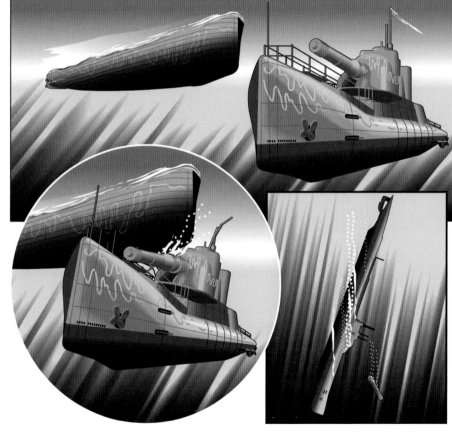

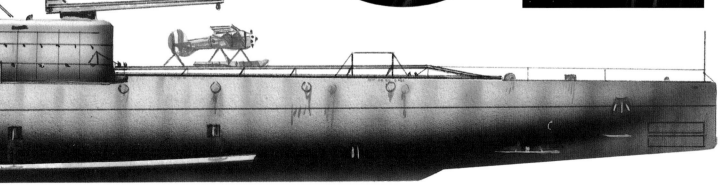

Submarine gun cruisers - powerful commerce raiders?

During the First World War, Germany produced three powerful submarine cruisers *U139-141* armed with two 5.9-inch guns, designed as commerce raiders, with 12,630 nm range at eight kts and a surface speed of up to 15.8 kts. Their performance impressed the Allied powers and Britain, France and the United States all produced designs for boats with the same role, limited in armament by naval treaty.

The Royal Navy produced the experimental *X1*, designed to destroy all armed merchant ships, armed with the new semi-automatic 5.2-inch/42 cal. Mk 1 quick-firing gun in two twin bulbous turrets mounted fore and after of the conning tower. A total of 104 rounds were carried per gun. The double-hulled boat, commissioned in 1925, was budgeted to cost £942,000 but after a series of mishaps, including an engine room fire under construction, the final cost was £1,044,158.

The boat was manpower-intensive: 58 crew were required to man the guns and reload them with ammunition hoists that proved problematical. Reports of engine problems were probably officially exaggerated; the boat was reported to handle well on the surface and whilst submerged. The Admiralty laid her up and scrapped her in 1936.

France meanwhile had hit on the same requirement and produced the monstrous *Surcouf*, armed with a turret forward of the conning tower armed with the new twin eight-inch/50 cal Model 1924 guns designed for surface cruisers. The guns could hurl a 271lb shell 34,340 yards and *Surcouf* managed a rate of fire of three rounds a

	X1	Surcouf	Argonaut	Type XI
Length (ft)	363.5	360.8	381.0	360.8
Beam (ft)	29.83	29.52	33.83	N/K
Displacement				
Surface	2,780	3,304	2,710	3,800
Submerged	3,600	4,218	4,080	4,750
Speed (kts)				
Surface	20	18	15	15
Dived	9	8.5	8	8
Armament				
	2 x 2 5.2-inch/42 guns	2 x 8-inch/50 guns	2 x 6-inch guns	2 x twin 5-inch guns
	2 x .303 machine guns	2 x 37mm AA		2 x 88 mm AA guns
		2 twin 13.2 mm MGs		
		Besson MB.411		Arado Ar 231 seaplane
		Scout seaplane		
	6x21-inch bow tubes	6 x 550 mm bow tubes	4x21-inch bow tubes	4 x 21" bow tubes
	6 reloads	4 x 400mm stern tubes	2 x 21" stern tubes	2 stern minelaying tubes
Engines				
	2 x 5,445 bhp diesel **	2 x 7,600 hp diesel	2 diesels, 6000 hp	8 diesels, 17,600 hp
	2,600 hp electric	2 electric 3,400 hp	2 electric, 2400 hp	2 electric 2,200 hp
	2 shafts	2 shafts		
Range				
Surfaced	12,400 nm at 12 kts	10,000 nm at 10 kts	16,000 nm at 8 kts	13,200 nm at 10 kts
Submerged	50 nm at 4 kts	70 nm at 4.5 kts	10 nm at 8 kts	50 nm at 4 kts
Diving depth	200 ft	250 ft	250 ft	N/K
Complement	109	120	89	110

* Torpedo tubes taken from cancelled 'L' class boat.

** Auxiliary MAN diesels taken from surrendered *U 126*.

Left: X1, the *Royal Navy's* venture into submarine gun cruisers. She was scrapped in 1936 after problems with ammunition hoists.

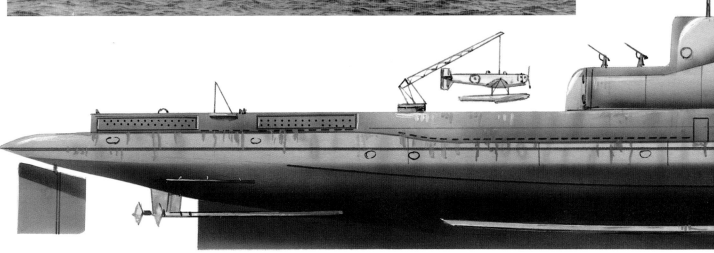

minute. Six hundred rounds were carried, but reportedly, the guns were never fired in anger. The boat also carried a Besson/ANF Mureaux MB 411 scout seaplane, in a hanger behind the conning tower, for target reconnaissance fall of shot spotting. *Surcouf* also had a special compartment to hold up to 40 prisoners - crews from captured prizes.

The boat was in refit at Brest in June 1940, when German troops occupied France. She escaped to Plymouth on the surface on only one engine. At 03.00 on July 3, when British forces, (fearing a hand-over of French ships to Germany,) boarded those sheltering in UK bases to seek their surrender, (in OPERATION CATAPULT) two British naval officers and one Frenchmen died when the *Surcouf* crew resisted.

In December 1940, the boat crossed the Atlantic and was involved in the controversial Free French operation to seize the islands of St Pierre and Miquelon, off the Atlantic coast of Canada. She was sunk by an American army transport on February 18 1941, in the Gulf of Panama, *en route* to Tahiti while only one engine was working. All 159 on board were lost - the world's worst submarine disaster.

The US Navy also was interested in submarine gun cruisers. The *Argonaut,* exempt from treaty armament and tonnage limitations, and designed mainly as a minelayer, was armed with two six-inch unprotected guns fore and aft of the conning tower, and was fitted with more powerful diesel engines than earlier boats of the 'V' class. She proved slow to dive with poor underwater manoeuvrability. *Argonaut* was damaged by depth charges during an attack on a five-cargo ship Japanese convoy, between New Britain and Bougainville on January 10 1943. Ironically, she was sunk by surface gunfire by the convoy escorts.

Germany produced the Type XI design, initially armed with four 15 cm guns, later changed to four 12.7 cm guns in twin turrets, fore and aft of the conning tower. The class was conceived with an armament capable of engaging an auxiliary cruiser at ranges greater than 30,000 yards with rapid fire immediately on surfacing. The class was also to carry an Ar 231 seaplane for reconnaissance. The 'Z' construction plan, of January 1939, envisaged seven Type XI boats operational by the end of 1941 and orders for the first four, *U112-115*, were placed with A.G.Weser of Bremen on January 17 1939, but were cancelled in May 1940. Any hulls that had been laid down were broken up.

Between the wars submarine gun cruisers

Boat	Builder	Laid down	Commissioned	Fate
X1	HM Dockyard, Chatham	02-11-1921	12-1925	In reserve, 1933. Up for disposal, 1936. Scrapped, 12-12-1936
Surcouf	Cherbourg Dockyard	12-1927*	05-1934	Sunk by US army transport *Thomson Sykes*, 18-02-1941.
Argonaut (ex-V4)	Portsmouth Navy Yard, Portsmouth, New Hampshire	01-05-1925	02-04-1928	Damaged by depth-charges and sunk by gunfire during attack on Japanese convoy, between New Britain and Bougainville, Pacific, 10-01-1943.
Type XI U Boat				
U 112	AG Weser, Bremen	N/K	-	Ordered 17-01-1939. Cancelled 05-1940.
U 113	AG Weser, Bremen	-	-	Ordered 17-01-1939. Cancelled 05-1940.
U 114	AG Weser, Bremen	-	-	Ordered 17-01-1939. Cancelled 05-1940.
U 115	AG Weser, Bremen	-	-	Ordered 17-01-1939. Cancelled 05-1940.

* Launched 18-10-1929.

Right: Surcouf in happier days before the Second World War. She sank later in a collision with an American troop ship in the worst submarine disaster.

Below: France's *Surcouf*, armed with a cruiser's twin eight-inch 50 cal model 1924 guns in a turret forward of the conning tower she also carried a Besson/ANF Mureaux MB 411 scout aircraft.

WORLD WAR II DESIGN & CONSTRUCTION

AS HOSTILITIES AT SEA INTENSIFIED, NEW DESIGNED MODIFICATIONS

were rushed into production, some successful, like the US Navy's *Gato* class;

some unsuccessful, such as the ill-conceived *Flak* U Boats.

This abandoned the submarines most important asset – the ability

to hide – to fight it out with enemy aircraft on the surface.

Inevitably, the submarine lost.

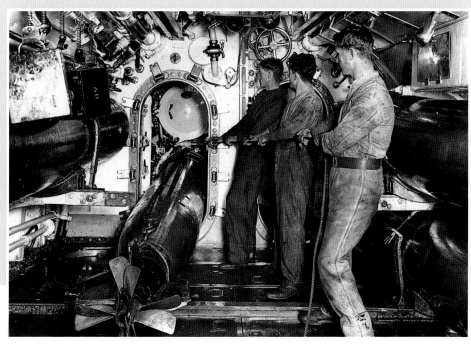

Type IXB - most successful convoy hunter

Germany's Type IXB submarine was the most successful of all U Boat classes in World War II, sinking 282 ships displacing a total of 1,526,510 tons. *U 107*, under Kptlt Günther Hessler, mounted the most successful U Boat patrol between March 29 and July 2, 1941, sinking 14 ships, totalling 86,699 tons, between the Canary Islands and the west coast of Africa.

U 123 was one of five Type IX boats that took part in the first stage of OPERATION PAUKENSCHLAG ('Drumbeat') off the East coast of the USA in January

Right: The crew of a departing U-Boat in a wartime propoganda photograph. This vessel was lost with all hands shortly afterwards.

Length (ft)	250.92 oa
Beam (ft)	22.17 oa
Displacement (tons)	
Surfaced	769
Submerged	871
Speed (kts)	
Surfaced	18.2
Dived	7.3
Armament	4 x 21" bow tubes, 2x21" stern tube
	16 reloads
	1 x 105 mm 5 calibre deck gun. 110 rounds
	44 TMA mines
Engines	4400 hp diesel
	1000 hp electric
Range	
Surfaced	12,000 nm at 10 kts
Submerged	65 nm at 4 kts
Diving depth	755 ft
Complement	54

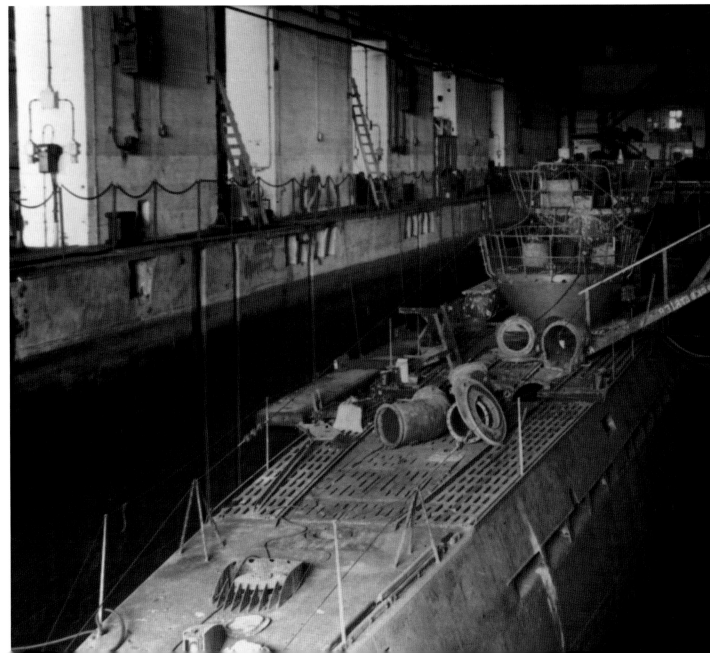

1942. The boat was the first to sink a ship, *Cyclops,* on January 11 and when the first phase of the operation ended on February 6, *U123* had sunk nine ships displacing 52,173 tons.[1]

The class had an additional range of 1,500 nm over the earlier Type IX, more powerful propulsion and carried extra torpedoes. During 'Drumbeat' operations they were refuelled by tanker U Boats, the so-called 'Milch cows' off Bermuda, which extended their time on patrol by eight weeks.

Only one Type IXB survived the war to become the French submarine *Blaison. U 110* was captured by British warships (contrary to Hollywood's perception) during an attack on convoy OB 318, south of Iceland on May 9, 1941. The boat was forced to surface after depth charging by the corvette *Aubretia* and was abandoned as *Bulldog* appeared to be on course for ramming her. During the rapid clearing of the boat's equipment and documents by British personnel, her enigma cipher machine was recovered which provided the last link in Britain's efforts

Type IXB long range U Boat

Boat	Builder	Laid down	Commissioned	Fate
U 64	AG Weser, Bremen	15-12-1938	16-12-1939	Sank in bombing by Swordfish aircraft of 700 sqd., based on battleship *Warspite,* in Herjangsfjord during second Battle of Narvik, 13-04-1940. 38 survivors. Raised, 1957, but sank under tow off Norway. Wreck raised 1957 but again sank under tow off Norway.
U 65	AG Weser, Bremen	06-12-1938	15-02-1940	Sunk by corvette *Gladiolus* SE of Iceland during attack on convoy HM.121. 28-04-1941.
U 103	AG Weser, Bremen	06-09-1939	05-07-1940	Sunk by bombs during USAAF attack on Kiel, 15-04-1945.
U 104	AG Weser, Bremen	10-11-1939	19-08-1940	Mined, NW of Iceland, 12-1940.
U 105	AG Weser, Bremen	16-11-1939	10-09-1940	Sunk by depth charges dropped by a Free French Navy flying boat off Dakar, 02-06-1943.
U 106	AG Weser Bremen	26-11-1939	24-09-1940	Sunk by depth charges from RAF Sunderland aircraft N/228 and Australian Sunderland M/461, SW Approaches, 02-08-1943.
U 107	AG Weser Bremen	06-12-1939	08-10-1940	Sunk by RAF Sunderland W/201, Bay of Biscay, 18-08-1944.
U 108	AG Weser Bremen	27-12-1939	22-10-1940	Sunk in bombing raid on Stettin, 11-04-1944, raised and scuttled 24-04-1945.
U 109	AG Weser Bremen	09-03-1940	05-12-1940	Sunk by depth charges dropped by Australian Sunderland aircraft W/10, Bay of Biscay, 07-05-1943.
U 110	AG Weser Bremen	01-02-1940	21-11-1940	Captured by corvette *Aubrieta* and escorts *Broadway* and *Bulldog* during attack on convoy OB.318, S. of Iceland, 09-05-1941. Sank under tow, 10-05-1941. 15, dead 32 captured.
U 111	AG Weser Bremen	20-02-1940	19-12-1940	Sunk by gunfire after depth charge attack by trawler *Lady Shirley,* 470 tons, WSW of Tenerife, 04-10-1941. 7 dead and 45 captured
U 122	AG Weser Bremen	05-03-1939	30-03-1940	Missing, 22-06-1940
U 123	AG Weser Bremen	15-04-1939	30-05-1940	Surrendered to French Navy at end of war and became French boat *Blaison.* Scrapped as Q 165, 09-1959.
U 124	AG Weser Bremen	11-08-1939	11-06-1940	Sunk by depth charges from corvette *Stonecrop* and sloop *Black Swan* during attack on convoy OS.45, off Oporto, 02-04-1943.

to decode German naval signal traffic. *U 110* sank the following day whilst under tow.

One of the strangest actions involved *U 111* caught on the surface WSW of Tenerife in the Canary Islands on October 4, 1941.

The boat dived when the armed trawler *Lady Shirley,* 470 tons, approached, but was located using asdic at 1,800 yards. The trawler dropped five depth charges and

Left and below: Only one example of this class survived the war and was amalgamated into the French Navy. Many boats were stationed within U-Boat 'pens' such as this along the Atlantic coast.

forced the submarine to the surface. The boat opened fire with her rapid-firing 105 mm deck gun, but unfortunately, the muzzle was still blocked by a tampion and the gun exploded. The trawler returned five, hitting the U Boat nine times with four-inch shells, and holing her pressure hull at the stern. *U 111* sank stern first, with 45 of her crew taken prisoner.

1 THE FIRST PHASE CLAIMED 25 SHIPS TOTALLING 156,940 TONS. TOTAL SHIPPING LOSSES IN THE DRUMBEAT CAMPAIGN THAT ENDED ON JULY 19, 1942, WERE MORE THAN 400 SHIPS TOTALLING MORE THAN TWO MILLION TONS AT THE COST OF 5,000 MERCHANT SEAMEN'S LIVES. THE US NAVY INSTITUTED CONVOYS IN MAY. SEVEN U BOATS WERE LOST.

U *Flak* Boats - gun platforms to trap Allied aircraft

The year 1943 saw mounting - and unacceptable - losses of U Boats in the Bay of Biscay, caught in a killing zone by Allied aircraft while departing or returning to their bases at Brest, Lorient, St. Nazaire and Bordeaux.. Twenty-eight boats were lost in this sea area - which became known as the 'Valley of Death" to U Boat crews, - in 1943 alone, 11% of total U Boat losses that year.

By the end of the war, the toll had risen to 65 as the Bay of Biscay became an ever more fruitful hunting ground for patrol aircraft, later joined by surface warship hunter-killer groups.

To counter the aircraft threat, the Kriegsmarine decided to convert four Type VIIC boats into formidable gun platforms to escort U Boats transiting the Bay of Biscay. *U441*, which had completed three patrols out of Brest, was converted to a U *flak* boat in April-May 1943; *U256*, damaged by aircraft attack in July 1942, began conversion in May at the same time as *U953*. The fourth U *flak* boat, *U621*, began conversion the following month, completing on July 7. Work began on modifying a further three Type VIIC boats, (*U211, U263, U271*) but this was abandoned when the tactic was discredited.

In the conversion, an additional sponson was built forward of the conning tower and fitted with a quick-firing 2.2 cm 38/43U four-barrelled cannon, with an armoured shield protecting its crew. Another was positioned aft of the bridge. The armament was also increased by a 3.7 cm automatic cannon and MG 42 machine guns mounted on the bridge. A small battery of 86 mm rockets was also fitted but these were found to be ineffective. The complement was increased from 48 to 67, by extra gunners and ammunition handlers, and standing orders decreed a bridge watch of 14 (with extra look-outs and gunners) instead of the regular four. The torpedo armament was reduced to five held in the four bow and single stern tubes for self defence against enemy escorts and submarines.

U441, now renamed *U flak 1*, departed Brest on her first patrol after conversion on May 22 1943. Two days afterwards, she was damaged by depth charges dropped by an RAF Sunderland flying boat which crashed moments after its attack. It was the only aircraft lost in action with a flak boat. *U flak 1* was forced to return to Brest for repair.

The Kriegsmarine, encouraged by the action, ordered U boats to transit the Bay of Biscay in surface groups. It was a fatal mistake. Sinkings continued to mount.

U441, now repaired, left Brest on July 8, 1943 and three days later was attacked from three directions by three Beaufighters from the RAF's 248 Squadron. The bridge watch and its replacements lost 10 men killed and 13 wounded in an action that lasted only a few minutes before the U Boat was forced to dive to escape. *U441* limped back to Brest.

U256, recommissioned on August 16 1943, was intended to safeguard, with *U271*, the Atlantic U boat refuelling area, north west of the Azores. She, like *U621* and *U953*, only mounted one patrol as a U *flak* boat.

It became painfully obvious to the German High Command that *flak* boats were alone not the answer to the Bay of Biscay killing ground in the teeth of overwhelming orchestrated attacks by groups of Allied attack.

Korvkpt Adolf Piening, commander of *U155*, conceived a route in and out of the Atlantic bases that hugged the coastlines of France and neutral Spain - where Allied aircraft were operating at the limit of their range

Above: The concept of transiting the Bay of Biscay at speed on the surface was soon demonstrated to be flawed following the increase in sinkings in late 1943, despite these heavily armed escorts.

and so had only short patrol endurance. However, Britain put diplomatic pressure on Spain to clear her waters of U boats and surface warship hunter killer groups were created to block the route off France. First successes to these anti-submarine groups came on June 23 1943, when the Royal Navy sloops *Wild Goose*, *Woodpecker* and *Kite* sank *U449* and sister ship *Starling* rammed and depth-charged *U119* in the Bay of Biscay.

With new anti-aircraft guns being fitted to all U boats, including the twin-barrel 2.0 cm 38 M II mounted on the workhorse Type VIIC submarines, the flak boat concept was abandoned. All the boats were converted back after November 1943.

A total of 125 Allied aircraft were shot down by German boats during World War II. The RAF alone sank 218 U boats, which demonstrated the efficacy of air attack against submarines. After the snorkel was fitted to frontline boats in 1944, losses from aircraft declined as U Boats spent less time on the surface.

U441 was sunk by depth-charges dropped by a Polish-manned Wellington aircraft off Ushant on June 18, 1944. *U621* was sunk by the Canadian destroyers *Kootenay*, *Chaudière* and *Ottawa* in the Bay of Biscay, on August 18 1944. *U256* was scuttled after shooting down three British and Canadian aircraft in 1944, and surrendering, in deep water off Ireland in 1945 during OPERATION DEADLIGHT - the destruction of captured U Boats. *U953* was broken up after Royal Navy trials in 1950.

Gato class - US Pacific warhorse

The US Navy's *Gato* class, rushed into production in late 1940, was the forerunner of all US World War II submarine designs and became the workhorse of the Pacific campaign. The 73-strong class sunk more than 1,700,000 tons of Japanese shipping - over 30% of the total destroyed by all hostile action.

With the war in Europe escalating, the US Navy needed increased submarine production rates - so new construction began in June, 1941 at Manitowoc Shipbuilding at Manitowoc, Wisconsin, under licence from Electric Boat at Groton, Connecticut.

More than half the class were built at Electric Boat, with three slipways added in a new North Yard. The Wisconsin boats were loaded onto barges or floating dry-docks for transit, via the Chicago Drainage Canal and the Mississippi River, to New Orleans for final fitting out. Additional construction lines were opened in early 1941 at Portsmouth and Mare Island Navy Yards.

Although the Pacific was the main theatre of operations for the class, *Gato* boats also operated for periods in the Caribbean and the Atlantic, in the latter case in support of TORCH, the Allied landings in North Africa in 1942, and in a campaign against blockade runners. *Herring* is credited by the US Navy for the sinking of the German *U 163* NW of Cap Finisterre, on March 21 1943.[1] *Dorado* was lost in the Caribbean in October 1943, during her maiden war patrol, possibly in a friendly fire incident involving a US naval patrol aircraft based at Guantanamo Bay, Cuba.

In the Pacific, the class took a heavy toll of Japanese shipping. In the league table of confirmed sinkings by US submarines in World War II, *Gato* boats occupy the first three places: *Flasher* (100,231 tons), *Rasher* (99,901 tons) and *Barb* (96,928 tons.) Lieut. Cmdr. Dudley 'Mush' Morton, in *Wahoo* became known as the 'One Boat Wolf Pack' because of his prowess. [His claimed sinkings totalled 17 ships amounting to 100,000 tons - more than any other American skipper - but the US Navy confirmed 19 ships, totalling 55,000 tons after post-war analysis of Japanese records.] In one attack on a small trawler, *Wahoo* opened fire with her four-inch deck gun and secondary armament of three 20mm cannon. When the cannon all jammed, the submarine's crew hurled home-made petrol bombs, or 'Molotov cocktails', aboard the target to set her ablaze.

In an engagement with a Japanese gunboat, *Growler* lost her heroic commanding officer after machine gun fire raked the bridge. Severely wounded, Lieut. Cmdr. Howard Gilmore cleared the bridge and ordered a crash-dive to save the boat - even though he would not have time to get below himself.

Boats of the class sank three Japanese submarines: *Sawfish* fired four torpedoes at *I-29* when she was caught on the surface on July 18, 1944. The enemy submarine exploded and sank within minutes. *Scamp* also expended four torpedoes to sink *I-168* on July 27, 1943.[2] *Bluefish* sank *I-351* on July 15, 1945. Conversely, *Corvina* became

Below: The advent of the submarine bathothermograph (SBT) in 1942 provided the submarine force with an important tool for covert patrol operations and attacks. *Herring (SS-233)*, pictured, was an early example of the successful application of the SBT.

Length (ft)	311.75		
Beam (ft)	27.25		
Displacement (tons)			
Surfaced	1,526		
Submerged	2,424		
Speed (kts)			
Surfaced	20.25 design; 17 operational average		
Dived	8.75		
Armament	10 x 21" tubes (6 bow, 4 stern) 14 reloads		
	2 x.50 cal, 2 x.30 cal machine guns*		
	1 x 3-inch deck gun**		
Engines	4 x diesel 5,400 hp		
	4 x electric motors 2,740 hp		
	2 shafts		
Range			
Surfaced	12,000 nm at 10 kts		
Submerged	95 nm at 5 kts		
Diving depth	300 ft†		
Complement	60		

* Only 2 x.50 cal or 2 x.30 cal in some.

** 4-inch gun mounted in *Grunion*, *Barb*, *Bluefish*, *Bonefish*, *Bashaw*, *Bluegill*, *Wahoo*, *Rock* and *Tullibee*. 5-inch deck gun in *Angler*, *Gabilan*, *Lapon*, *Pogy*, *Pompon* and *Tunny*. Additional 40 mm AA gun in *Angler*, *Pompon*, *Puffer*, *Rock*, *Tunny*. Additional 20 mm gun in *Albacore*, *Growler*, and *Tunny*. *Rock* was fitted with 2x20 mm AA guns in additional to its 40 mm mounting. *Wahoo* had three 20 mm cannon.

† *Albacore* dived to 450 ft after being bombed mistakenly by an American aircraft in the Pacific on November 10, 1943.

1 Some reports suggest that the Canadian escort *Prescott* sank the U Boat with depth charges.

2 *Wahoo* also claimed the sinking of *I-2* after she fired three torpedoes at a range of 800 yards but this was not officially confirmed.

101

Gato class - US Pacific warhorse

US Gato class patrol submarine

Boat	Builder	Laid down	Commissioned	Fate
Gato (SS-212)	Electric Boat Co, Groton, Connecticut	05-10-1940	31-12-1941	Struck from Navy List, 01-03-1060. Sold for scrap, 25-07-1960.
Greenling (SS-213)	Electric Boat Co, Groton, Connecticut	12-11-1940	21-01-1942	Sold for scrap, 16-06-1960.
Grouper (SS-214)	Electric Boat Co, Groton, Connecticut	28-12-1940	12-02-1942	Reclassified AGSS-214, 17-05-1958, converted into research boat, 11-1959. Scrapped 1970.
Growler (SS-215)	Electric Boat Co, Groton, Connecticut	10-02-1941	20-03-1942	Missing after attacking convoy near Luzon, Philippines, 08-11-1944.
Grunion (SS-216)	Electric Boat Co, Groton, Connecticut	01-03-1941	11-04-1942	Lost off Kiska, Aleutian Islands, 05-10-1942, cause unknown.
Guardfish (SS-217)	Electric Boat Co, Groton, Connecticut	01-04-1941	08-05-1942	Struck from Navy List, 13-06-1960. Sunk in torpedo trials as target off New London, 10-10-1961.
Albacore (SS-218)	Electric Boat Co, Groton, Connecticut	21-04-1941	01-06-1942	Mined off NE Hokkaido, 07-11-1944.
Amberjack (SS-219)	Electric Boat Co, Groton, Connecticut	15-05-1941	19-06-1942 ?	Sunk in depth charge attack, off Solomon Islands, 16-02-1943.
Barb (SS-220)	Electric Boat Co, Groton, Connecticut	07-06-1941	08-07-1942	Decommissioned 05-02-1954 for conversion to Guppy standard. Recommissioned 03-08-1954, decommissioned 13-12-1954 and loaned to Italy as *Enrico Tazzoli* (511). Scrapped 1975.
Blackfish (SS-221)	Electric Boat Co, Groton, Connecticut	01-07-1941	22-07-1942	Reserve training, 05-05-1949-02-02-1954. Scrapped 1960.
Bluefish (SS-222)	Electric Boat Co, Groton, Connecticut	05-06-1942	24-05-1943	Decommissioned 20-11-1953. Scrapped 1960.
Bonefish (SS-223)	Electric Boat Co, Groton, Connecticut	25-06-1942	31-05-1943	Lost off Toyama Wan, Honshu Island, Japan, 18-06-1945.
Cod (SS-224)	Electric Boat Co, Groton, Connecticut	21-07-1942	21-06-1943	Decommissioned, 22-06-1946. On display, Cleveland, Ohio.
Cero (SS-225)	Electric Boat Co, Groton, Connecticut	24-08-1942	04-07-1943	Decommissioned, 23-12-1953. Scrapped 1971.
Corvina (SS-226)	Electric Boat Co, Groton, Connecticut	21-09-1942	06-08-1943	Torpedoed by Japanese submarine *I-176* south of Truk Island, Caroline Islands, 16-11-1943 on maiden war patrol.
Darter (SS-227)	Electric Boat Co, Groton, Connecticut	20-10-1942	07-09-1943	Grounded on Bombay Shoal, Palawan Passage, Philippines, 24-10-1944. Attempts to scuttle failed, then bombed and destroyed by Japanese aircraft. Crew rescued by *Dace*.
Drum (SS-228)	Portsmouth Navy Yard, Portsmouth, New Hampshire	11-09-1940	01-11-1941	Decommissioned 16-02-1946. Reserve training role to 1962. Now on display, Mobile, Alabama.
Flying Fish (SS-229)	Portsmouth Navy Yard, Portsmouth, New Hampshire	06-12-1940	10-12-1941	Reclassified auxiliary AGSS-229, 29-11-1950. Decommissioned, 28-05-1954. Sold for scrap, 11-05-1959.
Finback (SS-230)	Portsmouth Navy Yard, Portsmouth, New Hampshire	05-02-1041	31-01-1942	Decommissioned 21-04-1950, New London. Scrapped 1960.
Haddock (SS-231)	Portsmouth Navy Yard, Portsmouth, New Hampshire	31-03-1941	14-03-1942	Reserves training boat, 08-1948. Struck from Navy List, 06-1956. Sold for scrap 23-08-1960.
Halibut (SS-232)	Portsmouth Navy Yard, Portsmouth, New Hampshire	16-05-1941	10-04-1942	Badly damaged by depth charges during attack on convoy in Luzon Strait, Philippines, 14-11-1944. Decommissioned 18-07-1945 and sold for scrap 10-01-1947.
Herring (SS-233)	Portsmouth Navy Yard, Portsmouth, New Hampshire	14-07-1941	04-05-1942	Sunk by gunfire from Japanese shore batteries, Matsuwa Island, Kurile Islands, 01-06-1944.
Kingfish (SS-234)	Portsmouth Navy Yard, Portsmouth, New Hampshire	29-08-1941	20-05-1942	Decommissioned, 09-03-1946. Sold for scrap, 06-10-1960.
Shad (SS-235)	Portsmouth Navy Yard, Portsmouth, New Hampshire	24-10-1941	12-06-1942	Used to train reservists ton 1960. Struck from Navy List, 01-04-1960. Sold for scrap 07-1960.
Silversides (SS-236)	Mare Island Navy Yard, Vallejo, California	04-11-1940	15-12-1941	Reclassified as auxiliary submarine AGSS-236, 06-11-1962. Struck from Navy List, 30-06-1969. On display at Muskegon, Michigan, from 1973.
Trigger (SS-237)	Mare Island Navy Yard, Vallejo, California	01-02-1941	30-01-1942	Sunk in depth charge attack off Okinawa, 28-03-1945
Wahoo (SS-238)	Mare island Navy Yard, Vallejo, California	28-06-1941	15-05-1942	Sunk by bombs dropped by Japanese aircraft, Soya Strait, Sea of Japan, 11-10-1943
Whale (SS-239)	Mare Island Navy Yard, Vallejo, California	28-06-1941	01-06-1942	Struck from Navy List, 01-03-1960. Sold for scrap, New Orleans, 29-09-1960.
Angler (SS-240)	Electric Boat Co, Groton, Connecticut	09-11-1942	01-10-1943	Re-designated SSK-240, 02-1953. Reclassified as auxiliary boat AGSS-240, 1963. Struck from Navy List, 15-12-1971. Sold for scrap 01-02-1974.
Bashaw (SS-241)	Electric Boat Co, Groton, Connecticut	04-12-1942	25-10-1943	Designated SSK-241, 18-02-1953. Scrapped 1973.
Bluegill (SS-242)	Electric Boat Co, Groton, Cannecticut	07-12-1942	11-11-1943	Reclassified as SSK-242, recommissioned 02-05-1953. Scrapped 1971.
Bream (SS-243)	Electric Boat Co, Groton, Connecticut	05-02-1943	24-02-1944	Converted to SSK-243, 18-02-1953. Sunk as target, 11-1969.
Cavalla (SS-244)	Electric Boat Co, Groton, Connecticut	04-03-1943	29-02-1944	Reclassified SSK-244, 18-02-1953. Reverted to SS-244, 15-08-1959. Now on display at Pelican Island, Galveston, Texas.
Cobia (SS-245)	Electric Boat Co, Groton, Connecticut	17-03-1943	29-03-1944	Decommissioned, 19-03-1954. Now on display, Manitowoc, Wisconsin.
Croaker (SS-246)	Electric Boat Co, Groton, Connecticut	01-04-1943	21-04-1944	Reclassified SSK-246 09-04-1953. Struck from Navy List, 20-12-1971. On display, Groton, Connecticut.
Dace (SS-247)	Electric Boat Co, Groton, Connecticut	22-07-1942	23-07-1943	Transferred to Italian Navy, 1955 as *Da Vinci*. Stricken from Navy List, 15-10-1972. Scrapped 1978.
Dorado (SS-248)	Electric Boat Co, Groton, Connecticut	27-08-1942	28-08-1943	Sunk, possibly by US naval aircraft from Guantanamo Bay, Cuba, 12-10-1943 during maiden war patrol.
Flasher (SS-249)	Electric Boat Co, Groton, Connecticut	30-09-1942	25-09-1943	Decommissioned, 16-03-1946. Scrapped 1964.
Flier (SS-250)	Electric Boat Co, Groton, Connecticut	30-10-1942	18-10-1943	Sunk by mine, Balabac Strait, Philippines, 13-08-1944. 13 survivors.
Flounder (SS-251)	Electric Boat Co, Groton, Connecticut	05-12-1942	29-11-1943	Scrapped, 1960.
Gabilan (SS-252)	Electric Boat Co, Groton, Connecticut	05-12-1942	28-12-1943	Decommissioned 23-02-1946. Sold for scrap 15-12-1959.
Gunnel (SS-253)	Electric Boat Co, Groton, Connecticut	21-07-1941	20-08-1942	Decommissioned, 01-09-1958. Sold for scrap 01-12-1959.
Gurnard (SS-254)	Electric Boat Co, Groton, Connecticut	02-09-1941	18-09-1942	Reservist training boat, 1949-60. Sold for scrap 09-1961.
Haddo (SS-255)	Electric Boat Co, Groton, Connecticut	09-10-1942	08-10-1942	Decommissioned, 16-02-1946. Sold for scrap 30-04-1959.
Hake (SS-256)	Electric Boat Co, Groton, Connecticut	01-11-1941	30-10-1942	Reclassified as auxiliary boat, AGSS-256, 06-11-1962. Scrapped 1972.
Harder (SS-257)	Electric Boat Co, Groton, Connecticut	01-12-1941	02-12-1942	Sunk in depth charge attack off Dasol Bay, Philippines, 24-08-1944.
Hoe (SS-258)	Electric Boat Co, Groton, Connecticut	02-01-1942	16-12-1942	Decommissioned 07-08-1946. Sold 23-08-1960 for scrapping.
Jack (SS-259)	Electric Boat Co, Groton, Connecticut	02-02-1942	06-01-1943	Decommissioned 08-06-1944. Loaned to Greek Navy as *Amfitriti*, 21-045-1958. Stricken from Navy List, 01-09-1967. Expended as target 09-1967.
Lapon (SS-260)	Electric Boat Co, Groton, Connecticut	21-02-1942	23-01-1943	Placed in reserve, 25-07-1946. Loaned to Greek Navy, 08-08-1957 as *Poseidon*. Purchased by Greece, 04-1976 for spare parts.
Mingo (SS-261)	Electric Boat Co, Groton, Connecticut	21-03-1942	12-02-1943	Decommissioned 01-1947. Loaned to Japanese Navy as *Kuroshio*, 15-08-1955. Decommissioned 31-03-1966.
Muskallunge (SS-262)	Electric Boat Co, Groton, Connecticut	07-04-1942	15-03-1943	Decommissioned 29-01-1947. Loaned to Brazilian Navy, 18-01-1957 as *Humaita*. Returned 03-1968 and sunk as target.
Paddle (SS-263)	Electric Boat Co, Groton, Connecticut	01-05-1942	29-03-1943	Decommissioned 01-02-1946. Transferred to Brazilian Navy as *Riachuelo*, 18-01-1957. Decommissioned 03-1968. Stricken from Navy List, 30-06-1968. Scrapped 1969.
Pargo (SS-264)	Electric Boat Co, Groton, Connecticut	21-05-1942	26-04-1943.	Decommissioned 12-06-1946. Sold for scrap 17-04-1961.

US Gato class patrol submarine (continued)

Boat	Builder	Laid down	Commissioned	Fate
Peto (SS-265)	Manitowoc Shipbuilding, Manitowoc, Wisconsin	18-06-1941	21-11-1942	In reserve, 25-06-1946. Reservist training boat, 11-1956. Struck from Navy List, 01-08-1960. Sold for scrap 10-11-1960.
Pogy (SS-266)	Manitowoc Shipbuilding, Manitowoc, Wisconsin	15-09-1941	10-01-1943	In reserve, 20-07-1946. Sold for scrap 01-05-1959.
Pompon (SS-267)	Manitowoc Shipbuilding, Manitowoc, Wisconsin	26-11-1941	17-03-1943	In reserve, 11-05-1946. Converted to radar picket boat, SSR-267, 11-12-1951. Struck from Navy List, 01-04-1960. Sold for scrap 25-11-1960.
Puffer (SS-268)	Manitowoc Shipbuilding, Manitowoc, Wisconsin	16-02-1942	27-04-1943	In reserve, 28-06-1946. Reservists training boat, 1946-1960. For scrap 04-11-1960.
Rasher (SS-269)	Manitowoc Shipbuilding, Manitowoc, Wisconsin	04-05-1942	08-06-1943	Recommissioned as radar picket boat, SSR-269, 22-07-1953. Reclassified as auxiliary boat, AGSS-269, 01-07-1960. Decommissioned 27-05-1967. Struck from Navy List, 20-12-1971. Scrapped 1975.
Raton (SS-270)	Manitowoc Shipbuilding, Manitowoc, Wisconsin	29-05-1942	13-07-1943	Decommissioned 11-03-1949. Converted into radar picket boat, SSR-270, 1952, recommissioned 21-09-1953. Reclassified auxiliary boat AGSS-270, 01-07-1960. Decommissioned 1969. Hull sunk as gunnery target.
Ray (SS-271)	Manitowoc Shipbuilding, Manitowoc, Wisconsin	20-07-1942	27-07-1943	Converted into radar picket boat, SSR-271, 12-1950, recommissioned, 13-08-1952. In reserve, 30-09-1958. Sold for scrap 18-12-1960.
Redfin (SS-272)	Manitowoc Shipbuilding, Manitowoc, Wisconsin	03-09-1942	31-08-1943	Converted in radar picket boat, SSR-272, 1951. Recommissioned 09-01-1953. Reclassified auxiliary boat, AGSS-272, 28-06-1963. Struck from Navy List, 01-07-1970. Sold 03-03-1971.
Robalo (SS-273)	Manitowoc Shipbuilding, Manitowoc, Wisconsin	24-10-1942	28-09-1943	Mined or sunk in battery explosion, 26-07-1944 off Palawan Island, Philippines. 4 survivors.
Rock (SS-274)	Manitowoc Shipbuilding, Manitowoc, Wisconsin	23-12-1942	26-10-1943	Converted into radar picket boat, SSR-274, 1951. Recommissioned, 12-10-1953. Re-designated auxiliary boat AGSS-274, 31-12-1959. Decommissioned 13-09-1969. Sunk as target.
Runner (SS-275)	Portsmouth Navy Yard, Portsmouth, New Hampshire	08-12-1941	30-07-1942	Lost, 07-1943, off Hokkaido, Japan. Cause unknown.
Sawfish (SS-276)	Portsmouth Navy Yard, Portsmouth, New Hampshire	20-01-1942	26-08-1942	Decommissioned 20-06-1946. Reservist training boat. Struck from Navy List 01-04-1960 and sold for scrap.
Scamp (SS-277)	Portsmouth Navy Yard, Portsmouth, New Hampshire	06-03-1942	18-09-1942	Sunk in depth charge attack, 11-11-1944, south of Tokyo Bay.
Scorpion (SS-278)	Portsmouth Navy Yard, Portsmouth, New Hampshire	20-03-1942	01-10-1942 ?	Mined 27-02-1944, Pacific.
Snook (SS-279)	Portsmouth Navy Yard, Portsmouth, New Hampshire	17-04-1942	24-10-1942	Lost 04-1945. Pacific. Cause unknown.
Steelhead (SS-280)	Portsmouth Navy Yard, Portsmouth, New Hampshire	01-06-1942	07-12-1942	Struck from Navy List, 01-04-1960. Scrapped 1962.
Sunfish (SS-281)	Mare Island Navy Yard, Vallejo, California	26-09-1941	15-07-1942	Decommissioned 26-12-1945. Struck from Navy List, 05-1960. Scrapped 1961.
Tunny (SS-282)	Mare Island Navy Yard, Vallejo, California	10-11-1941	01-09-1942	Converted to carry Regulus missile as SSG-282, 1953, commissioning 06-03-1953. Re-designated SS-282, 05-1965. Converted to troop-carrying boat, APSS-282, 1967. Decommissioned 28-06-1969. Sunk as torpedo target 19-06-1970.
Tinosa (SS-283)	Mare Island Navy Yard, Vallejo, California	21-02-1942	15-01-1943	Decommissioned 02-12-1953. Struck from Navy List, 01-09-1958. Scuttled off Hawaii, 11-1960.
Tullibee (SS-284)	Mare Island Navy Yard, Vallejo, California	01-04-1942	15-02-1943	Sunk after own torpedo circled and hit her, 26-03-1944, off Palau Islands. 1 survivor.

the only US submarine sunk by a Japanese counterpart when she was hit twice by torpedoes fired by *I-176* south of Truk island on November 16, 1943.[3]

The class had numerous problems with its torpedoes - running at the wrong depth or exploding prematurely. Among the class's 19 war casualties, *Tullibee* was sunk by one of her own torpedoes after it circled back during an attack on a transport ship off Palau Island on March 26, 1944. There was just one survivor, who was on the bridge when the torpedo hit. *Greenling* nearly suffered the same fate during an attack on October 18, 1942 on a large freighter: her second torpedo travelled a complete circle and nearly hit its launching boat. *Pompon*'s own torpedo just missed her stern after an attack on the Sea of Okhotsk in July, 1944.

Several new items of equipment were fitted to the class before the end of hostilities and just afterwards. *Herring* demonstrated the success of the submarine bathothermograph in covert operations; *Haddock* was the first to be fitted with the Type SJ surface surveillance radar and *Muskallunge* was the first US boat to be armed with electrically-powered torpedoes.

Barb became the first submarine to deploy rockets in the shore bombardment role when she launched salvoes of five-inch rockets in attacks on three Japanese towns in June 1945.[4]

Grouper was fitted with the first, primitive, combat information centre, in 1946 and a year later, became the first submarine to discharge and recover men whilst submerged and underway.

After the war, some of the class were converted into radar picket boats before moving into training roles, particularly with reservists. *Rasher*, however, saw active service with the US 7th Fleet off Vietnam in 1966 and

Tunny was converted to carry the nuclear-armed Regulus missile and served in the Pacific from 1953-1965. *Redfin* was used in trials of inertial guidance systems for Polaris strategic missile submarines after 1959. The last active boat, *Rock*, was decommissioned in September 1969 and sunk as a target.

3 THIS WAS *CORVINA*'S MAIDEN WAR PATROL.
4 SHE ALSO LANDED VOLUNTEERS WHO BLEW UP A RAILWAY TRAIN.

Below: Gato (SS 212) provided the prototype design for the World War II vintage submarine. Construction of this class was accelerated in 1940 due to the escalation of the war in Europe. In order to increase production capability, the Manitowoc Shipbuilding Company in Wisconsin was contracted to build submarines under licence from Electric Boat.

Type XXI U Boats - Silent runners that came too late

The German Type XXI electro U Boats brought dramatically increased battery power to produce higher underwater speeds in the campaign against Allied convoys. If they had been built earlier, their impact on the war's outcome would have been considerable. However, their technology revolutionised design and became the forerunner to submarines of the 1950s and early 1960s.

A total of 119 Type XXIs were commissioned by the end of the war - a tribute to new pre-fabrication construction techniques that allowed boats to be assembled at three yards in five and a half months from first steel cutting. However, because lengthy training was constantly disrupted by RAF Bomb Command's mining operations in the Baltic, only two boats became operational by the end of hostilities, *U 2511* and *U 3008*.

The concept was based on the need for greater range and speeds with which to escape attacking Allied escorts. The answer was the provision of increased battery power by installing 372 44 MAL 740 battery cells producing 33,900 A/h - three times the electrical power available to

the Type VIIC. The design allowed 51 hours underwater running at full power or 100 hours at half, yielding submerged speeds of more than 17 kts, enough to evade most surface escorts. Moreover, the Type XXI needed just three hours cruising a day using the new schnorkel to recharge the batteries.

Approval for the new class was given in July 1943, and work stopped on building older designs to switch resources to the Type XXI. First of class, *U 2501*, was laid down on April 3 1944, launched on May 12 and commissioned on June 27.

The class was fitted with new hydrophones to locate convoys, new depth-keeping equipment, radar detection devices and rubber coatings to reduce radar signature. A new hydraulic torpedo loading system was fitted to enable all six tubes to be rearmed in 10 minutes.

More than 380 Type XXI were planned for delivery by May 1945, but a combination of disruption caused by repeated Allied air raids and early design faults meant that only 98 were training or fitting out at the time of the German surrender.

Length (ft)	251.58 oa
Beam (ft)	21.65 oa
Displacement (tons)	
Surfaced	1,621
Submerged	1,819
Speed (kts)	
Surfaced	15.75
Dived	17.2
Armament	6x21" bow tubes. 17 reloads
	2 x twin barrel 20 cm AA gun
Engines	2 diesels, 4,000 hp
	2 electric motors, 4,800 hp
	1 silent running electric, 226 hp
Range	
Surfaced	15,500 nm at 10 kts
Submerged	385 nm at 5 kts
Diving depth	850 ft (crush depth 1,200 ft)
Complement	57

Left and below: The Type XXI U-2518 commissioned in November 1944 and joined the 11th flotilla in Norway in April 1945. It never made a war patrol and was transferred to the French Navy and commissioned as the Roland Morillot, serving until 1967.

Both operational boats were at sea when the surrender order was radioed on May 4, 1945. *U 2511* sighted a Royal Navy cruiser, *Suffolk* and moved, undetected, into a firing position within the target's protective screen of destroyer escorts. She did not fire. *U 3008* located a convoy but passed beneath.

U 2540 was scuttled off the Flensburg lightship on May 4 1945, after an attack by RAF Beaufighters but was raised in 1957 and converted at Kiel to the research boat *Wilhelm Bauer*, commissioning in the Bundesmarine on September 1 1960. She decommissioned on December 15 1982, and is now on display at the German Maritime Museum at Bremerhaven.

German Type XXI Electro U Boats

Boat	Builder	Laid down	Commissioned	Fate	Boat	Builder	Laid down	Commissioned	Fate
U 2501	Blohm & Voss, Hamburg	03-04-1944	27-06-1944	Scuttled 03-05-1945, Hamburg.	U 2530	Blohm & Voss, Hamburg	01-10-1944	30-12-1944	Sunk in bombing raid on Hamburg, 31-12-1944.
U 2502	Blohm & Voss, Hamburg	25-04-1944	19-07-1944	Surrendered. Sunk off Ireland 02-01-1946.					Raised and sunk again by RAF raid on Hamburg
U 2503	Blohm & Voss, Hamburg	20-05-1944	01-08-1944	Scuttled off Horsens, Denmark, 04-05-1945.					17-01-1945.
				Thirteen crew killed after attack by RAF	U 2531	Blohm & Voss, Hamburg	03-10-1944	18-01-1945	Scuttled 03-05-1945.
				Beaufighters of 236 and 254 Sqdns.	U 2532	Blohm & Voss, Hamburg	10-10-1944	-	Sunk in raid on yard, 31-12-1944.
U 2504	Blohm & Voss, Hamburg	20-05-1944	12-08-1944	Scuttled, Hamburg, 03-05-1945.					Never completed.
U 2505	Blohm & Voss, Hamburg	23-05-1944	07-11-1944	Abandoned in 'Elbe II' U boat bunker, Hamburg.	U 2533	Blohm & Voss, Hamburg	13-10-1944	18-01-1945	Scuttled 03-05-1945.
U 2506	Blohm & Voss, Hamburg	29-05-1944	31-08-1944	Surrendered. Sunk off Ireland, 05-01-1946.	U 2534	Blohm & Voss, Hamburg	23-10-1944	17-01-1945	Scuttled 03-05-1945.
U 2507	Blohm & Voss, Hamburg	04-06-1944	08-09-1944	Scuttled 05-05-1945.	U 2535	Blohm & Voss, Hamburg	19-10-1944	28-01-1945	Scuttled 03-05-1945.
U 2508	Blohm & Voss, Hamburg	13-06-1944	26-09-1944	Scuttled, Kiel, 03-05-1945.	U 2536	Blohm & Voss, Hamburg	21-10-1944	06-02-1945	Scuttled 03-05-1945.
U 2509	Blohm & Voss, Hamburg	17-06-1944	21-09-1944	Sunk in bombing raid on shipyard, 08-04-1945.	U 2537	Blohm & Voss, Hamburg	22-10-1944	-	Sunk in bombing raid on yard, 31-12-1944.
U 2510	Blohm & Voss, Hamburg	05-07-1944	27-09-1944	Scuttled 02-05-1945.					Never completed.
U 2511	Blohm & Voss, Hamburg	07-07-1944	29-09-1944	Surrendered, Bergen, Norway. Scuttled off	U 2538	Blohm & Voss, Hamburg	24-10-1944	16-02-1945	Scuttled 08-05-1945.
				Ireland 07-01-1946.	U 2539	Blohm & Voss, Hamburg	27-10-1944	21-02-1945	Scuttled 03-05-1945.
U 2512	Blohm & Voss, Hamburg	13-07-1944	10-10-1944	Scuttled 03-05-1945.	U 2540	Blohm & Voss, Hamburg	28-10-1944	24-02-1945.	Sunk by RAF Beaufighters, in Kattegat,
U 2513	Blohm & Voss, Hamburg	19-07-1944	12-10-1944	Surrendered 08-05-1945. Transferred to US Navy,					04-05-1945. Raised, 1957 to become research
				08-1945. Sunk off Key West, Florida, in missile					boat Wilhelm Bauer, 1960. Decommissioned,
				trials 07-10-1951.					1982. Now on display at German Maritime
U 2514	Blohm & Voss, Hamburg	24-07-1944	17-10-1944	Sunk in bombing raid 08-04-1945.					Museum, Bremerhaven.
U 2515	Blohm & Voss, Hamburg	28-07-1944	19-10-1944	Sunk in bombing raid on Hamburg, 17-01-1945.	U 2541	Blohm & Voss, Hamburg	31-10-1944	01-03-1945	Scuttled 05-05-1945.
U 2516	Blohm & Voss, Hamburg	03-08-1944	24-10-1944	Sunk in bombing raid on Kiel, 09-04-1945.	U 2542	Blohm & Voss, Hamburg	10-11-1944	05-03-1945	Sunk by bombs 03-04-1945.
U 2517	Blohm & Voss, Hamburg	08-08-1944	31-10-1944	Scuttled 05-05-1945.	U 2543	Blohm & Voss, Hamburg	13-11-1944	07-03-1945	Scuttled 03-05-1945.
U 2518	Blohm & Voss, Hamburg	16-08-1944	04-11-1944	Surrendered 08-05-1945. Transferred to French	U 2544	Blohm & Voss, Hamburg	15-11-1944	10-03-1945	Scuttled 05-05-1945.
				Navy, 17-02-1945 as Roland Morillot; later	U 2546	Blohm & Voss, Hamburg	20-11-1944	21-03-1945	Scuttled 03-05-1945.
				renamed Q246. Decommissioned 17-10-1967.	U 2547	Blohm & Voss, Hamburg	27-11-1944	-	Sunk in bombing raid 11-03-1945.
				Scrapped 1969.					Never completed.
U 2519	Blohm & Voss, Hamburg	24-08-1944	15-11-1944	Scuttled 03-05-1945, Kiel.	U 2548	Blohm & Voss, Hamburg	30-11-1944	09-04-1945	Scuttled 03-05-1945.
U 2520	Blohm & Voss, Hamburg	24-08-1944	14-11-1944.	Scuttled 03-05-1945.	U 2549	Blohm & Voss, Hamburg	03-12-1944	-	Sunk in bombing raid, 11-03-1945.
U 2521	Blohm & Voss, Hamburg	31-08-1944	21-11-1944	Sunk by RAF Liberator K/547,					Never completed.
				Kattegat 05-05-1945.	U 2550	Blohm & Voss, Hamburg	05-12-1944	-	Sunk in bombing raid, 11-03-1945.
U 2522	Blohm & Voss, Hamburg	28-08-1944	22-11-1944	Scuttled 05-05-1945.					Never completed.
U 2523	Blohm & Voss, Hamburg	06-09-1944	26-12-1944	Sunk in bombing raid on shipyard 17-01-1945.	U 2551	Blohm & Voss, Hamburg	08-12-1944	24-04-1945	Scuttled 05-05-1945.
U 2524	Blohm & Voss, Hamburg	06-09-1944	16-01-1945	Sunk by RAF Beaufighters of 236 and 254 Sqdns,	U 2552	Blohm & Voss, Hamburg	10-12-1944	21-04-1945	Scuttled 03-05-1945, Kiel.
				Kattegat 03-05-1945.	U 2553	Blohm & Voss, Hamburg	12-12-1944	-	Never completed. Broken up.
U 2525	Blohm & Voss, Hamburg	13-09-1944	12-12-1944	Scuttled 05-05-1945.	U 2554	Blohm & Voss, Hamburg	14-12-1944	-	Never completed. Broken up.
U 2526	Blohm & Voss, Hamburg	16-09-1944	15-12-1944	Scuttled 02-05-1945.	U 2555	Blohm & Voss, Hamburg	20-12-1944	-	Never completed. Broken up.
U 2527	Blohm & Voss, Hamburg	20-09-1944	23-12-1944	Scuttled 02-05-1945.	U 2556	Blohm & Voss, Hamburg	23-12-1944	-	Never completed. Broken up.
U 2528	Blohm & Voss, Hamburg	25-09-1944	09-12-1944	Scuttled 02-05-1945.	U 2557	Blohm & Voss, Hamburg	30-12-1944	-	Never completed. Broken up.
U 2529	Blohm & Voss, Hamburg	29-09-1944	22-02-1944	Surrendered. Recommissioned in Royal Navy as	U 2558	Blohm & Voss, Hamburg	01-02-1945	-	Never completed. Broken up.
				N 28. Transferred to Soviet Navy as B 28,	U 2559	Blohm & Voss, Hamburg	04-02-1945	-	Never completed. Broken up.
				commissioning 02-1946. Scrapped 1958.	U 2560	Blohm & Voss, Hamburg	12-02-1945	-	Never completed. Broken up.

Continued on following page

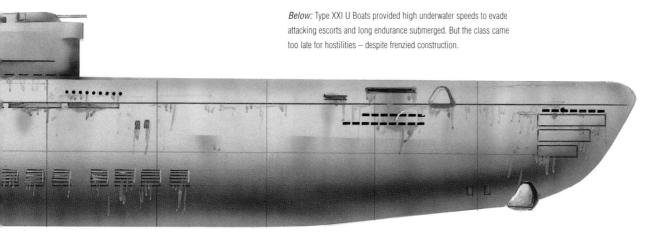

Below: Type XXI U Boats provided high underwater speeds to evade attacking escorts and long endurance submerged. But the class came too late for hostilities – despite frenzied construction.

Type XXI U Boats - Silent runners that came too late

German Type XXI Electro U Boats (continued)

Boat	Builder	Laid down	Commissioned	Fate	Boat	Builder	Laid down	Commissioned	Fate
U 2561	Blohm & Voss, Hamburg	15-02-1945	-	Never completed. Broken up.	U 3503	F Schichau, Danzig	7-06-1944	09-09-1944	Sunk by RAF Liberator G/86 Kattegat..
U 2562	Blohm & Voss, Hamburg	24-02-1945	-	Never completed. Broken up.	U 3504	F Schichau, Danzig	30-06-1944	23-09-1944	Scuttled 02-05-1945.
U 2563	Blohm & Voss, Hamburg	25-02-1945	-	Never completed. Broken up.	U 3505	F Schichau, Danzig	09-07-1944	07-10-1945	Sunk in bombing raid 03-05-1945.
U 2564	Blohm & Voss, Hamburg	29-03-1945	-	Never completed. Broken up.	U 3506	F Schichau, Danzig	14-07-1944	19-10-1944	Abandoned in 'Elbe II' U boat bunker, Hamburg.
U 3001	A.G.Weser, Bremen	15-04-1944	20-07-1944	Scuttled 03-05-1945.	U 3507	F Schichau, Danzig	19-07-1944	19-10-1944	Scuttled 03-05-1945.
U 3002	A.G.Weser, Bremen	23-04-1944	06-08-1945	Scuttled 02-05-1945.	U 3508	F Schichau, Danzig	25-07-1944	02-11-1944	Sunk in bombing raid on Wilhelmshaven 04-03-
U 3003	A.G.Weser, Bremen	27-05-1944	22-08-1944	Sunk in bombing raid, Kiel, 04-04-1945.	1945.				
U 3004	A.G.Weser, Bremen	04-06-1944	30-08-1944	Abandoned in 'Elbe II' U boat bunker, Hamburg.	U 3509	F Schichau, Danzig	29-07-1944	29-01-1945	Scuttled 03-05-1945.
U 3005	A.G.Weser, Bremen	21-06-1944	20-09-1944	Scuttled 03-05-1945.	U 3510	F Schichau, Danzig	06-08-1944	11-11-1944	Scuttled 05-05-1945.
U 3006	A.G.Weser, Bremen	12-06-1944	05-10-1944	Scuttled 01-05-1945.	U 3511	F Schichau, Danzig	14-08-1944	18-11-1945	Scuttled 03-05-1945.
U 3007	A.G.Weser, Bremen	09-07-1944	22-10-1944	Sunk in bombing raid 24-02-1945.	U 3512	F Schichau, Danzig	15-08-1944	27-11-1944	Sunk in air raid on Kiel 08-04-1945.
U 3008	A.G.Weser, Bremen	02-07-1944	19-10-1944	Transferred to US Navy, 1945 as trials boat.	U 3513	F Schichau, Danzig	20-08-1944	02-12-1944	Scuttled 03-05-1945.
				Scrapped Puerto Rico, 1955.	U 3514	F Schichau, Danzig	21-08-1944	09-12-1944	Scuttled off NW coast of Ireland 12-02-1946.
U 3009	A.G.Weser, Bremen	21-07-1944	10-11-1944	Scuttled 01-05-1945.	U 3515	F Schichau, Danzig	27-08-1944	14-12-1944	Surrendered. Transferred to Royal Navy as N 30.
U 3010	A.G.Weser, Bremen	13-07-1944	11-11-1944	Scuttled 03-05-1945.					Transferred to Soviet Navy as B 28, 02-1946.
U 3011	A.G.Weser, Bremen	14-08-1944	21-12-1944	Scuttled 03-05-1945.					Scrapped 1973.
U 3012	A.G.Weser, Bremen	26-08-1944	04-12-1944	Scuttled 03-05-1945.	U 3516	F Schichau, Danzig	28-08-1944	18-12-1944	Scuttled 02-05-1945.
U 3013	A.G.Weser, Bremen	18-08-1944	22-11-1944	Scuttled 03-05-1945.	U 3517	F Schichau, Danzig	12-09-1944	22-12-1944	Scuttled 02-05-1945.
U 3014	A.G.Weser, Bremen	28-08-1944	17-12-1944	Scuttled 03-05-1945.	U 3518	F Schichau, Danzig	12-09-1944	29-12-1944	Scuttled 03-05-1945.
U 3015	A.G.Weser, Bremen	25-08-1944	17-12-1944	Scuttled 05-05-1945.	U 3519	F Schichau, Danzig	19-09-1944	06-01-1945	Mined and sunk off Warnemünde,
U 3016	A.G.Weser, Bremen	06-09-1944	05-01-1945	Scuttled 02-05-1945.					Baltic 02-03-1945.
U 3017	A.G.Weser, Bremen	02-09-1944	05-01-1945	Surrendered. Transferred to Royal Navy to	U 3520	F Schichau, Danzig	20-09-1944	12-01-1945	Sunk in Baltic 31-01-1945.
				become N 41 trials boat. Scrapped 1949.	U 3521	F Schichau, Danzig	24-09-1944	14-01-1945	Scuttled 02-05-1945.
U 3018	A.G.Weser, Bremen	18-09-1944	07-01-1945	Scuttled 02-05-1945.	U 3522	F Schichau, Danzig	25-09-1944	21-01-1945	Scuttled 02-05-1945.
U 3019	A.G.Weser, Bremen	10-09-1944	23-12-1944	Scuttled 02-05-1945.	U 3523	F Schichau, Danzig	07-10-1944	23-01-1945	Sunk by depth charges dropped by RAF Liberator
U 3020	A.G.Weser, Bremen	01-10-1944	23-12-1945	Scuttled 02-05-1945.					T/224 in Kattegat 05-05-1945.
U 3021	A.G.Weser, Bremen	26-09-1944	12-02-1945	Scuttled 02-05-1945.	U 3524	F Schichau, Danzig	08-10-1944	26-01-1945	Scuttled 05-05-1945.
U 3022	A.G.Weser, Bremen	06-10-1944	22-01-1945	Scuttled 03-05-1945.	U 3525	F Schichau, Danzig	17-10-1944	31-01-1945	Scuttled 03-05-1945.
U 3023	A.G.Weser, Bremen	03-10-1944	22-01-1945	Scuttled 03-05-1945.	U 3526	F Schichau, Danzig	18-10-1944	22-03-1945	Scuttled 05-05-1945.
U 3024	A.G.Weser, Bremen	14-10-1944	13-01-1945	Scuttled 03-05-1945.	U 3527	F Schichau, Danzig	25-10-1944	10-03-1945	Scuttled 05-05-1945.
U 3025	A.G.Weser, Bremen	12-10-1944	20-01-1945	Scuttled 03-05-1945.	U 3528	F Schichau, Danzig	26-10-1944	18-03-1945	Scuttled 05-05-1945.
U 3026	A.G.Weser, Bremen	19-10-1944	22-01-1945	Scuttled 03-05-1945.	U 3529	F Schichau, Danzig	02-11-1944	22-03-1945	Scuttled 05-05-1945
U 3027	A.G.Weser, Bremen	18-10-1944	25-01-1945	Scuttled 03-05-1945.	U 3530	F Schichau, Danzig	03-11-1944	22-03-1945	Scuttled 03-05-1945.
U 3028	A.G.Weser, Bremen	26-10-1944	27-01-1945	Scuttled 03-05-1945.	U 3531	F Schichau, Danzig	09-11-1944	-	Never completed. Broken up.
U 3029	A.G.Weser, Bremen	28-10-1944	05-02-1945	Scuttled 03-05-1945.	U 3532	F Schichau, Danzig	09-11-1944	-	Never completed. Broken up.
U 3030	A.G.Weser, Bremen	02-11-1944	14-02-1945	Scuttled 08-05-1945.	U 3533	F Schichau, Danzig	16-11-1944	-	Never completed. Broken up.
U 3031	A.G.Weser, Bremen	30-10-1944	28-02-1945	Scuttled 03-05-1945.	U 3534	F Schichau, Danzig	17-11-1944	-	Never completed. Broken up.
U 3032	A.G.Weser, Bremen	09-11-1944	12-02-1945	Sunk by aircraft of 2nd Tactical Air Force, in	U 3536	F Schichau, Danzig	26-11-1944	-	Never completed. Broken up.
				Kattegat 03-05-1945.	U 3536	F Schichau, Danzig	27-11-1944	-	Never completed. Broken up
U 3033	A.G.Weser, Bremen	06-11-1944	27-02-1945	Scuttled 04-05-1945.	U 3537	F Schichau, Danzig	20-12-1944	-	Never completed. Broken up.
U 3034	A.G.Weser, Bremen	14-11-1944	31-03-1945	Scuttled 04-05-1945.	U 3546	A.G.Weser, Bremen	29-12-1944	-	Damaged in bombing raid on yard 30-03-1945.
U 3035	A.G.Weser, Bremen	11-11-1944	01-03-1945	Surrendered, Norway. Transferred to Royal Navy,					Never completed.
				1945. Transferred to Soviet Navy,	U 3547	A.G.Weser, Bremen	03-01-1945	-	Never completed. Broken up.
				1945 to become B 29. Scrapped 1958.	U 3548	A.G.Weser, Bremen	31-12-1944	-	Never completed. Broken up.
U 3036	A.G.Weser, Bremen	22-11-1944	-	Never completed. Broken up.	U 3549	A.G.Weser, Bremen	30-12-1944	-	Never completed. Broken up.
U 3037	A.G.Weser, Bremen	18-11-1944	03-03-1945	Scuttled 03-05-1945.	U 3550	A.G.Weser, Bremen	09-01-1945	-	Never completed. Broken up.
U 3038	A.G.Weser, Bremen	01-12-1944	04-03-1945	Scuttled 03-05-1945.	U 3551	A.G.Weser, Bremen	08-01-1945	-	Never completed. Broken up.
U 3039	A.G.Weser, Bremen	29-11-1944	08-03-1945	Scuttled 03-05-1945.	U 3552	A.G.Weser, Bremen	22-01-1945	-	Never completed. Broken up.
U 3040	A.G.Weser, Bremen	09-12-1944	08-03-1945	Scuttled 03-05-1945.	U 3553	A.G.Weser, Bremen	25-01-1945	-	Never completed. Broken up.
U 3041	A.G.Weser, Bremen	07-12-1944	10-03-1945	Surrendered. Transferred to Royal Navy as N 29,	U 3554	A.G.Weser, Bremen	27-01-1945	-	Never completed. Broken up.
				then transferred to Soviet Navy as B 30.	U 3555	A.G.Weser, Bremen	25-01-1945	-	Never completed. Broken up.
				Scrapped 1959.	U 3556	A.G.Weser, Bremen	07-02-1945	-	Never completed. Broken up.
U 3042	A.G.Weser, Bremen	11-12-1944	-	Damaged in air raid on yard, 22-02-1945.	U 3557	A.G.Weser, Bremen	04-02-1945	-	Never completed. Broken up.
				Never completed. Broken up.	U 3558	A.G.Weser, Bremen	17-02-1945	-	Never completed. Broken up.
U 3043	A.G.Weser, Bremen	14-12-1944	-	Never completed. Broken up.	U 3559	A.G.Weser, Bremen	17-02-1945	-	Never completed. Broken up.
U 3044	A.G.Weser, Bremen	21-12-1944	27-03-1945	Scuttled 05-05-1945.	U 3560	A.G.Weser, Bremen	25-02-1945	-	ever completed. Broken up.
U 3045	A.G.Weser, Bremen	20-12-1944	-	Sunk in bombing raid on yard 30-03-1945.	U 3561	A.G.Weser, Bremen	24-02-1945	-	Never completed. Broken up.
U 3501	F Schichau, Danzig	20-05-1944	29-07-1944	Scuttled 05-05-1945.	U 3562	A.G.Weser, Bremen	09-03-1945	-	Never completed. Broken up.
U 3502	F Schichau, Danzig	16-04-1944	19-08-1944	Damaged by bomb attack 05-1945.	U 3563	A.G.Weser, Bremen	07-03-1945	-	Never completed. Broken up.

Japan's *Sen Toku* seaplane carriers - giants to attack the Panama Canal

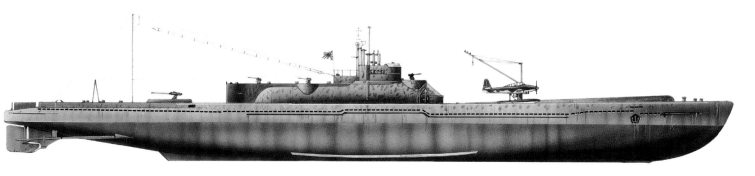

Length (ft)	400.3 oa
Beam (ft)	39.3 oa
Displacement (tons)	
Surfaced	5,233
Submerged	6,520
Speed (kts)	
Surfaced	18.75
Dived	6.5
Armament	8 x 21" bow tubes, 12 reloads
	1 x 140 mm 50 calibre deck gun.
	3 x 25 mm triple barrel AA cannon;
	1 x 25 mm AA cannon.
	3 Aichi M6A1 Seiran seaplanes, armed
	with torpedo or 800 kg bomb
Engines	4 x diesels, 7,700 hp
	2,400 hp electric
	2 shafts
Range	
Surfaced	37,500 nm at 14 kts
Submerged	60 nm at 3 kts
Diving depth	330 ft
Complement	144

The largest submarines in World War II were the Japanese *Sen Toku* seaplane carriers, designed to bomb the Panama Canal and West coast US cities. Development of the giant boats began in 1942 and construction of the first boat in January 1943. The design had double hulls, side by side, (a configuration adopted by the Soviet 'Typhoon' boats three decades later) and carried three Aichi M6A1 Seiran seaplanes with parts for a fourth airframe.

Eighteen boats in the class were planned but 13 were cancelled before construction began and work was halted on the final two before the surrender: *I-404* was then 90% complete.

The aircraft folded to fit into the 115-feet long cylindrical hangar that opened forward to allow access to an 80-feet long catapult-launching ramp which ended just aft of the bows. The tall conning tower was positioned offset to port above the hangar entrance to accommodate the bulky superstructure.

The boat carried four air-dropped torpedoes, twelve 250 kg and three 800 kg bombs to arm the aircraft, which could be launched within 45 minutes.

The first two units, *I-400* and *I-401* were tasked to launch aircraft attacks on US fleet positions at Ulithi on

August 17 1945, co-ordinated with *Kaiten* human torpedo attacks but the operation was overtaken by the Japanese surrender on August 15. Both boats were examined by the US Navy before being scuttled in the Pacific in 1946. The third of class, *I-402* had been converted into a tanker to carry much-needed petrol from the East Indies to Japan - but never undertook a mission.

Japan began building aircraft carrying submarines in 1940 with the B1 class boats, carrying one seaplane.[1] Twenty were built up to 1943, displacing 2,584 tons, surfaced and 3,654 tons submerged. Curiously, their successes came via the boat's own torpedo armament, with *1-26* damaging the carrier USS *Saratoga* on August 31 1942. *I-19* hit the carrier *Wasp* and with the same salvo, damaged the battleship *North Carolina* and sank the destroyer *O'Brien* on September 15 1942.

The aircraft capability was removed from some of the class and two boats were modified to carry *Kaiten* human torpedo craft in 1944.

Japan continued to build aircraft-carrying boats with the three (2,919 ton surface displacement, 4,149 tons submerged,) of Type A1, (*I-9, I-10, I-11*) based on the 'J3' design, fitted with a hangar for one seaplane, completing in 1942. A single, slower boat. *I-12,* of the A2 type, followed in 1944 and the two much larger (3,603 ton surface/4,762 tons submerged displacement) boats (*I-13* and *I-14*) of the Modified Type A in 1944-45 which carried two seaplane bombers.

Two classes, building on the Type B1, were constructed in 1943-44. All six boats of Type B2 were all sunk by US vessels. Type B3 numbered three boats with enhanced range. Both classes carried one aircraft.

Japanese *Sen Toku* submarine seaplane carrier

Boat	Builder	Laid down	Commissioned	Fate
I-400	Kure Naval Arsenal, Honshu	18-01-1943	30-12-1944	Surrendered to US Navy and scuttled in Pacific 1946.
I-401	Sasebo Naval Arsenal, Kyushu	1944*	08-01-1945	Surrendered to US Navy and scuttled in Pacific 1946.
I-402	Sasebo Naval Arsenal, Kyushu	1944*	24-07-1945	Converted into fuel carrier.
				Scuttled off Goto Island 1946.
I-403	Kawasaki Heavy Industries, Kobe	-	-	Cancelled 03-1945
I-404	Kure Naval Arsenal, Honshu	07-07-1944	-	Work stopped 03-1945 when 90% complete.
I-405	Kawaksaki Heavy Industries, Senshu Dockyards, near Osaka	-	-	Work stopped before completion. Cancelled 03-1945.

* Launch dates

1 *I-15*, FIRST OF CLASS, WAS COMPLETED ON SEPTEMBER 30 1940.

World War II submarine warfare; the grim Battle of the Atlantic

The beginning of World War II saw Britain prepared for unrestricted U Boat warfare and committed to operating a convoy system to protect merchant shipping - even though it reduced potential imports by a third. Royal Navy anti-submarine warfare capability against Germany's 57 operational U Boats in September 1939, had been enhanced by fully functional Asdic sonar but the full benefits of radar were yet to be enjoyed.

The first British merchant ship convoy left the USA on September 6 1939 - 36 slow-moving ships in nine parallel rows of four each, protected by three escorts, in front and on the flanks. It was a pattern to be repeated hundreds of times in the coming years.

The U Boat campaign got into its stride following the fall of France and the creation of new bases on the French coast, shortening transit time to the hunting grounds of the Atlantic. By September 1940, enough U Boats were operational to change tactics into co-ordinated group attacks by Wolfpacks, travelling on the surface at night to avoid detection. Around 130 such groups were set up between 1940 and 1943, each operational for two weeks and sometimes amounting to around 20 U Boats each.

By October 1940, the U Boats had notched up average sinkings of 60,000 tons of shipping per month, per submarine. On October 16-19, a six strong Wolfpack sank 36 ships in two Allied convoys totalling 79 vessels. Only 24 U Boats were sunk in 1940, on top of the 9 destroyed in 1939. The strategy was working: the U Boats were beginning to sink merchant ships faster than Britain could build them.

The next year, 1941, saw a new phase in the Battle of the Atlantic with 35 U Boats at sea and more than 400,000 tons of Allied cargo ships lost. Overall, the most successful U Boat skipper during World War II was Kptlt Otto Kretschmer in the Type VIIB boat *U99* who sank 30 ships displacing 175,804 tons, followed by Kptlt Joachim Schepke in the sister boat *U100* who accounted for 24 ships totalling 121,712 tons.[1] The most successful single U Boat patrol was mounted by Kptlt Günther Hessler in *U107* who sank 14 ships totalling 87,000 tons between March and July 1941.

Above: This boat sank 26 minutes after being damaged by depth charges from an RAF Coastal Command Sunderland in 1944.

Below: This unidentified U-Boat was also attacked by an RAF Sunderland in the Bay of Biscay in June 1942. It's final fate is unclear, but the boat eventually submerged leaving a wide trail of oil.

1 Schepke sank seven ships in three hours during a patrol in September 1940.

Radar Interception

After many experiments with airborne radar, the first effective systems to detect U Boats on the surface was the H2S, first installed in a Wellington at the end of 1942, with the first attack on a target in March 1943.

For night attacks, some method of illuminating the target was required for aircraft. The 'Leigh Light' a 20 million candlepower searchlight, mounted in a retractable pod beneath the fuselage, was fitted to Coastal Command aircraft. The advent of the schnorkel, which enabled U Boats to stay submerged much longer, handed the advantage back to the Kriegsmarine boats.

But new technology was coming to the aid of the allies. The first operational detection of a U-Boat on the surface by radar came on March 17 1941, when HMS *Walker* sank *U99* and with *Vanoc* sank *U100* off the Faeroes Islands while defending convoy HX.112. In a single day the Royal Navy had destroyed Germany's two most successful U Boats and their skippers.

On May 9 1941, three British escorts *Aubretia, Broadway* and *Bulldog* captured *U110* in the North Atlantic after she attacked convoy OB.318. With her, by good fortune, they captured a complete Enigma encryption machine which provided the last piece in the jigsaw for British code-breakers to read German high level signals traffic.

But the tide was still running in favour of the U Boats. 1942 was their most successful year with 1,664 Allied ships sunk, 1,097 vessels in the North Atlantic alone totalling 6,266,000 tons. After the USA's entry into the war on December 12 1941, the submarines headed for America's east coast, increasing their time on patrol by taking on fuel, supplies and munitions reloads from so-called 'Milch Cows' - a class of specially built U boat freighters. The US Navy did not institute convoy protection until May 14 1942, and a black-out of US cities along the eastern sea board was not ordered until the following June, so ships were easily targeted - frequently silhouetted against the bright lights of the shore. A total of 216 ships were sunk between January and March off the east coast, mainly oil tankers. June saw the worst shipping losses of the war - 834,196 tons sunk.

Convoy SC.94 suffered one third of its original strength in attacks by 18 U Boats, in August 1942. The Canadian destroyer *Assiniboine* swapped gunfire with *U210* and finally sunk her by ramming the boat twice on August 6. Badly damaged, she was forced to head home, leaving three 'Flower' class corvettes to protect the convoy's 32 ships. They staved off the attacks until August 8, when six ships were torpedoed, one of them a straggler, picked off away from the protective escort screen. *Dianthus* managed to sink *U379* after depth charge attacks and ramming her five times. Two destroyers arrived that night and fog cleared enough to allow air patrols to be mounted - but not before another four merchantmen were sunk.

The most desperate time for the convoys was during the four or five days in mid-Atlantic in the so-called 'Air Gap' where anti-submarine aircraft did not have the endurance to patrol. New air bases set up in Iceland and the Faeroes eventually helped close that gap.

At the Allied leaders' conference in Casablanca in January 1943, the war against the U Boats was given highest priority. The USA allocated 250 patrol aircraft for the Atlantic and added more escorts for convoy protection.

In March 1943, convoys HX.229 and SC.122 with 88 merchantmen and 15 escorts left New York for England via Halifax. In mid-Atlantic, they were attacked by 45 U Boats who sank 21 ships, displacing 141,000 tons with 90 torpedoes. The escorts expended 298 depth charges to

World War II submarine warfare; the grim Battle of the Atlantic

Schnorkel

The schnorkel, first tested by the Dutch Navy, allowed U Boat commanders to charge their batteries while submerged by drawing air to allow diesel motor operation.

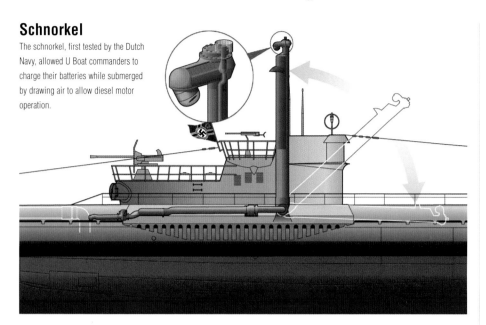

sink one U Boat and to damage two others. That month, 627,377 tons of shipping were sunk.

New Allied tactics were deployed. Long-range Liberator aircraft were deployed to provide air cover, new surface radar was introduced and the sea areas around the U Boat bases at Lorient, Brest, Nazaire and Bordeaux were targeted by aircraft and dedicated hunter-killer groups of destroyers, frigates and corvettes.

Twenty-eight boats were lost in the transit area of the Bay of Biscay - which became known as the 'Valley of Death' to U Boat crews - in 1943 alone, 11% of the total 242 U Boat losses that year. In May, the German Navy lost 43 U Boats, twice the replacement rate for sinking 34 ships. U Boat sinkings of merchantmen began to decline: 327,943 tons in April, 264,852 in May and 95,753 in June.

New weapons were arriving in the Allied arsenal. High Frequency Direction Finders, introduced in 1942, picked up Wolfpack radio messages and enabled their positions to be located. Magnetic anomaly detectors could spot submerged submarines. The US Navy introduced the air-launched Mk24 Fido acoustic torpedo in 1943 with the first kill, of *U657*, coming on May 17. Thirty-seven Axis submarines were eventually sunk by this weapon. Finally, new 'hedge-hog' depth charge throwers hurled 24 depth charges *ahead* of escorts, providing no clue to the submerged U Boat as to the direction of attack.

The U Boat command retaliated with the development of the schnorkel, first experimented by the Dutch Navy in 1938, which drew in air through a raised pipe to allow diesels to operate while submerged at periscope depth and enabling batteries to be recharged. The idea was taken up by U Boat designers and fitted in the Type VIIC and IXC classes in 1943 with at least 95 equipped by the end of 1945. It enabled the submarines to increase both

Below: April 1944. The crew of a stricken U-Boat attempt to escape into their one-man dinghies as the boat sinks by the stern.

their endurance at sea and time charging their batteries while submerged, undetected.

By the end of the war, 6,439 Allied merchant ships had been sunk, totalling 21,570,000 tons, of which the UK lost 3,194 ships, totalling 12,251,000 tons. Of this, 2,775 had been lost to submarines. In return, Germany had lost 782 U Boats and the average life expectancy of a U Boat crewman was around 30 days by the end of hostilities.

In the Pacific, the submarine war was completely different. Japanese submarines failed to target merchant shipping, focusing on high-value warships like carriers and battleships. Conversely, Allied boats were particularly effective in sinking Japanese cargo vessels - despite prolonged and fierce anti-submarine attacks by escorts. Japan lost 1,178 ships displacing 5,053,491 tons and ended the war with just 12% of her merchant fleet remaining. More than 55% were sunk by US boats. It was only in early 1944, that the Japanese Navy ordered convoying for merchantmen, and launched a huge building programme of more than 150 escorts. By then it was too late and US submarines countered by operating in their own wolfpacks.

Right: The last minutes of a Japanese merchant ship as seen through the periscope of a US Navy submarine.

World War II British, Allied & Neutral Merchant losses all theatres of war, gross registered tons

	1939	1940	1941	1942	1943	1944	1945	Total
By submarine	421,156	2,186,158	2,171,754	6,266,215	2,586,905	773,327	281,716	14,687,231
Total	755,237	3,991,641	4,328,558	7,790,697	3,220,137	1,045,629	438,821	21,570,720
% of losses caused by submarine	55.76	54.77	50.17	80.43	80.34	73.96	64.20	68.09

Source: *Official History of the Second World War: The War at Sea*, London, 1954-61.

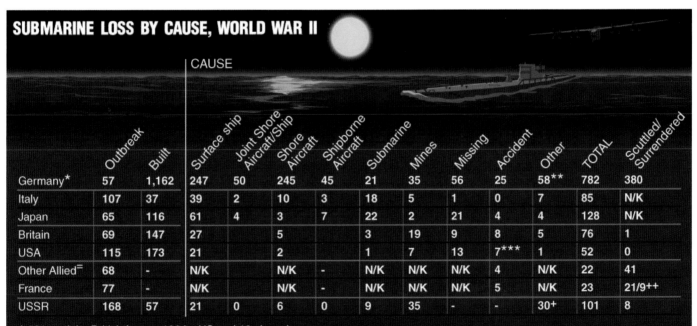

SUBMARINE LOSS BY CAUSE, WORLD WAR II

	Outbreak	Built	Surface ship	Joint Shore Aircraft/Ship	Shore Aircraft	Shipborne Aircraft	Submarine	Mines	Missing	Accident	Other	TOTAL	Scuttled/Surrendered
Germany*	57	1,162	247	50	245	45	21	35	56	25	58**	782	380
Italy	107	37	39	2	10	3	18	5	1	0	7	85	N/K
Japan	65	116	61	4	3	7	22	2	21	4	4	128	N/K
Britain	69	147	27		5		3	19	9	8	5	76	1
USA	115	173	21		2		1	7	13	7***	1	52	0
Other Allied=	68	-	N/K		N/K	-	N/K	N/K	N/K	4	N/K	22	41
France	77	-	N/K		N/K	-	N/K	N/K	N/K	5	N/K	23	21/9++
USSR	168	57	21	0	6	0	9	35	-	-	30+	101	8

* 521 sunk by British forces, 166 by US and 12 shared.

** Includes four boats in Japanese service and two boats interned in Spain. More than 60 were destroyed in allied bombing raids

*** Includes two US submarines sunk by their own torpedoes: Tullibee (SS-284) and Tang (SS-306)

\+ Includes accidents and missing.

\++ 36 were under construction at the fall of France, of which, only one, L 'Aurore entered service with the French Navy in 1940. Three incomplete boats were taken over by the Kriegsmarine after capture in 1940; L;Africaine, L'AndromÉde and L'Favorite became UF 1, UF 2 and UF 3, of which only UF 2 was commissioned and used for training, commissioning in November, 1942. She was scuttled in May 1945, but with the others, handed back to France after the war.

= Netherlands, Norway, Poland, Denmark, Yugoslavia, Greece.

Legacy of U-Boat Innovation

AT THE END OF WORLD WAR II, MORE THAN 20 SURRENDERED
completed U Boats were shared amongst the victorious Allies as war prizes, for use
in trials or as reparations. Of particular interest to the Allied navies were the
technological advances contained in the Type XXI electro-boats, their
smaller coastal counterparts, the Type XXIII, and the schnorkel,
allowing recharging of batteries while submerged.

The legacy of U Boat innovation

The concept of using the volatile and highly flammable chemical hydrogen peroxide as an air independent propulsion system also intrigued the British and Americans. This had been conceived by German engineer Professor Hellmuth Walter in 1934 and the Kriegsmarine had built 10 experimental and research boats between 1940 and 1943. One Type XVIIA boat, *U794*, had reached a submerged speed of 25 during trials in 1944.

Before hostilities ended all had been scuttled but two 310 ton Type VIIB boats were raised at Cuxhaven by the Americans and British. *U1406* was taken by transport ship to the USA and used in trials by the US Navy, who quickly abandoned the propulsion method as too dangerous. The boat was broken up in 1948.

U1407 became the British trials submarine *Meteorite* which produced some startling operating characteristics and was scrapped in 1949. Although the Royal Navy believed the system hazardous for combat, they went on to build two experimental boats to further assess the use of hydrogen peroxide to heat water for steam turbine

Below: The *Tang* was the first submarine designed for underwater performance rather than surfaced speed and handling. Key features included removing the deck guns, streamlining the outer hull, replacing the conning tower with a sail, installing new propellers designed for submerged operations, installing more air conditioning and a snorkel mast, and doubling the battery capacity.

propulsion. The streamlined *Explorer* (nicknamed, with black humour, 'Exploder') and *Exclaibur* were used as high-speed targets, producing underwater speeds of up to 30 kts. before experiments ended in 1968. Not only was hydrogen peroxide finally proved to be unstable, but nuclear power was clearly the route to take for submarine propulsion in the future.

A number of boats were taken on for weapons trials and experiments. The British took over 10 boats, including the Type VIIC class *U1105*, which had been coated with black rubber to test absorbance of sonar emissions[1] to become the 'N' trials class. Six (including five Type XXI electro-boats) were transferred to the Soviet Navy in 1946-47 to be recommissioned as Russian boats, serving up to the mid-1950s, in addition to the four Type VIICs which went direct as war prizes. Norway took four boats and France three, a Type VIIC[2], a Type XXIII electro coastal boat[3] and a Type XXI, *U2518*, recommissioned as *Roland Morillot*.[4]

Boat technologies less radical than the use of hydrogen peroxide were adopted. In the USA, the Type XXI boat *U3008* was commissioned into the US Navy on July 24, 1946[5] and became the genesis of the Navy's 'Guppy' (Greater Underwater Propulsive Power) programme, launched in 1946. The fleet submarines *Odax* (SS-484) and *Pomadon* (SS-486), were the first boats to be converted, incorporating Type XXI battery technology.

Above: Within two years of the end of the war, the U.S. Navy had a functional snorkel mast on an operational, high speed submarine-the *Irex* (SS 482).

The outer hull and conning tower were also streamlined with all features contributing to a new submerged speed of 18.2 kts. Twenty-four additional conversions were made under the 'Guppy II' project which included fitting schnorkels. In 1947, *Irex* (SS-482) became the first American boat to enter service with a schnorkel mast. Eventually, 50 boats were modified and some of these were transferred to friendly navies, some still serving into the 1990s.[6] In Britain, the schnorkel was fitted to boats in the new 'A' class delivered 1947-48.

Lessons learnt from the Type XXI continued to influence submarine design. The first US post-war design, the *Tang* class, incorporated such concepts, focussing on underwater performance rather than surface speed.

France assimilated lessons learned from the Type XXI in the six-boat *Narwhal* class of the late 1950s and in the

Soviet Union, large-scale construction programmes were launched with considerable influence in the submarines' design derived from captured U Boats. This was reflected in the long-range Project 611 boats (Nato codename 'Zulu') which had large battery capacity to double existing submerged speeds. The largest class was Project 613, displacing 1,050 tons, ('Whiskey') class. A total of 215 were built between 1950-1956, mimicking the capability of Type XXI high capacity batteries and slow speed motors for silent running and schnorkels.

U Boat operational service was not over, however. In 1956, the West German government raised two Type XXIII coastal electro-boats *U2365* and *U2367*. *U2365* had been scuttled in the Kattegat on May 8, 1945. After raising and refurbishment, she was recommissioned in the West German Navy as *U Hai* on August 15, 1957 but sank on September 14, 1966 in the North Sea. *U2367*, which had sunk off Denmark after a collision with another U boat on May 5, 1945. It was repaired and recommissioned as *U Hecht* on October 1, 1957, serving until September, 1968.[7] Finally, *U2540*, which was

scuttled near the Flensburg lightshipon May 4, 1945, was raised in 1957 to become the West German Navy's research boat *Wilhelm Bauer*. She is the last surviving Type XXI boat, now displayed at the German Maritime Museum at Bremerhaven.

1 LATER TRANSFERRED TO THE US NAVY AND SUNK DURING EXPLOSIVE TRIALS IN THE POTOMAC RIVER IN NOVEMBER, 1948.
2 RECOMMISSIONED AS *LAUBIE*, LATER *Q335*. DECOMMISSIONED 1963.
3 SANK AT TOULON, DECEMBER 6, 1946, WITH THE LOSS OF 17 CREW.
4 DECOMMISSIONED SEPTEMBER 30, 1967. SPAIN BOUGHT THE INTERNED *U 573*, RECOMMISSIONING IT AS *G 7*.
5 TAKEN OUT OF SERVICE ON JUNE 18, 1948. SOLD FOR SCRAP, SEPTEMBER 15, 1955 AFTER SERVING AS A TEST HULK AT ROOSEVELT ROADS. *U 2513* ALSO SAW SERVICE WITH THE US NAVY FROM SEPTEMBER 26, 1946 TO JULY 1949. SUNK BY GUNFIRE AFTER SEPTEMBER, 1951.
6 FOUR ARE STILL IN SERVICE. TWO, *HAI SINH* (EX-*CUTLASS, SS-478*), *HAI BAO* (EX-*TUSK,SS 426*) ARE USED FOR ANTI-SUBMARINE EXERCISES BY THE TAIWANESE NAVY AND A FURTHER TWO, *MARATREIS* (EX-*RAZORBACK, SS 394*) AND *ULUÇALIREIS* (EX-*THORNBACK, SS 418*) ARE OPERATIONAL IN THE TURKISH NAVY.
7 THE FIRST POST-WAR GERMAN SUBMARINE, *U1*, (TYPE 201,) WAS COMMISSIONED INTO THE BUNDESMARINE ON MARCH 20, 1962.

Albacore - prototype of modern submarine design

Length (ft)	203.8
Beam (ft)	27.25
Displacement (tons)	
Surfaced	1,692
Submerged	1,908
Speed (kts)	
Surfaced	15 design (26 achieved)
Dived	25+ (30 achieved)
Armament	Unarmed
Engines	various
Range	
Surfaced	various
Submerged	
Diving depth	N/K
Complement	36

US research into new submarine technologies began in 1944, focusing on new hull shapes and methods of propulsion. A major result landmark was *Albacore*, a floating test-bed that introduced the distinctive and highly-efficient hydrodynamic "teardrop" hull shape into submarine design, now adopted by most navies. After a host of wind-tunnel tests, the design, including a single screw, led to an experimental boat being authorised on November 25 1950, at a cost of $20 million.

Albacore (AGSS-569) was laid down at the Portsmouth Navy Yard in New Hampshire, on March 15 1952, launched on August 1 1953, and commissioned on December 6 1953. She was constructed of low carbon structural steel, (HY-80) with the sail positioned one third of the overall length from the bow. She had large rudders and stern planes placed aft of the small screw propeller with an additional rudder mounted on the aft section of the sail. Trials showed the design allowed fast underwater speeds and to be quieter in operation than expected.

The boat returned to Portsmouth in December 1955, for planned modifications including renewal of the stern section, moving the propeller aft of the control surfaces. The subsidiary rudder on the sail was removed. To

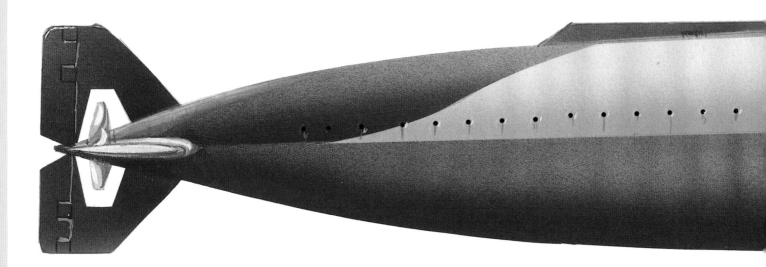

Left: In 1950 Langley tested the drag characteristics of what was then the world's fastest submarine, the Albacore, in the 30 x 60 Full Scale Tunnel. Water and air are both essentially fluids of different densities. Air traveling at high speed can simulate water traveling at lower speed for many purposes. *1/1/1958, NASA*

Right: The experimental submarine Albacore (AGSS-569) introduced the distinctive teardrop shape hull, which has influenced all follow-on submarine designs. This design provided for major advances in noise reduction, underwater speed and the use of low carbon (HY-80) as a structural steel. It also tested the first glassfibre sonar dome, installed in 1953.

reduce noise, the engines were isolated from the hull by rubber pads and free flooding areas coated with a new sound dampening elastic material called Aquaplas.

In 1959, a new 14-foot propeller was fitted and the bow diving planes removed to reduce cavitation noise, and on November 21 1960, *Albacore* began a major overhaul at Portsmouth Navy Yard, which included fitting a new 'X'-shaped stern (which improved agility,) a new bow and a bow dome housing BQS-4A active sonar and BQR-2B passive sonar. A towed array was also installed.

After further trials, the boat underwent another conversion at Portsmouth, beginning on December 7 1962. A pair of concentric, contra-rotating propellers replaced the single screw, a larger diesel motor was installed and a high-capacity silver-zinc battery replaced lead-acid models. A new ballast control system, designed in the wake of the loss of USS *Thresher*, was also tested. The final conversion began on January 1 1968, with further modifications to the propulsion system to produce even higher underwater speeds.

The boat was finally decommissioned on December 9 1972, and struck from the Navy List on May 1 1980. She is now on display at the Portsmouth Maritime Museum, New Hampshire.

As a result of the experiments involving *Albacore,* the tear drop design has influenced all modern submarine design. This hull form was first used in the three-strong US *Barbel* class, the last diesel-electric boats to be built for the US Navy.

Below: The US Navy's Albacore (AGSS-569), as first built, introduced the now familiar 'tear drop' shape to submarine hulls.

Nautilus - **first nuclear-powered submarine**

Length (ft)	323.75
Beam (ft)	27.66
Displacement (tons)	
Surfaced	3,533
Submerged	4,092
Speed (kts)	
Surfaced	22
Dived	25
Armament	6x21" bow tubes. 18 reloads.
Engines	1 S2Wa PWR
	2 shafts
Diving depth	600 ft
Complement	105

The world's first nuclear powered submarine was born out of a realisation in the later stages of the Second War World that this propulsion method would revolutionalise submarine warfare - no longer would boats' engines need oxygen to operate and endurance would not be constrained by fuel capacity. The Naval Reactors Branch of the US Atomic Energy Commission, under (then) Capt. Hyman G. Rickover, developed a successful pressurised water reactor (PWR) and construction of *Nautilus* was authorised by Congress in July 1951.

Her keel was laid at General Dynamic's Electric Boat Division's Groton, Connecticut, yard on June 14 1952, and she was commissioned on January 21 1954. *Nautilus* was underway on nuclear power on January 15 1955. The submarine went on to break endurance and speed records

- she remained submerged on passage to Puerto Rico, travelling 1,381 miles in 89.8 hours.

On August 3 1958, the boat became the first ship to reach the geographic North Pole and went on to travel a total of 1,830 miles under the ice - achieving a major objective, given the future importance of the Polar region in strategic ballistic missile submarine operations.

During 1962, she took part in the naval quarantine of Cuba during the Cuban Missile Crisis.

Nautilus decommissioned on March 30 1980, after a 25-year career covering half a million miles. She was designated a National Historic Landmark by the US Secretary of the Interior on May 20 1982, and was converted at Mare Island to become a museum ship at Groton, where she remains.

Left: Inside the combat information centre of Nautilus.

Seawolf , the second nuclear-propelled submarine, (3,765 tons surface displacement, 4,200 dived,) was initially fitted with a SIR MkII S2G liquid-sodium reactor which first went critical on June 25 1956. However, steam leaks developed during alongside testing and the reactor was shut down. After repairs and further testing, *Seawolf* completed two years of operation but went into Groton for removal of her liquid-metal reactor and a PWR substituted.

Above: USS *Nautilus*, pictured, represented a watershed for the U.S. Navy's submarine programme. This was the world's first nuclear-powered submarine, a design improvement which allowed for a dramatic increase in range and operational flexibility. The *Nautilus* is also credited with forcing shipbuilders to develop an improved quality control programme.

Below: Nautilus made history on January 15 1955 becoming the first-submarine to be underway on nuclear power.

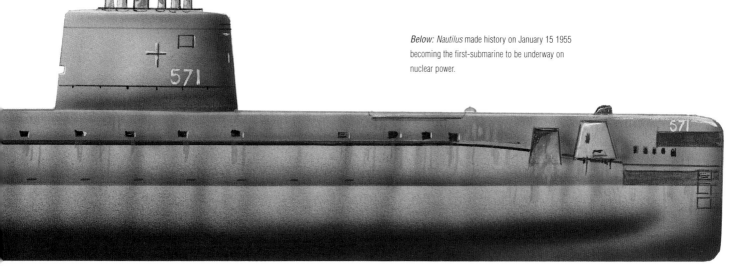

US 'Skipjack' class SSN

Length (ft)	251.7
Beam (ft)	31.5
Displacement (tons)	
Surfaced	3,075
Submerged	3,513
Speed (kts)	
Surfaced	16
Dived	30+
Armament	6x21 tubes
Engines	1 PWR , 15,000 shp
	1 shaft
Diving depth	700 ft
Complement	93

The US Navy's 'Skipjack' class combined the high speed and endurance benefits of nuclear propulsion with the streamlined 'tear-drop' shaped hull of the *Albacore* and so became the design-base of most modern SSNs. First-of-class *Skipjack* was authorised in the FY 1956 new construction programme, commissioning in April 1959.

Each hull cost around $40 million. *Scorpion*'s hull was laid down twice; the original (01-11-1957) was utilised for the Polaris submarine *George Washington* (*SSBN-598*) and the second for *SSN-589*. Similarly, material for *Scamp* was diverted for construction of *Patrick Henry,* (*SSBN-599*), delaying her progress.

The class had a single propeller shaft, as against two in earlier boats, and mounted diving planes on the sail. Because of the sharply tapering sterns, no aft torpedo tubes were fitted. Two Mk 45 ASTOR torpedoes, with low-yield tactical nuclear weapons were deployed in some boats.

Scamp saw service in fleet operations along the Vietnamese Coast during the Indo-China war in 1967 and in the South China sea in the first half of 1972. *Snook* served off Vietnam during the latter period.

Scorpion was lost with all hands *en-route* from a Mediterranean deployment to Norfolk, Virginia, in May 1968, 400 miles SW of the Azores.

US 'Skipjack' class SSN

Boat	Builder	Laid down	Commissioned	Fate
Skipjack (SSN-595)	General Dynamics Electric Boat, Groton, Connecticut	29-05-1956	15-04-1959	Decommissioned 19-04-1990. Scrapped 17-03-1996, Puget Sound.
Scamp (SSN-588)	Mare Island Navy Yard, Vallejo, California	23-01-1959	05-06-1961	Decommissioned early, 28-04-1988, after sail and planes damaged while assisting stricken freighter. Scrapped 09-09-1994, Puget Sound.
Scorpion (SSN-589)	General Dynamics Electric Boat, Groton, Connecticut	20-08-1958	29-07-1960	Lost 400 miles SW of Azores, 22-05-1968. 99 lost. Lies at 10,000ft depth in two major sections.
Sculpin (SSN-590)	Ingalls Shipbuilding, Pascagoula, Mississippi	03-02-1958	01-06-1961	Decommissioned 03-08-1990. Scrapped 30-09-1999, Puget Sound.
Shark (SSN-591)	Newport News Shipbuilding, Newport News, Virginia	24-02-1958	09-02-1961	Decommissioned 15-12-1989. Scrapped 28-06-1996, Puget Sound.
Snook (SSN-592)	Ingalls Shipbuilding, Pascagoula, Mississippi	07-04-1958	24-10-1961	Decommissioned 08-10-1986. Scrapped, 10-1996, Puget Sound.

Left: The USS *Skipjack* was the first nuclear-powered submarine built with the Albacore hull design. It also was the first nuclear submarine with a single propulsion shaft and screw. Another first was mounting bow planes on the sail which reduced flow noise at the bow-mounted sonar. Deep-diving and high speed capabilities were the result of HY-80 construction and a new reactor design, the S5W. This reactor became the U.S. Navy's standard until the *Los Angeles* class joined the fleet in the mid-1970's.

Right and Inset: Skipjack underway on the surface with distinctive tall sail with diving planes mounted at the tapering leading edge.

Below: SSN-589, USS *Scorpion* during her sea trials in 1960. She sank in 1968 with the loss of all hands.

British later Oberons - quietest SSKs of their time

The successful British *Oberon* class, born out of the earlier *Porpoise* class, had the reputation of being the quietest operational SSKs in the 1960s and 70s. Plastic was used in the superstructure and glass fibre laminate in the construction of the fin before and abaft the bridge, except in *Orpheus* where the superstructure was of light aluminium alloy and *Otter* which was reinforced with steel for her role as target.

First of class, *Oberon* was laid down at Chatham on November 28 1957, and built at a cost of £2.43 million, the price rising to £3.6 million for *Onyx*, last of the British boats. The Chilean and Brazilian boats suffered delays in fitting out because of electrical fires in the cabling. *Tonelero* suffered a serious fire at Vickers, which resulted in re-cabling of all *Oberons* then under construction. *Hyatt* also suffered a minor explosion while fitting out at Scott-Lithgow at Greenock and was delayed in delivery.

Substantial upgrade programmes lengthened the service life of all the boats. The British *Oberons* were retrofitted with the Type 2051/CSU 3-41 attack sonar, beginning with *Opossum,* weapons capability improved with the Tigerfish torpedo and Sub Harpoon anti-ship missile. *Oberon* was the first to have a modified, deeper casing to house equipment for initial training of SSN crews. *Olympus* was fitted with a 16-feet long exit chamber for the deployment of special forces personnel on covert missions.

	British/Australian	Canadian/Chilean	Brazilian
Length (ft)	295.25	295.25	295.25
Beam (ft)	26.5	26.5	26.5
Displacement			
Surface	2,030	2,030	2,030
Dived	2,410	2,410	2,410
Speed (kts)			
Surface	16	12	16
Dived	17	16	17
Armament			
	8x21" tubes (6 bow, 2 stern)	8x21" tubes (6 bow, 2 stern)*	8x21" tubes (6 bow, 2 stern)
	12 reloads†	22 reloads	12 reloads†
	Sub Harpoon SSM	Sub Harpoon SSM**	
Engines			
	2 diesels, 3680 bhp	2 diesels 3680 bhp	2 diesels 3680 bhp
	2 electric 6000 shp	2 electric 6000 shp	2 electric 6000 shp
	2 shafts	2 shafts`	2 shafts
Range			
Surfaced	9,000 at 10 kts	9,000 at 10 kts	9,000 at 10 kts
Submerged	N/K	N/K	N/K
Diving depth	900	656	600
Complement	69‡	65	70

* Stern tubes removed in Canadian boats, no longer used in Chilean hulls.

** Canada only

† Tigerfish Mk 24 torpedoes later in British and Brazilian boats.

‡ 62 in Australian Oberons

The Canadian boats underwent a SOUP (Submarine Operational Update Project) in 1982-84 with more modern sonar and fire control. A towed array was fitted in 1995. The Royal Australian Navy's boats had a new attack sonar, similar to their British counterparts, together with Mk 48 Mod 8 torpedoes and Sub Harpoon in the 1980s.

The last Canadian and Brazilian boats paid off in 2000. The two Chilean boats will pay off in 2004 and 2006 when the two new French design *Scorpene* SSKs enter service.

Right: In 1967 the Canadian fleet received a major update with the addition of four British-built Oberon class diesel submarines. Shown here is HMCS Ojibwa, just off the coast of Puerto Rico, exercising with other Canadian and American vessels, on 1 February 1967. *Canadian Forces Photo*

Below: The former Royal Australian Navy Oberon (Otway) pictured here in the process of being scrapped in 1995. The fin had already been removed to a museum.

British '*Oberon*' class SSKS, 1961-1978

Boat	Builder	Laid down	Commissioned	Fate
Royal Navy				
Oberon	HM Dockyard, Chatham	28-11-1957	24-02-1961	Paid off 1986.
Odin	Cammell Laird, Birkenhead	27-04-1959	03-05-1962	Paid off 18-09-1990. Sold for scrap, Greece, 09-1991.
Orpheus	Vickers, Barrow	16-04-1959	25-11-1960	Paid off 09-1992.
Olympus	Vickers, Barrow	04-03-1960	07-07-1962	Paid off, on disposal list, 08-1989. Alongside training in Canada from 1989.
Osiris	Vickers, Barrow	26-02-1962	11-01-1964	Paid off 28-05-1992. Sold to Canada for spare parts, 1992.
Onslaught	HM Dockyard, Chatham	08-04-1959	14-08-1962	Paid off 1990.
Otter	Scotts Shipbuilding, Greenock	14-01-1960	20-08-1962	Paid off 31-07-1991.
Oracle	Cammell Laird, Birkenhead	26-04-1960	14-02-1963	Paid off 18-09-1993.
Ocelot	HM Dockyard, Chatham	17-11-1960	31-02-1964	Paid off 08-1991. Sold 1992, Chatham Historic Dockyard, England.
Otus	Scotts Shipbuilding, Greenock	31-05-1961	05-10-1963	Paid off 04-1991.
Opossum	Cammell Laird, Birkenhead	21-12-1961	05-06-1964	Paid off 26-08-1993.
Opportune	Scotts Shipbuilding, Greenock	26-10-1962	29-12-1964	Paid off 02-06-1993.
Onyx	Cammell Laird, Birkenhead	16-11-1964	20-11-1967	Paid off 1990. Preserved at Birkenhead, England.
Canada				
Ojibwa (ex-Onyx)	HM Dockyard, Chatham	27-09-1962	23-09-1965	Decommissioned 1998.
Onondaga	HM Dockyard, Chatham	18-06-1964	22-06-1967	Paid off, 07-2000.
Okanagan	HM Dockyard, Chatham	25-03-1965	22-06-1968	Decommissioned 1998.
Australia				
Oxley	Scotts Shipbuilding, Greenock	02-07-1964	18-05-1967	Decommissioned 13-02-1992. Scrapped.
Otway	Scotts Shipbuilding, Greenock	29-06-1965	23-04-1968	Decommissioned 17-02-1994. Scrapped.
Onslow	Scotts Shipbuilding, Greenock	04-12-1967	22-12-1969	Decommissioned 1999.
Orion	Scotts Shipbuilding, Greenock	06-10-1972	15-06-1977	Decommissioned 1996. To be scrapped.
Otama	Scotts Shipbuilding, Greenock	25-05-1973	27-04-1978	In reserve, 1999.
Ovens	Scotts Shipbuilding, Greenock	17-06-1966	18-04-1969	Now museum boat at Fremantle.
Brazil				
Humaita	Vickers, Barrow	03-11-1970	18-06-1973	Decommissioned 1997.
Tonelero	Vickers, Barrow	18-11-1971	10-12-1977	Decommissioned 2000.
Riachuelo	Vickers, Barrow	26-05-1973	12-03-1977	Decommissioned 1997. Now museum boat.
Chile				
O'Brien	Scott-Lithgow, Greenock	17-01-1971	04-1976	Still operational, to be decommissioned in 2004.
Hyatt (ex-Condell)	Scott-Lithgow, Greenock	10-01-1972	27-09-1976	Still operational, to be decommissioned in 2005.

Japan's *Yuushio* class SSKs

Japanese post-war submarine design and construction began with the 1,420 ton submerged displacement *Oyashio*, launched in 1957. Quickly adapting new technologies, the Japanese Maritime Self-defence Force produced the single shaft, teardrop hulled *Uzushio* class between 1971-1978. The 10-boat *Yuushio* class is an enlarged version of this, with a double-hull, and with a much improved underwater speed and diving depth.

First of class entered service in 1980. Hydroplanes are fitted to the very tall sail. A very low frequency ZQR 1 passive towed array, housed in a conduit on the starboard side of the casing, was fitted in *Okishio* in 1987 and retrofitted in the sister boats. The Sub Harpoon anti-ship missile arms all except *Yuushio*, which was deleted in 1998.

Sonar fit is the medium/low frequency Hughes/Oki ZQQ 5 bow-mounted, active/passive search and attack.

Mochishio converted into a training submarine in 1997 and was decommissioned in 2000. Sister boats *Setoshio* moved into the training role on March 10 1999, and *Okishio* followed in 2000.

The class was followed by seven boat *Harushio* class between 1987 and 1997, which achieved substantial gains in noise reduction, aided by anechoic coating. Diving depth for this class is 1,150-feet.

Length (ft)	249.3
Beam (ft)	32.5
Displacement (tons)	
Surfaced	2,200*
Submerged	2,450
Speed (kts)	
Surfaced	12
Dived	24
Armament	6 x 21" amidships tubes,
	16 Type 89 torpedo reloads
	Sub Harpoon Block 1C anti-surface ship
	missile (except *Yuushio*)
Engines	2x diesels 6,800 hp (m)
	2 x electric motors, 7,200 hp (m)
	1 shaft
Range	
Surfaced	N/K
Submerged	N/K
Diving depth	900 ft
Complement	75

* 2,250 tons surface displacement for *Mochishio* and *Nadashio*, *Hamashio*, *Akishio*, *Takeshio*, *Yukishio* and *Sachishio*. 2,300 tons surface displacement for *Okishio*.

Above: The Nadashio surfacing at speed circa 1997.

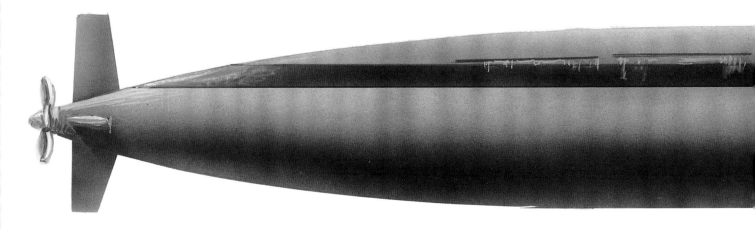

Japanese *Yuushio* Class SSK

Boat	Builder	Laid down	Commissioned	Fate
Yuushio	Mitsubishi, Kobe	03-12-1976	26-02-1980	Deleted from active service 1998.
Mochishio	Kawasaki, Kobe	09-05-1978	05-03-1981	Converted into training boat, 1997. Deleted from active service 2000.
Setoshio	Mitsubishi, Kobe	17-04-1979	17-03-1982	Converted into training boat 10-03-1999.
Okishio	Kawasaki, Kobe	17-04-1980	01-03-1983	Converted into training boat 2000.
Nadashio	Mitsubishi, Kobe	16-04-1981	06-03-1984	In service.
Hamashio	Kawasaki, Kobe	08-04-1982	05-03-1985	In service.
Akishio	Mitsubishi, Kobe	15-04-1983	05-03-1986	In service.
Takeshio	Kawasaki, Kobe	03-04-1984	03-03-1987	In service.
Yukishio	Mitsubishi, Kobe	11-04-1985	11-03-1988	In service.
Sachishio	Kawasaki, Kobe	11-04-1986	24-03-1989	In service.

Below: Japan's *Yuushio* class of diesel submarines brought much improved underwater speeds and diving depths to Maritime Self-Defence Force operations.

Australia's *Collins* class SSKs

Length (ft)	255.2 oa
Beam (ft)	25.6 oa
Displacement (tons)	
Surfaced	3,051
Submerged	3,353
Speed (kts)	
Surfaced	10
Dived	20
Armament	6x21" forward tubes,
	12 Mk 48 Mod 4 torpedo reloads
	Sub Harpoon Block 1C
	anti-surface ship missile
	44 mines instead of torpedoes
Engines	3 x diesels Type V18B/14 6,020 hp
	1x electric motors, 7,344 hp (m)
	3 x generators (4.3 MW)
	1 emergency hydraulic motor
	1 shaft
Range	
Surfaced	11,500 nm at 10 kts
Submerged	400 nm at 4 kts
Diving depth	985 ft
Complement	42

Australia's new class of SSK, the *Collins* class, is a Kockums Type 471 design with the bow and midships sections of the first two submarines built in Sweden. Six were ordered as replacements for the Royal Australian Navy's elderly *Oberons* but options for a further two were not taken up. Because of problems with high-speed underwater noise levels and software connected with the boat's command and control system, full operational service was delayed.

The single-hull class is distinguished by a prominent sonar pod positioned above the hemispherical bows, containing the Thomson Sintra active/passive intercept array and by the hydroplanes mounted forward almost halfway up the fin. A long thin tube above the stern streams the Kariwarra towed-array in the first two boats and the Narama or TB 23 in the rest of the class. TSM 225 surveillance and ranging arrays are mounted within six shallow rectangular blisters along the casing, three on each side.

With the exception of *Collins*, all the boats were built fitted with anechoic tiles; the first of class being retrofitted.

The class was built to couple the capacity for short coastal patrols with a requirement for long-endurance ocean operations in the Pacific, Indian and Antarctic Oceans of more than 70 days.

A Kockums Stirling Mk 1 Air-Independent Propulsion (AIP) has been tested on a shore rig and the *Collins* design allows for a plug containing an AIP plant to be inserted into the hull. AIP allows a diesel-electric submarine to operate at low speeds, up to five knots, submerged for more than two weeks without having to resort to snorting to operate its propulsion system. This is based on an air-dependent diesel providing energy to a lead-acid secondary battery system or an energy converter.

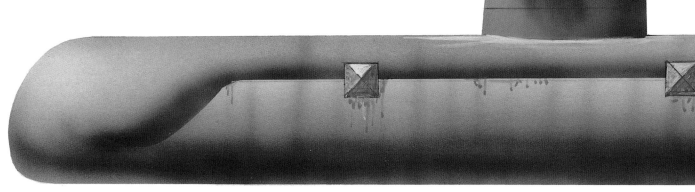

Above: HMAS *Collins*, the first of the class, during sea trials in 1996.

Below: The rectangular blisters containing the *TSM* 225 surveillance and ranging arrays are prominent on the casing.

Above: Pictured here in 1993 before the fitting of the distinctive mounting for the Karriwarra towed array.

Australian Collins Class SSK

Boat	Builder	Laid down	Commissioned	Fate
Collins	Australian Submarine Corp., Adelaide	14-02-1990	27-07-1996	In service
Farncomb	Australian Submarine Corp., Adelaide	01-03-1991	31-01-1998	In service
Waller	Australian Submarine Corp., Adelaide	19-03-1992	10-07-1999	In service
Dechaineux	Australian Submarine Corp., Adelaide	04-03-1993	06-2000	In service
Sheean	Australian Submarine Corp., Adelaide	17-02-1994	10-2000	In service
Rankin	Australian Submarine Corp., Adelaide	12-05-1995	-	Commissioning due 2001.

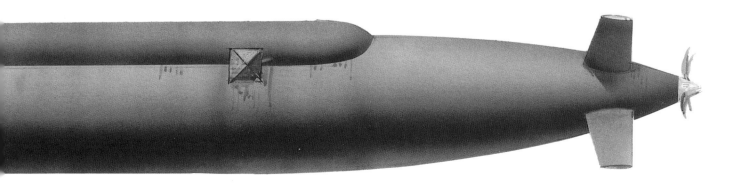

Kilo - exporting power-projection

Russia's 'Kilo' or 'Vashavyanka' class of diesel electric patrol submarines has provided potent power projection capabilities for a number of export customers, through the design's high survivability and flexible weapon systems. Twelve remain operational with the Russian fleet but the class has been exported to China (four, with a further two more of the more advanced Type 636 'Amur' class), India, (eight, with two ordered), Algeria, (two), Poland, (one), Romania (one), and Iran (three).

The design has a 32% buoyancy reserve (compared with the 13% of US SSNs) and meets requirements to remain afloat with a compartment and two adjacent main ballast tanks flooded. Thus, it is likely to survive the pressure hull being holed in an attack.

An unusual design feature is the surface-to-air missiles stored in a ready-to-use watertight compartment between the snorkel and radio antenna masts in the submarine sail. The shoulder-launched missiles, eight Strela in Type 877 boats, and six later Gimlets in the Type 636. A SA-N-10 system may be fitted to Iranian boats in the future.

One reported problem area in the export versions is the three groups of 120 batteries with 9700 kWh capacity. Iranian boats have had these replaced with Indian batteries; Indian, with ones of German design. Anechoic tiles have been fitted on the fins and casings of the Indian boats.

One of the Russian 'Kilos' was reported to be trialling water-jet propulsion in the Black Sea in 1998.

First of the Type 877/Type 877M/Type 877MK class was launched in 1979 and commissioned on September 12 1982. Twenty-four were built for the Russian Navy and those in reserve could be sold off for export after refit, or reactivated for Russian service. Type 877EM were export versions. The Type 877EMK design was supplied to the Iranian Navy and two to the Russian Navy. India's *Sindhushastra* is believed to be a Type 636, as are the third and fourth Chinese boats.

	Type 877/M/EM/MK	Type 636 'Amur'
Length (ft)	238.2 oa	242.1 oa
Beam (ft)	32.5 oa	32.5 oa
Displacement (tons)		
Surfaced	2,325	2,325
Submerged	3,076	3,076
Speed (kts)		
Surfaced	10	10
Dived	17	19
Armament	6x21" tubes, 12 reloads*	
	SA-N-5 Strela 2 SAM	SA-N-8 Gimlet SAM
	Maximum 24 AM-1 mines as replacement for torpedoes	Maximum 24 AM-1 mines as replacement for torpedoes
Engines	2 x 1,500 hp diesel	2 x 1,500 hp diesel
	1 x 5,590 hp electric	1 x 5,500 hp electric
	Cruise: 1x 190hp	Cruise: 1x 190 hp
	Reserve: 2 x 102 hp	Reserve: 2x 102 hp
	6 blade propeller	7 skewed-blade propeller
Range		
Surfaced	6,000 nm at 7 kts (snorting)	7,500 nm at 7 kts (snorting)
Submerged	400 nm at 3 kts.	400 nm at 3 kts.
Diving depth	787 ft (985 ft max)	787 ft (985 ft max)
Complement	52	52

* Novator SS-N-27 SLCM in three Indian 'Sindhughosh' class

Below: Orzel - the Polish Navy's single Kilo photographed visiting Kiel Naval Base in Germany during exercises in the Baltic.

Above: Iran's third Kilo *Yunes* is towed by a support vessel in the central Mediterranean Sea en route to Iran in January 1997.

Right: Built in St Petersburg, Russia, this Kilo was photographed being loaded aboard a floating transport for delivery to its final customer, Iran.

NUCLEAR AGE 1: THE HUNTER KILLERS

THE US NAVY'S NAUTILUS DEMONSTRATED THE RELIABILITY, INDEPENDENCE

and long endurance that nuclear power could bring to submarine operations.

It was not long before all the major naval powers produced their own

nuclear boats (SSNs) equipped with a wide range of weapons

and sensor fits, both for strategic and tactical purposes.

US 'Thresher/Permit' class SSNs

The US's 'Thresher' class SSNs provided greater depth capabilities than its predecessors, with 1,300-feet for operations, and 1,950-feet as a crush depth. First of class, *Thresher*, was lost off the New England coast in April 1963, during deep-diving trials following an overhaul.

Following the accident, *Flasher, Gato* and *Greenling* were modified during construction to include heavier machinery and a larger sail structure, 20-feet tall, compared to the 13.75 to 15-feet height of earlier boats.

Jack was fitted with an experimental direct drive power plant, two smaller propellers and a contra-rotating turbine to reduce operating noise. Power efficiency was also increased by 10% but this did not yield greater speeds. The arrangement was deemed unsuccessful and was removed.

Permit became the first submarine to successfully fire the SUBROC anti-submarine weapon in January 1963. The class was equipped with the bow-mounted BQQ-2 sonar suite comprising BSQ-6 active and BSQ-7 passive and the BQQ-5A-E series. Later boats also had the TB-126 towed array.

	Class	Jack	Greenling, Gato & Flasher
Length (ft)	278.5	297.4 oa	292.2
Beam (ft)	31.7	31.7	31.7
Displacement (tons)			
Surfaced	3,750	3,750	3,800
Submerged	4,300	4,470	4,600
Speed (kts)			
Surfaced	20+	20+	20+
Dived	30+	30+	30+
Armament	4 x Sub-Harpoon anti-ship missile*	4 x Sub-Harpoon anti-ship missile*	4 x Sub-Harpoon anti-ship missile*
	4-6 SUBROC anti-submarine missile	4-6 SUBROC anti-submarine missile	4-6 SUBROC anti-submarine missile
	4 x 21" amidship tubes, 12-18 reloads	4 x 21" amidship tubes, 12-18 reloads	4 x 21" amidship tubes, 12-18 reloads
Engines	1 PWR, 2 steam turbes, 15,000 shp	1 PWR, 2 steam turbes, 15,000 shp	1 PWR, 2 steam turbes, 15,000 shp
	1 shaft*	1 shaft**	1 shaft*
Diving depth	1,300	1,300	1,300
Complement	112	112	112

* Except *SSN-604-606, 612, 614-15.*

** *Jack* fitted with two propellers on one shaft and a contra-rotating turbine.

US 'Thresher/Permit' class SSN

Boat	Builder	Laid down	Commissioned	Fate
Thresher (SSN-593)	Portsmouth Navy Yard, New Hampshire	28-05-1958	03-08-1961	Lost 220 miles E of Boston while on post overhaul sea trials, 10-04-1963. 129 lost. Submarine broken up at depth of 8,400 ft.
Permit (SSN-594)	Mare Island Navy Yard, Vallejo, California	16-07-1959	29-05-1962	Decommissioned 12-06-1991. Scrapped 05-1993 Puget Sound.
Plunger (ex-Pollack) (SSN-595)	Mare Island Navy Yard, Vallejo, California	02-03-1960	21-11-1962	Decommissioned 03-01-1990. Scrapped 03-1996 Puget Sound.
Barb (ex-Pollack,ex-Plunger) (SSN-596)	Ingalls Shipbuilding, Pascagoula, Mississippi	09-11-1959	24-08-1963	Decommissioned 20-12-1989. Scrapped 03-1996, Puget Sound.
Pollack (ex-Barb) (SSN-603)	New York Shipbuilding, Camden, New Jersey	14-03-1960	26-05-1964	Decommissioned 01-03-1989. Scrapped 02-1995 Puget Sound.
Haddo (SSN-604)	New York Shipbuilding, Camden, New Jersey	09-09-1960	16-12-1964	Decommissioned 12-06-1991. Scrapped 08-1992 Puget Sound.
Jack (SSN-605)	Portsmouth Navy Yard, New Hampshire	16-09-1960	31-03-1967	Decommissioned 11-07-1990. Scrapped 09-1992 Puget Sound.
Tinosa (SSN-606)	Portsmouth Navy Yard, New Hampshire	24-11-1959	17-10-1964	Decommissioned 15-01-1992. Scrapped 06-1992 Puget Sound.
Dace (SSN-607)	Ingalls Shipbuilding, Pascagoula, Mississippi	06-06-1960	04-04-1964	Decommissioned 02-12-1988. Scrapped 01-1997 Puget Sound.
Guardfish (SSN-612)	New York Shipbuilding, Camden, New Jersey	28-02-1961	20-12-1966	Decommissioned 04-02-1992. Scrapped 07-1992 Puget Sound.
Flasher (SSN-613)	General Dynamics Electric Boat, Groton, Connecticut	14-04-1961	22-07-1966	Decommissioned 14-09-1992. Scrapped 05-1994 Puget Sound.
Greenling (SSN-614*	General Dynamics Electric Boat, Groton, Connecticut	15-08-1961	03-11-1967	Decommissioned 18-04-1993. Scrapped 09-1994 Puget Sound.
Gato (SSN-615)*	General Dynamics Electric Boat, Groton, Connecticut	15-12-1961	25-01-1968	Decommissioned 25-04-1993. Scrapped 04-1996 Puget Sound.
Haddock (SSN-661)	Ingalls Shipbuilding, Pascagoula, Mississippi	24-04-1961	22-12-1967	Decommissioned 07-04-1993.

* Greenling and Gato were launched at Groton and towed to Quincy Division, Massachusetts, for lengthening and completion.

Below left: SSN-613 'Flasher', pictured in 1982. The distinctive camouflage pattern applied to the masts is still used on many modern boats.

Below: SSN-595 'Plunger'. The distinctive extended teardrop hull was to set the pattern for US boats for decades to come.

Below: The first vessel in the class, 'Thresher', was lost in deep water less than two years after she was commissioned. There were no survivors.

US *'Sturgeon'* class SSN

The USA's 'Sturgeon' class was an improved version of the 'Thresher' class, fitted with acoustic tiles to reduce the boats' target strength and their own radiated noise. Although built for an operational life of at least 30 years, the class fell foul of military expenditure reductions and the later hulls decommissioned very early.

The sail in the class was taller than the 'Thresher' with the diving planes positioned lower to improve control at periscope depth. In the 'Sturgeon' class, the planes rotated to vertical for breaking through the Polar ice when surfacing. *Whale* and *Pargo* staged exercises in the Arctic ice pack in March-April 1969 with *Whale* surfacing at the geographic North Pole on the 60th anniversary of Peary's arrival there.

SSN-678-87 were built with an extra 10 ft in length to improve habitability. *Archerfish, Tunny, Cavalla* and *L Mendel Rivers* were converted to take on a special forces mission, with a dry-dock shelter mounted on the hull for a swimmer delivery vehicle, inflatable boats or a platoon of SEALs. *Hawkbill, Pintado, Billfish,* and *William H Bates* were modified to carry and support Deep Submergence Rescue Vehicles. *Parche* was converted in 1987-91 for seabed research operations.

	Class	SSN-678-687
Length (ft)	292.25	302.25
Beam (ft)	31.7	31.7
Displacement (tons)		
Surfaced	3,640	3,640
Submerged	4,640	4,640
Speed (kts)		
Surfaced	20+	20+
Dived	30+	30+
Armament (all)		
	Sub-Harpoon anti-ship missile.	
	Tomahawk Land Attack Missile/Tomahawk anti-ship missile	
	4x21" amidship tubes, 15 reloads plus 4 Sub Harpoon or up to	
	8 Tomahawks instead of equiavlent number of torpedoes or Sub Harpoons.	
	Minelaying configuration: Mk 67 Mobile or Mk 60 CAPTOR mines instead of torpedoes	
Engines (all)		
	1 PWR, 11.2 MW 2 steam turbines	
	1 shaft	
Diving depth	1,320	1,320
Complement	107	107

US *'Sturgeon'* Class SSNs

Boat	Builder	Laid down	Commissioned	Fate
Sturgeon (SSN-637)	General Dynamics Electric Boat, Groton, Connecticut	10-08-1963	03-03-1967	Scrapped 11-09-1995 Puget Sound.
Whale (SSN-638)	General Dynamics, Quincy, Massachusetts	27-05-1964	12-10-1968	Decommissioned, 25-06-1996. Scrapped 29-09-1997 Puget Sound.
Tautog (SSN-639)	Ingalls Shipbuilding, Pascagoula, Mississippi	27-01-1964	17-08-1968	Decommissioned 31-03-1997.
Grayling (SSN 646)	Portsmouth Navy Yard, New Hampshire	12-05-1964	11-10-1969	Decommissioned 18-07-1997
Pogy (SSN 647)	Ingalls Shipbuilding, Pascagoula, Mississippi	04-05-1964	15-05-1971	Decommissioned 04-01-1999
Aspro (SSN-648)	Ingalls Shipbuilding. Pascagoula, Massachusetts	23-11-1964	20-02-1969	Decommissioned 31-03-1995.
Sunfish (SSN 649)	General Dynamics, Quincy, Massachusetts	15-01-1965	15-03-1969	Decommissioned 31-03-1997
Pargo (SSN-650)	General Dynamics Electric Boat, Groton, Connecticut	03-06-1964	05-01-1968	Decommissioned 14-04-1992. Scrapped 14-04-1996, Puget Sound.
Queenfish (SSN-651)	Newport News Shipbuilding, Newport News, Virginia	11-05-1964	06-12-1966	Decommissioned 08-11-1991. Scrapped 07-04-1993, Puget Sound.
Puffer (SSN-652)	Ingalls Shipbuilding, Pascagoula, Mississippi	08-02-1965	09-08-1969	Decommissioned 12-08-1996. Scrapped, 03-1997, Puget Sound.
Ray (SSN-652)	Newport News Shipbuilding, Newport News, Virginia	01-04-1965	12-04-1967	Decommissioned 16-03-1993.
Sand Lance (SSN 660)	Portsmouth Navy Yard, New Hampshire	15-01-1965	25-09-1971	Decommissioned 07-08-1998
Lapon (SSN-661)	Newport News Shipbuilders, Newport News, Virginia	26-07-1965	14-12-1967	Decommissioned 08-1992.
Gurnard (SSN-662)	Mare Island Navy Yard, Vallejo, California.	22-12-1964	06-12-1968	Decommissioned 28-04-1992. Scrapped 10-1006, Puget Sound.
Hammerhead (SSN-663)	Newport News Shipbuilding, Newport News, Virginia	29-11-1965	28-06-1968	Decommissioned 05-04-1995. Scrapped 11-1995, Puget Sound.
Sea Devil (SSN-664)	Newport News Shipbuilding, Newport News, Virginia	12-04-1966	30-01-1969	Decommissioned 16-10-1992. Scrapped 09-1999, Puget Sound.
Guitarro (SSN-665)	Mare Island Navy Yard, Vallejo, California	09-12-1965	09-09-1972	Decommissioned 29-05-1992. Scrapped 10-1994, Puget Sound.
Hawkbill (SSN-666)	Mare Island Navy Yard, Vallejo, California	12-09-1966	04-02-1971	Modified for Deep Submergence Rescue Vehicle role Decommissioned 1999.
Bergall (SSN-667)	Mare Island Navy Yard, Vallejo, California	16-04-1966	13-06-1969	Decommissioned 06-06-1996. Scrapped 09-1997, Puget Sound.
Spadefish (SSN-668)	Newport News Shipbuilding, Newport News, Virginia	21-12-1966	14-08-1969	Decommissioned 11-04-1997. Scrapped 10-1997, Puget Sound.
Seahorse (SSN-669)	General Dynamics, Electric Boat, Groton, Connecticut	13-08-1966	19-09-1969	Decommissioned 11-04-1997. Scrapped 09-1996, Puget Sound.
Finback (SSN-670)	Newport News Shipbuilding, Newport News, Virginia	26-06-1967	04-02-1970	Decommissioned 28-03-1997. Scrapped 01-1997, Puget Sound.
Pintando (SSN-672)	Mare Island Navy Yard, Vallejo, California	27-10-1967	11-09-1971	Modified for Deep Submergence Rescue Vehicle role Decommissioned 26-02-1998. Scrapped 10-1998, Puget Sound.
Flying Fish (SSN-673)	General Dynamics Electric Boat, Groton, Connecticut	30-06-1967	29-04-1970	Decommissioned 16-05-1996. Scrapped 10-1996, Puget Sound.
Trepang (SSN-674)	General Dynamics Electric Boat, Groton, Connecticut	28-10-1967	14-08-1970	Decommissioned 01-07-1999.
Bluefish (SSN-675)	General Dynamics Electric Boat, Groton, Connecticut	13-03-1968	08-01-1971	Decommissioned 01-07-1996.
Billfish (SSN-676)	General Dynamics Electric Boat, Groton, Connecticut	20-09-1968	12-03-1971	Modified for Deep Submergence Rescue Vehicle role Decommissioned 31-05-1996.
Drum (SSN-677)	Mare Island Navy Yard, Vallejo, California	20-08-1968	15-04-1972	Decommissioned 31-03-1998
Archerfish (SSN-678)	General Dynamics Electric Boat, Groton, Connecticut	19-06-1969	17-12-1971	Modified for special forces role. Decommissioned 31-03-1998. Scrapped 11-1998, Puget Sound
Silversides (SSN-679)	General Dynamics Electric Boat, Groton, Connecticut	13-10-1969	05-05-1974	Decommissioned 21-07-1994.
William H Bates (ex-Redfish) (SSN-680)	Ingalls Shipbuilding, Pascagoula, Mississippi.	04-08-1969	05-05-1973	Modified for Deep Submergence Rescue Vehicle role Removed from service, 1999.
Batfish (SSN-681)	General Dynamics Electric Boat, Groton, Connecticut	09-02-1970	01-09-1972	Decommissioned 17-03-1999.
Tunny (SSN-682)	Ingalls Shipbuilding, Pascagoula, Mississippi	25-05-1970	26-01-1974	Modified for special forces role Decommissioned 13-03-1998. Scrapped 10-1998, Puget Sound.
Parche (SSN-683)	Ingalls Shipbuilding, Pascagoula, Mississippi	10-12-1970	17-08-1974	Modified with 100 ft section for seabed research, 1987-1991. To be decommissioned, end 2003.
Cavalla (SSN-684)	General Dynamics Electric Boat, Groton, Connecticut	04-06-1970	09-02-1973	Modified for special forces role, 1982. Decommissioned 30-03-1998.
L Mendel Rivers (SSN-686)	Newport News Shipbuilding, Newport News, Virginia	26-06-1971	01-02-1975	Modified for special forces role Decommissioned late 2000.
Richard B Russell (SSN-687)	Newport News Shipbuilding, Newport News, Virginia	19-10-1971	16-08-1975	Decommissioned 24-06-1994. To be scrapped end 2001.

Left: USS *Hawkbill* in 1999 on SCICEX (SCience ICe EXpedition). Arctic operations began just after World War II. Almost every year since then, U.S. submarines have deployed to the Arctic on classified missions designed to improve their proficiency in arctic operations. These Ice Exercises (or ICEX missions) continue today. In 1993 the U.S. Navy decided to share its submarines with the world scientific community in a series of Science Ice Expedition cruises. USS *Hawkbill* was decomissioned soon after returning from this mission.

Below: The Sturgeon class was an extension and improvement on the *Thresher/Permit* design. This class of 37 submarines became the workhorse of the fleet from the mid-1960s through to 1980s when the *Los Angeles* class entered the fleet in large numbers. Here, Drum shows the tailfin with diving planes fitted lower than the earlier *Thresher/Permit* class to improve control at periscope depth.

Below: SSN-665, USS *Guitarro*,
seen during a visit to a Royal
Australian Naval Base in 1983.

Russia's '*Sierra*' class - deep diving attack submarine

Russia's small and expensive 'Sierra' class was the successor to the ill-fated 'Alfa' class, built from the mid-1960s to 1981 and all are now deleted. It's two light and strong titanium hulls enabled it to operate at great depths and provided reduced radiated noise levels as well an increased resistance to damage in torpedo attacks.

The first 'Sierra I' boat, was laid down in May 1982, at the Gorky Shipyard, launched in August 1983, and was fitted out at Severodvinsk. It was laid up in 1997. The survivor, *Tula* (ex-*Karp*) was launched in July 1986, and commissioned in September 1987. This class was the first fitted with a releasable escape pod for the crew, covered by a V-shaped casing on the port side of the sail.

The follow-class, 'Sierra II' has a considerably larger sail, (16.5 ft longer than 'Sierra I') which is squat, but with a curious flat, square leading edge, which must impact hydrodynamic quietening. Masts are offset on the starboard side to make way for two escape pods in the sail. On the starboard side, is a 10-point environment sensor fitted at right angles to the front end of the sail. A prominent, much larger, pod on the after fin houses the Skat 3 passive, very low frequency towed array.

Two *Pskon* and *Nizny-Novgorod* remain operational at Russia's Northern Fleet. A third of class, *Mars*, was scrapped before completion in July 1992.

Soviet titanium technology was far in advance of the West requiring fewer passes to achieve a successful weld, but the cost of the hulls limited the numbers built, despite advantages in depth and underwater speed.

	Sierra II	Sierra I
Length (ft)	364.2	351
Beam (ft)	46.6	41
Displacement (tons)		
Surfaced	7,600	7,200
Submerged	9,100	8,100
Speed (kts)		
Surfaced	10	10
Dived	32	34
Armament (IIand I)	SS-N-21 Sampson SLCM with	
	200kT nuclear warhead	
	SS-N-15 Starfish anti-submarine weapon:	
	200kT depth charge or	
	90 kg HE Type40 torpedo.	
	SS-N-16 Stallion, 200 kT depth-charge or	
	90kg HE Type 40 torpedo	
	4 x 25.6" and 4x21" tubes	
	Minelaying configuration: 42 instead of	
	torpedoes	
Engines (IIand I)	1 PWR, 190MW output	
	2 x 1,002 hp emergency motors	
	1 shaft, 2 spinners	
Diving depth	2,460 ft	2,460 ft
Complement	61	61

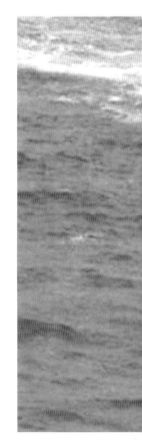

Below and right:
Aerial shots taken by NATO patrol aircraft during the mid-1980s. The use of titanium in Soviet boats enabled them to descend to unprecedented depths.

Russian '*Akula I* and *II*' Type 971/971M SSNs

The Russian 'Akula' class, follow-ons to the prolific 'Victor III' SSNs, have produced very significant reductions in noise levels, both by using suppression technologies, such as double-laying the silence system around the power train and in active sound cancellation, some based on Western commercial developments. The 'Improved Akulas' and the 'Akula IIs' now have noise levels at slow speeds equal to, if not better than, some Western boats, eroding the advantage long enjoyed by NATO submarines.

Eight steel-hulled boats were built between July 1984 and December 1991 - in the 'Akula I' group, and a further four 'Improved Akula Is' between May 1992 and July 1995. A final hull, *Nerpa*, was launched in May 1994, and has still to be completed.

All share a very long, low rounded sail, faired into the hull, containing a U-shaped rescue pod for crew members. A number of non-acoustic sensors are located on the leading-edge of the sail and on the forward casing on the 'Improved Akulas.' All boats have a large pod on the vertical stern containing the thin-wire Skat-3 passive, very low frequency towed array.

A new variant, the 'Akula II' began with the launch, on December 10 1994, of *Viper* which was commissioned in July the following year. A second 'Akula II,' *Gepard*, was launched on August 18 1999 and commissioned in June 2000. No more are expected to be built.

Both 'Improved Akulas' and 'Akula IIs' are fitted with six additional 21" bow tubes mounted externally. These are probably for SS-N-15 Starfish anti-submarine weapons and their position precludes reloading from

within the pressure hull. The addition of these tubes probably enables a greater number of torpedo reloads to be embarked.

Four 'Akula Is' paid off 1996-1999. The remainder serve with the Northern and Pacific Fleets.

	Akula I	Akula II
Length (ft)	360.1 oa	372.2 oa
Beam (ft)	45.9	45.9
Displacement (tons)		
Surfaced	7,500	7,500
Submerged	9,100	9,500
Speed (kts)		
Surfaced	10	10
Dived	28	30
Armament		
	SS-N-21 Sampson SLCM with 200kT nuclear warhead	SS-N-21 Sampson SLCM with 200kT nuclear warhead
	SS-N-15 Starfish anti-submarine weapon:	SS-N-15 Starfish anti-submarine weapon:
	200kT depth charge or 90 kg HE Type 40 torpedo.	200kT depth charge or 90 kg HE Type 40 torpedo.
	SS-N-16 Stallion, 200 kT depth-charge	SS-N-16 Stallion, 200 kT depth-charge
	or 90kg HE Type 40 torpedo	or 90kg HE Type 40 torpedo
	4 x 25.6" and 4x21" tubes	10 x 21" and 4 x 25.6" tubes
	SA-N-5/8 Strela SAM, shoulder-launched	SA-N-5/8 Strela SAM, shoulder-launched
Engines		
	1 PWR, 190MW output	1 PWR, 190MW output
	2 x 750 hp emergency motors	2 x 750 hp emergency motors
	1 shaft, 2 spinners	1 shaft, 2 spinners
Diving depth	1,480 ft	1,480 ft
Complement	62	62

Below and Right: Inevitably, most photos of Soviet attack submarines were taken from patrol aircraft. Both of these images were released by the US Navy in 1988.

Below: One of the earlier photographs, released by the Pentagon, of an Akula I off the Northern Cape.

'Oscar' class - leviathan of the deep

The massive 'Oscar' class submarines, with potent surface-to-surface weapons, succeeded the 'Echo II' as primary submarine-launched cruise missile platforms, designed to destroy large enemy surface combatants, particularly aircraft carriers. Two earlier boats, *Archangelysk* and *Murmansk* formed the 'Oscar I' class, 36 ft shorter and with a displacement of 1,400 tons less. Both are now laid up in the Northern Fleet.

'Oscar II' carries 24 missiles in two banks of 12, inclined in pairs at 40° outside the 27.9ft pressure hull, creating an important 13ft gap between outer and inner hulls, producing the very wide beam but more importantly, the ability to sustain battle damage. All but the first of class were equipped with a tube on the rudder fin, which dispenses a thin-line Pelamida passive very low frequency towed array. Other sonar fits are Shark Gill, hull-mounted passive/active search and attack; Shark Rib, passive flank array and Mouse Roar, hull-mounted high frequency active attack.

Eleven 'Oscar II' boats were built at Severodvinsk; the first three are now laid up awaiting disposal. The 12th, *Belgorod*, was launched in August 1999 but is unlikely to be completed, given current financial constraints.

Four are based with the Northern Fleet, one of which the ill-fated *Kursk* deployed to the Mediterranean in 1999, the first such Russian deployment for a decade. A further four serve with the Pacific Fleet, based at Tarya Bay. One of these was despatched to the USA's West Coast at the same time as the Mediterranean detachment, as a demonstration to Washington of the Russian Navy's remaining operational capability.

Kursk sank in the Barents Sea during naval exercises on August 12 2000, with the loss of the 118 on board. There has been much speculation as to the cause - sabotage, poor maintenance, collision with a Western submarine, or loss by World War II vintage mine. All these seem unlikely.

Kursk was a proficient submarine. She had earlier deployed to the Mediterranean and her captain had commanded her since 1995. Shortly before the accident, she had successfully fired an unarmed Chelomey Granit SS-N-19 (Shipwreck) anti-ship cruise missile from one of her 24 external tubes. Firing a Shkval WA III rocket propelled torpedo may have been her next serial in the exercise.

It was then that events went suddenly and terribly wrong. Sonar recordings by US SSN *Memphis* suggest the most likely cause of the catastrophe was that the torpedo, in the forward compartment exploded. Possibly a nickel battery began "cooking off" and a warning light in the control room triggered a desperate attempt to dispose of the torpedo through the forward tubes.

The explosion partially triggered the 210kg warhead which in turn, 135 seconds later, set off the warheads of the munitions stored in the compartment. The resultant blast destroyed the forward part of the submarine killing everyone forward of the reactor department, including those in the control room. There was no time to blow the main ballast tanks to surface. The reactor automatically shut down, killing power throughout the submarine whose stern had probably reared 150-feet above the surface as

Oscar II	
Length (ft)	505.2
Beam (ft)	59.7
Displacement (tons)	
Surfaced	13,900
Submerged	18,300
Speed (kts)	
Surfaced	15
Dived	28
Armament	
	24 SS-N-19 Shipwreck surface-to-surface
	missiles with 500 kT nuclear warhead
	or 350 kg HE. SS-N-15 Starfish
	anti-submarine weapon: 200 kT depth charge
	or 90 kg HE Type 40 torpedo.
	SS-N-16 Stallion, 200 kT depth-charge
	or 90 kg HE Type 40 torpedo
	2 x 25.6" and 4 x 21" tubes
	Minelaying configuration: 32 instead of torpedoes
Engines	2 PWR, 380 MW output
	2 shafts, 2 spinners
Diving depth	1,000 ft
Complement	107

flooding dragged down its destroyed bows. Probably around a dozen survivors remained alive in the spaces at the stern surround the shaft for as long as two days.

With the exception of the remaining 'Oscar' boat and the completion of an Akula II unit in June 2000, the only Russian SSN construction activity is that of the first of a new class at Severodvinsk. The 'Yasen' class (Type 855) will have a 8,600 dived displacement, be armed with the SS-N-27 in eight vertical launch tubes together with the SS-N-15 Starfish anti-submarine weapons and eight 21-inch torpedo tubes.

First-of-class, *Severodvinsk* was laid down on December 21 1993, but has still to be launched. Work is said to be progressing very slowly, if at all, on the hull. Assuming that new funding becomes available, the boat will not be commissioned before 2005-06.

Right and Below: The wide 59·7 feet beam of the Oscar II class is well seen here. Missiles are carried in two banks on either side of the sail and outside the pressure hull.

Below: The hatches covering the tubes holding SS-N-19 Shipwreck anti-ship missiles can be seen here. Hatches aft of the blister on top of the sail hide, communication and radar masts.

UK's *Trafalgar* class SSNs

Britain's ultra-quiet *Trafalgar* class was a development of the older *Swiftsure* boats producing big benefits in underwater speed, endurance and noise reduction. Since coming into service in 1983, the class has been progressively upgraded with new sonar fits, the Tomahawk land-attack cruise missile and the autonomous 70 kt, 14 nm range Spearfish torpedo, for which *Trafalgar* was the trials boat.

Pressure hulls and outer surfaces are coated with conformal anechoic noise reduction coatings. A non-hull penetrating optronic mast was trialled in *Trenchant* in 1998. All the class have special under-ice operational features: the sail is strengthened; the forward hydroplanes are retractable and Type 778 and Type 780 echo-sounders are mounted vertically to establish depth.

During modernisation, the class is receiving a new Type 2076 sonar fit to replace the Type 2074 hull-mounted passive/active search and attack and the Type 2046 towed array. The update also includes installation of the Type 2077 short-range classification sonar and the SMCS tactical data handling system.

Length (ft)	280.1
Beam (ft)	32.1
Displacement (tons)	
Surfaced	4,740
Submerged	5,208
Speed (kts)	
Surfaced	12
Dived	32
Armament	
	Tomahawk Block IIIC SLCM, range 918 nm.
	5x21" bow tubes, 20 Spearfish /Tigerfish
	Mk 24 Mod 2 torpedo reloads
	Sub Harpoon Block 1C anti-surface ship
	missile, range 70 nm.
	Mine-laying capability instead of torpedoes
Engines	1 Rolls-Royce PWR 1 nuclear reactor;
	2 turbines, 15,000 hp
	1 pump-jet propulsor
	1 motor for emergency drive
	1 shaft
Range	
Surfaced	N/K
Submerged	N/K
Diving depth	>1,000 ft
Complement	130

Above: HMS *Torbay* at her launch. Note the panelling around her bow, designed to prevent 'prying eyes' getting a good look at her sonar sensors.

Right: A clear demonstration of the endurance of nuclear-powered submarines is their ability to transit under the ice of the Arctic. This photo, taken through the HMS *Superb*'s periscope, shows HMS *Turbulent* surfacing at the North Pole.

British *Trafalgar* class SSN

Boat	Builder	Laid down	Commissioned	Status
Trafalgar	Vickers Shipbuilding, Barrow-in-Furness	25-04-1979	27-05-1983	In service. Modernisation and first refuel 12-1995.
Turbulent	Vickers Shipbuilding, Barrow-in-Furness	08-05-1980	28-04-1984	In service. Modernisation and first refuel 1997.
Tireless	Vickers Shipbuilding, Barrow-in-Furness	06-06-1981	05-10-1985	In service. Modernisation and first refuel 01-1999.
Torbay	Vickers Shipbuilding, Barrow-in-Furness	03-12-1982	07-02-1987	Modernisation and refuel completed 02-2001.
Trenchant	Vickers Shipbuilding, Barrow-in-Furness	28-10-1985	14-01-1989	In service.
Talent	Vickers Shipbuilding, Barrow-in-Furness	13-05-1986	12-05-1990	In service.
Triumph	Vickers Shipbuilding, Barrow-in-Furness	02-02-1987	12-10-1991	In service.

Above: HMS *Trafalgar* in the Mediterranean in 1998.

Left and below: First of class *Trafalgar* commissioned in May 1983.

US *Los Angeles* class - Carrier Battle Group escort

Length (ft)	362
Beam (ft)	33
Displacement (tons)	
Surfaced	6,082*
Submerged	6,927
Speed (kts)	
Surfaced	20
Dived	32
Armament	
	Tomahawk land attack Block III SLCM, range 1,700 nm.**
	4 x 21" bow tubes, 10 Mk 48 ADCAP torpedo reloads
	Harpoon anti-surface ship missile, range 70 nm.
	Mine-laying: Mk 67 Mobile and Mk 60 Captor mines
Engines	
	1 GE PWR S6G nuclear reactor; 2 turbines, 35,000 hp
	1 auxiliary motor 325 hp
	1 shaft
Range	
Surfaced	N/K
Submerged	N/K
Diving depth	950 ft. 1,475 ft crush depth.
Complement	129

*Design improvements have increased displacement of boats *SSN-668-773* by 220 tons.

** Normally eight Tomahawk carried internally in addition to 12 in Vertical Launch Tubes positioned
  outside the pressure hull in *SSN-719* onwards.

Below: The *Los Angeles* class attack submarine USS *Scranton* (SSN 756) surfaces in the North Arabian
Sea while the aircraft carrier USS *George Washington* (CVN 73) cruises in the background on May 9, 1996.
The carrier and its battle group were operating in the Arabian Gulf where they conducted air patrols in
support of Operation Southern Watch, the enforcement of the no-fly-zone over Southern Iraq.

US Los Angeles Class SSN

Boat	Builder	Laid down	Commissioned	Status
Los Angeles (SSN- 688)	Newport News Shipbuilding	8-01-1972	13-11-1976	Pacific Fleet.
Baton Rouge (SSN-689)	Newport News Shipbuilding	18-11-1972	25-06-1977	Collision with Russian 'Sierra' class SSN off Severomorsk, 11-02-1992. Decommissioned 13-01-1995. Scrapped Puget Sound, 1997.
Philadelphia (SSN- 690)	General Dynamics Electric Boat Division	12-08-1972	25-06-1977	Atlantic Fleet.
Memphis (SSN- 691)	Newport News Shipbuilding	23-06-1973	17-12-1977	Research platform for submarine technology late 1989. Atlantic Fleet.
Omaha (SSN-692)	General Dynamics Electric Boat Division	27-01-1973	11-03-1978	Decommissioned 05-10-1995. To be scrapped
Cincinnati (SSN- 693)	Newport News Shipbuilding	06-04-1974	10-06-1978	Decommissioned 29-07-1996. To be scrapped.
Groton (SSN-694)	General Dynamics Electric Boat Division	03-08-1973	08-07-1978	Decommissioned 07-11-1997. To be scrapped.
Birmingham (SSN- 695)	Newport News Shipbuilding	26-04-1975	16-12-1978	Decommissioned 22-12-1997. To be scrapped.
New York City (SSN-696)	General Dynamics Electric Boat Division	15-12-1973	03-03-1979	Decommissioned 30-04-1997. To be scrapped.
Indianapolis (SSN- 697)	General Dynamics Electric Boat Division	19-10-1974	05-01-1980	Decommissioned 17-02-1998. To be scrapped.
Bremerton (SSN- 698)	General Dynamics Electric Boat Division	08-05-1976	28-03-1981	Pacific Fleet. Decommissioned 2001.
Jacksonville (SSN- 699)	General Dynamics Electric Boat Division	21-02-1976	16-05-1981	Atlantic Fleet. Decommissioned 2001.
Dallas (SSN-700)	General Dynamics Electric Boat Division	09-10-1976	18-07-1981	Atlantic Fleet.
La Jolla (SSN-701)	General Dynamics Electric Boat Division	16-10-1976	24-10-1981	Pacific Fleet.
Phoenix (SSN- 702)	General Dynamics Electric Boat Division	30-07-1977	19-12-1981	Decommissioned 29-07-1998. To be scrapped.
Boston (SSN-703)	General Dynamics Electric Boat Division	11-08-1978	30-01-1982	Decommissioned 18-01-1999. To be scrapped.
Baltimore (SSN- 704)	General Dynamics Electric Boat Division	21-05-1979	24-07-1982	Decommissioned 10-07-1998. To be scrapped.
City of Corpus Christi (SSN-705)	General Dynamics Electric Boat Division	04-09-1979	08-01-1983	Atlantic Fleet.
Albuquerque (SSN- 706)	General Dynamics Electric Boat Division	27-12-1979	21-05-1983	Atlantic Fleet.
Portsmouth (SSN- 707)	General Dynamics Electric Boat Division	08-05-1980	01-10-1983	Pacific Fleet.
Minneapolis-Saint Paul (SSN-708)	General Dynamics Electric Boat Division	30-01-1981	10-03-1984	Atlantic Fleet.
Hyman G Rickover (SSN-709)	General Dynamics Electric Boat Division	24-07-1981	21-07-1984	Atlantic Fleet.
Augusta (SSN- 710)	General Dynamics Electric Boat Division	01-04-1982	19-01-1985	Trials platform for BQQ-5D wide aperture array passive sonar. Atlantic Fleet. To be decommissioned FY 2008.
San Francisco (SSN-711)	Newport News Shipbuilding	26-05-1977	24-04-1981	Pacific Fleet.
Atlanta (SSN-712)	Newport News Shipbuilding	17-08-1978	06-03-1982	Decommissioned 22-01-1999. To be scrapped.
Houston (SSN- 713)	Newport News Shipbuilding	29-01-1979	25-09-1982	Decommissioned FY 2000.
Norfolk (SSN-714)	Newport News Shipbuilding	01-08-1979	21-05-1982	Atlantic Fleet. Decommissioned FY 2001.
Buffalo (SSN-715)	Newport News Shipbuilding	25-01-1980	05-11-1983	Pacific Fleet.
Salt Lake City (SSN-716)	Newport News Shipbuilding	26-08-1980	12-05-1984	Pacific Fleet. To be decommissioned FY 2005.
Olympia (SSN- 717)	Newport News Shipbuilding	31-03-1981	17-11-1983	Pacific Fleet. To be decommissioned FY 2006.
Honolulu (SSN- 718)	Newport News Shipbuilding	10-11-1981	06-07-1985	Pacific Fleet. To be decommissioned FY 2007.
Providence (SSN- 719)	General Dynamics Electric Boat Division	14-10-1982	27-07-1985	Atlantic Fleet.
Pittsburgh (SSN- 720)	General Dynamics Electric Boat Division	15-04-1983	23-11-1985	Atlantic Fleet.
Chicago (SSN- 721)	Newport News Shipbuilding	05-01-1983	27-09-1986	Pacific Fleet
Key West (SSN- 722)	Newport News Shipbuilding	06-07-1983	12-09-1987	Atlantic Fleet.
Oklahoma City (SSN-723)	Newport News Shipbuilding	04-01-1984	09-07-1988	Atlantic Fleet.
Louisville (SSN- 724)	General Dynamics Electric Boat Division	16-09-1984	08-11-1986	Pacific Fleet.
Helena (SSN-725)	General Dynamics Electric Boat Division	28-03-1985	11-07-1987	Pacific Fleet.
Newport News (SSN-750)	Newport News Shipbuilding	03-03-1984	03-06-1989	Atlantic Fleet.

Improved 688I

Boat	Builder	Laid down	Commissioned	Status
San Juan (SSN- 751)	General Dynamics Electric Boat Division	16-08-1985	06-08-1988	Atlantic Fleet.
Pasadena (SSN- 752)	General Dynamics Electric Boat Division	20-12-1985	11-02-1989	Pacific Fleet.
Albany (SSN-753)	Newport News Shipbuilding	22-04-1985	07-04-1990	Atlantic Fleet.
Topeka (SSN-754)	General Dynamics Electric Boat Division	13-05-1986	21-10-1989	Atlantic Fleet.
Miami (SSN-755)	General Dynamics Electric Boat Division	24-10-1986	30-06-1990	Atlantic Fleet.
Scranton (SSN-756)	Newport News Shipbuilding	29-06-1986	26-01-1991	Atlantic Fleet.
Alexandria (SSN-757)	General Dynamics Electric Boat Division	19-06-1987	29-06-1991	Atlantic Fleet.
Asheville (SSN-758)	Newport News Shipbuilding	01-01-1987	28-09-1991	Pacific Fleet.
Jefferson City (SSN-759)	Newport News Shipbuilding	21-09-1987	29-02-1992	Atlantic Fleet.
Annapolis (SSN-760)	General Dynamics Electric Boat Division	15-06-1988	11-04-1992	Atlantic Fleet.
Springfield (SSN-761)	General Dynamics Electric Boat Division	29-01-1990	09-1-1993	Pacific Fleet.
Columbus (SSN-762)	General Dynamics Electric Boat Division	07-01-1991	24-07-1993	Pacific Fleet.
Santa Fe (SSN-763)	General Dynamics Electric Boat Division	09-07-1991	08-01-1994	Atlantic Fleet.
Boise (SSN-764)	Newport News Shipbuilding	25-08-1988	07-11-1992	Atlantic Fleet.
Montpelier (SSN-765)	Newport News Shipbuilding	19-05-1989	13-03-1993	Atlantic Fleet.
Charlotte (SSN-766)	Newport News Shipbuilding	17-08-1990	16-09-1994	Pacific Fleet.
Hampton (SSN-767)	Newport News Shipbuilding	02-03-1990	06-11-1993	Atlantic Fleet.
Hartford (SSN-768)	General Dynamics Electric Boat Division	27-04-1992	10-12-1994	Atlantic Fleet.
Toledo (SSN-769)	Newport News Shipbuilding	06-05-1991	24-02-1995	Atlantic Fleet.
Tucson (SSN-770)	Newport News Shipbuilding	15-08-1991	09-09-1995	Pacific Fleet.
Columbia (SSN-771)	General Dynamics Electric Boat Division	24-04-1993	09-10-1995	Pacific Fleet.
Greeneville (SSN-772)	Newport News Shipbuilding	28-02-1992	16-02-1996	Pacific Fleet.
Cheyenne (SSN-773)	Newport News Shipbuilding	06-07-1992	13-09-1996	Pacific Fleet.

Above: The *Los Angeles* class currently serves as the "backbone" of the US submarine fleet and is likely to remain so well into the 21st Century. These submarines are faster, quieter and far more capable than any of their predecessors. Later ships in the class have incorporated design improvements especially in sonar and electronics areas as well as the addition of external cruise missile launch tubes. This is first-of-class, Los Angeles, commissioned in November, 1976.

The US Navy's *Los Angeles* class of SSN, originally 62 strong, were designed and built as anti-submarine escorts for carrier battle groups and to attack and destroy distant Soviet surface action groups at a cost of $900 million each.[1] In the aftermath of the Cold War, land attack Tomahawk cruise missiles have been fitted to support American and allied military operations around the world with an endurance of more than 90 days.

From *San Juan* onwards, the Improved 688 class has enhanced noise reduction features and includes the BQQ-5E passive/active spherical search and attack sonar and TB 29 thin line towed array, together with a tube minelaying capability. New emphasis on Arctic under-ice operations means that forward diving planes were moved forward from the sail to the bow and the sail strengthened. The MIDAS (Mine and Ice Detection

1 1990 PRICES.

US *Los Angeles* class - Carrier Battle Group escort

Left: Pearl Harbor, Hawaii, Feb. 21, 2001 — USS Greeneville (SSN 772) sits atop blocks in Dry Dock #1 at the Pearl Harbor Naval Shipyard and Intermediate Maintenance Facility. The Los Angeles-class attack sub is dry-docked to examine damage and perform necessary repairs following a tragic Feb. 9 collision at sea with the Japanese fishing vessel Ehime Maru approximately nine miles off the coast from Diamond Head. The Japanese ship sank in 2,000 feet of water and nine persons remain missing and presumed dead.

Right: USS *Greeneville* (SSN 772) is the 61st *Los Angeles* Class submarine and the 22nd Improved *Los Angeles* Class Attack submarine. *Greeneville* moved to its new homeport at Submarine Base Pearl Harbor in April 1997.

Below: Crewmembers man the sail as *Greeneville* comes to the surface following a submerged run.

Above: The Korean submarine *Choi Moo Sun* makes its way past the *Helena* (SSN 725) and into the Sembawang port facilities in Singapore during Exercise Pacific Reach 2000. The Republic of Singapore Navy, the Japanese Maritime Self Defense Force, the Republic of Korea Navy and the U.S. Navy took part in this first cooperative regional submarine rescue exercise.

Avoidance System) has also been fitted in these boats, as well as improved navigation and communications equipment.

With the withdrawal of the Subroc anti-submarine weapon system in 1990, nuclear weapons are no longer carried but are still available for use. In 1996-97, trials of the Predator and Sea Ferret unmanned aerial vehicles were conducted in two of the class. These reconnaissance vehicles may become available for launching in Harpoon canisters eventually.

Improvements continue. The Acoustic Rapid COTS[2] Insertion (ARCI) programme underway in 1997-2001, retrofits BQQ-5 sonars with open system architecture, allowing annual updates to software and hardware to keep pace with threats presented by increasingly sophisticated foreign submarines.

The US Navy retired 11 *Los Angeles* by 2000 with three others planned to decommission in FY 2001-2002. The class is planned to comprise 68% of the Navy's nuclear submarine attack force in 2015.

2 COTS - COMMERCIAL OFF THE SHELF.

Above: Key West (SSN 722) cruises on the surface of the Pacific Ocean as part of the USS *Constellation* (CV 64) battle group.

US *Seawolf* - last Cold War warrior

With Soviet submarines steadily reducing the 30-year-old Western advantage in low noise submarines operations in the late 1980s, the *Seawolf* class was designed to recapture that lead. The platform was also designed to be a potent strike weapon with twice as many torpedo tubes and 30% more weapons capacity than a *Los Angeles* class SSN as well as possessing a special forces role.

But the stealth characteristics and the new PWR proved expensive to develop: more than one billion dollars was spent on research and development on the class, which will end after completion of the third boat, *Jimmy Carter.* The design has put emphasis on under-ice operations, including the provision of retractable bow diving planes.

Commissioning of the first of class, *Seawolf* was delayed because panels were pulled away from the wide aperture sonar array during sea trials and problems were also experienced with the torpedo tube doors.

Full acoustic cladding has been applied to the boat and hydrodynamics improved by avoiding external weapons. The US Navy claims its running noise levels at tactical speeds are quieter than a *Los Angeles* class SSN moored alongside.

Length (ft)	353
Beam (ft)	40
Displacement (tons)	
Surfaced	8,600
Submerged	9,142
Speed (kts)	
Surfaced	18
Dived	39, 20 (silent speed)
Armament	
	Tomahawk cruise land attack missile
	(200 kt nuclear warhead/454 kg HE warhead,
	range: 1,400 nm)
	Tomahawk anti-ship missile
	(454 kg HE warhead, range 250 nm)
	8 x 26" tubes. 40 torpedo reloads
	Minelaying configuration:
	100 instead of torpedoes
Engines	
	1 S6W PWR , 45,000 hp
	1 secondary propulsion submerged motor
	1 shaft, 1 pumpjet propulsor
Diving depth	1,950 ft
Complement	134

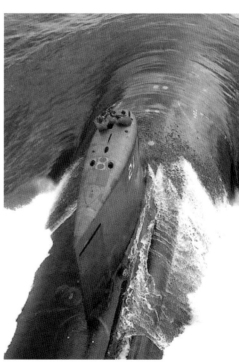

Left: Seawolf (SSN 21) puts to sea in the Narragansett Bay operating area for her first at-sea trial operations on July 3, 1996.

Right: Commissioned on July 19, 1997 is the first completely new design in thirty years. It is the fastest, quietest and most heavily armed submarine in the world. The Seawolf class can carry up to 50 torpedoes/missiles, or 100 mines. Armed with Tomahawk cruise missiles, Seawolf can target about 75 percent of the earth's land mass for strike missions and can target surface ships at long range. The *Seawolf* is significantly quieter and faster than any *Los Angeles* class submarine, and has twice as many torpedoes tubes and a 30 percent increase in weapons magazine size.

US Seawolf SSN

Boat	Builder	Start date	Commissioned	Fate
Seawolf (SSN-21	General Dyanmics Electric Boat, Groton, Connecticut	25-10-1989	19-07-1997	Operational.
Connecticut (SSN-22)	General Dyanmics Electric Boat, Groton, Connecticut	14-09-1992	11-12-1998	Operational.
Jimmy Carter (SSN-23)	General Dyanmics Electric Boat, Groton, Connecticut	12-12-1995	12-2005	Due to be launched 06-2004.

Right: Personnel man the underway main control watch, aboard.

Left: More than $1 billion was spent on research and development of the *Seawolf* class.

US *Seawolf* - last Cold War warrior

UK's new *Astute* class SSN

The UK Royal Navy's new *Astute* class, due to enter service late in 2005, is a development of the *Trafalgar* class, including the upgrades provided by modernisation. Invitations to tender were issued on July 14, 1994 to build the first three boats with options on two more, with confirmation of the latter coming in June, 1998.

First steel was cut in late 1999 for construction of *Astute* at Barrow which will follow modular pre-outfitting techniques. The fixed price prime contract, awarded in March, 1997, totalled £1.9 billion, which also included assuming responsibilities for the Royal Navy's *Swiftsure* and *Trafalgar* class SSN Final Phase updates

The *Astute* class will have increased weapon load, reduced noise radiation but with overall performance similar to modernised *Trafalgars*. Two CM10 non-hull penetrating optronic masts will be fitted. Nuclear refuelling will not have to be undertaken during the life cycle of each boat.

There may be plans for a sixth of class depending on budget availability.

Britain's Astute Class SSNS

Boat	Builder	Start date	Commissioned	Fate
Astute	BAE Systems Marine, Barrow-in-Furness	10-1999	06-2005	Building
Ambush	BAE Systems Marine, Barrow-in-Furness	2001	2007	Ordered
Artful	BAE Systems Marine, Barrow-in-Furness	2002	2008	Ordered
?	BAE Systems Marine, Barrow-in-Furness	?	?	Planned
?	BAE Systems Marine, Barrow-in-Furness	?	?	Planned

Length (ft)	318.2
Beam (ft)	35.1
Displacement (tons)	
Surfaced	6,500
Submerged	7,200
Speed (kts)	
Surfaced	12
Dived	32+

Armament

Tomahawk Block III C SLCM, range 918 nm.
6x21" bow tubes, 20 Spearfish torpedo reloads
Sub Harpoon Block 1C anti-surface ship missile,.
range 70 nm.
Mine-laying capability instead of torpedoes

Engines

1 Rolls-Royce PWR 2 nuclear reactor;
2 turbines, 15,000 hp
1 pump-jet propulsor
2 motors for emergency drive
1 shaft

Range

Surfaced	N/K
Submerged	N/K
Diving depth	>1,000 ft
Complement	98

Left and below:
Computer-generated impressions
of the Astute class underway.

China's '*Han*' class (Type 091) SSN

Problems beset China's five-boat 'Han' class from construction of the first hull. First of class, *401*, was laid down at Huludao Shipyard in 1967, with commissioning on August 1 1974, but she did not become fully operational until the early 1980s because of problems with the nuclear reactor. More recently, the class was not seen much at sea with the first pair non-operational in the late 1980s.

After refits to *403* and *404*, four out of the five are now operational with the North Sea Fleet. A US carrier battle group operating off North Korea was tracked by a 'Han' class on October 27-29 1994, coming within 21 nm of USS *Kitty Hawk*, in a Chinese People's Liberation Army (Navy) demonstration of new-found submarine capability.

Refits to the first four included replacement of the Russian ESM countermeasures with French equipment. A French DUUX-5 Fenelon low frequency passive ranging and intercept panoramic sonar has also been retrofitted, capable of tracking three targets simultaneously. The hull has been extended by 26ft in *403-405* for reasons which remain unclear.

The first of a new class of Chinese SSN, the Type 093, reportedly based on the Russian 'Victor III' design, is under construction at Huludao Shipyard, with the first-of-class expected to enter service in 2005. A second is predicted to follow in 2007.

	401-2	403-405
Length (ft)	321.5	347.5
Beam (ft)	32.8	32.8
Displacement (tons)		
Surfaced	4,500	4,500
Submerged	5,500	5,500
Speed (kts)		
Surfaced	12	
Dived	25	
Armament	YJ-82 surface to surface missile.	
	6 x 21" torpedo tubes. 12 reloads	
	Minelayer configuration: 36 instead of torpedoes	
Engines	1 PWR,	
	90 MW	
	1 shaft	
Diving depth	985 ft	
Complement	75	

Right: 'Han' class tracking a US carrier battle group in 1994. Her shallow depth is deliberate; the PLA Navy was seeking to demonstrate the capability of the class.

Below: The USS *Ohio* (SSBN 726) is the lead ship of the current fleet of eighteen ballistic missile submarines. This class incorporated tremendous improvements in noise quieting, ease of maintenance and performance over earlier designs. In addition, this class introduced a more accurate and longer range missile, the Trident D5/C4, that eliminated the need for these submarines to be homeported overseas.

NUCLEAR AGE 2: THE BOOMERS

WITH INCREASED ENDURANCE AND RANGE AVAILABLE SUBMARINES BECAME.
potent strategic weapons in the early 1960s with the advent of the US *Halibut*,
armed with a Regulus missile.

Halibut - first submarine to launch a guided missile

USS *Halibut* (*SSGN-587*) was the first submarine designed and built to launch guided missiles - the Regulus 1[1], armed with a 45 kT warhead. The single boat in the class was laid down at Mare Island Navy Yard on April 11 1957, and commissioned January 4 1960. Forward of the sail was a high casing to provide a dry launching platform for the cruise missile, raised by hydraulic rams.

Halibut became the first boat to launch a guided missile on March 25 1960, *en-route* to Australia and so became the first of the 'boomers' - missile firing submarines. She and four conventional submarines maintained the US's sea-borne nuclear deterrent, armed with Regulus, from 1959-1964 in the Pacific, completing a total of 40 patrols.[2] The last Regulus patrol was mounted by *Halibut* and departed Pearl Harbour on May 6 1964. The boat was re-designated SSN on August 15 1965, after removal of the Regulus equipment. In August 1968, she berthed at Mare Island Navy Yard for installation of side thrusters and equipment for a new role of oceanographic research. She decommissioned on June 30 1974, and was scrapped at Puget Sound, September 9 1994.

1 A REGULUS 2 PROGRAMME WAS CANCELLED IN 1958 FOR BUDGETARY REASONS AND BECAUSE OF THE ADVENT OF POLARIS.
2 THE OTHER SUBMARINES WERE *GROWLER (SSG-577), GRAYBACK (SSG-574) BARBERO (SSG-317)* AND *TUNNY, (SSG-282.)*

Length (ft)	350
Beam (ft)	29.5
Displacement (tons)	
Surfaced	3
Submerged	6,709
Speed (kts)	
Surfaced	18
Dived	22
Armament	
	1 Regulus I cruise missile (single W5 or W27
	45kT nuclear warhead, range: 500 nm)
	forward launching platform
	6 x2 1" bow torpedo tubes
Engines	
	1 PWR , 15,000 shp
	2 shafts
Diving depth	600 ft
Complement	111

Below: USS Halibut firing a Regulus surface-to-surface missle in 1961. The carrier in the background is USS Lexington.

Right: The single Regulus missile was in service for only five years before being superceded by the Polaris boats.

US *George Washington* class - first strategic ballistic missile submarine

The world's first submarine-launch of strategic ballistic missiles was from *George Washington* in the Atlantic Missile Test Range off Cape Canaveral, Florida, on June 28 1960. The successful submerged launch was followed by a second Polaris A1 two hours later. The submarine ballistic missile nuclear deterrent had arrived.

George Washington had originally been laid down as the *Skipjack* class SSN *Scorpion* at Electric Boat at Groton, Connecticut. But priorities were changed, and a 130-feet missile section was inserted to create the first nuclear-powered operational SSBN.

The second-of-class, *Patrick Henry,* completed an 18 month refit in June 1966, to re-equip with the longer range and more accurate Polaris A3 version, beginning her 18th patrol with this weapon in December 1966. *Roosevelt* and *Robert E Lee* were refitted with the A3 in the same year, *Abraham Lincoln* was recalled from a month-long upkeep period at Holy Loch Scotland during the Cuban Missile Crisis in October 1962, mounting a 65-day deterrent patrol at short notice. *Lincoln* became the first SSBN to complete 50 strategic patrols in 1977.

Like the *Ethan Allen* SSBN class, *Washington, Patrick Henry* and *Robert E Lee* were converted into SSNs by decommissioning the missile section and filling the tubes with cement blocks as ballast compensation. It was thought their remaining hull lives did not warrant conversion as platforms for the newer Poseidon C3 SLBM.

Length (ft)	381.7
Beam (ft)	33
Displacement (tons)	
Surfaced	5,959
Submerged	6,709
Speed (kts)	
Surfaced	18
Dived	25+
Armament	
	16 Polaris A1 missiles (W47-Y1 warhead, 600kT, range 2,200 km) later Polaris A3 (W58, warhead 200kT, range 4,630 km) 6 x 21" bow torpedo tubes
Engines	
	1 S5W PWR , 15,000 shp 1 shaft
Diving depth	700 ft
Complement	112

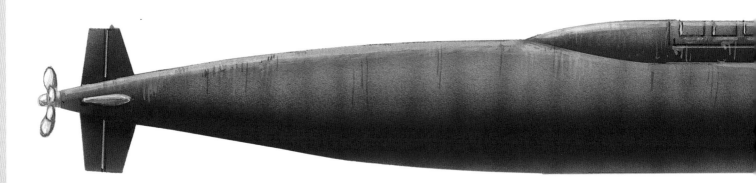

US *'George Washington'* class SSBNs

Boat	Builder	Laid down	Commissioned	Fate
George Washington (SSBN-598) (ex-Scorpion)	General Dynamics Electric Boat, Groton, Connecticut	01-11-1957	30-12-1959	Converted to SSN (SSN-598) 01-03-1982. Decommissioned 24-01-1985. Scrapped 09-1998, Puget Sound. Sail at Submarine Museum, New London, Connecticut.
Patrick Henry (SSBN-599)	General Dynamics Electric Boat, Groton, Connecticut	27-05-1958	09-04-1960	Converted to SSN (SSN-599). Decommissioned 25-05-1984. Scrapped 31-08-1997, Puget Sound.
Theodore Roosevelt (SSBN-600)	Mare Island Navy Yard, Vallejo, California	20-05-1958	13-02-1961	Decommissioned 28-02-1981. Scrapped 03-04-1995, Puget Sound.
Robert E Lee (SSBN-601)	Newport News Shipbuilding, Newport News, Virginia	25-08-1958	16-09-1960	Converted to SSN (SSN-601) 01-03-1982. Decommissioned 30-11-1983. Scrapped 30-09-1991, Puget Sound
Abraham Lincoln (SSBN-602)	Portsmouth Navy Yard, Portsmouth, New Hampshire	01-11-1958	08-03-1961	Decommissioned 28-02-1981. Scrapped 10-05-1994, Puget Sound.

Below: A Polaris missile being loaded aboard USS *George Washington* at Holy Loch Submarine base, Scotland, in 1964.

Left: The USS *George Washington* (SSBN 598) was the world's first nuclear powered ballistic missile submarine. Arguably, it can be considered the submarine that has most influenced world events in the 20th Century. With its entry into service in December 1959 the United States instantly gained the most powerful deterrent force imaginable, a stealth platform with enormous nuclear firepower.

Below: Sixteen tubes were positioned after of the sail for the Polaris A1/A3 missiles.

Delta SSBNs - still the mainstay of Russia's sea-launch nuclear deterrent

Russia's long-serving 'Delta' class of SSBNs, began with the Delta Is, based on the old 'Yankee' class, with the first hull laid down in 1969 and a class of 18 completed by 1972. The existing 7 'Delta III' (Kalmar) class evolved out of the now defunct 'Delta II' because of the need to accommodate the larger SS-N-18 Stingray SLBMs. The final manifestation, the 'Delta IVs,' began construction in February 1981, with the last commissioned on February 20 1992, all armed with the SS-N-23 Skiff SLBMs.

The last two Delta Is, *K 447* and *K 530* were paid off in 2000. Of the 'Delta IIIs,' four were decommissioned in 1996-97 and two more in 1998. Six more are laid up, with seven remaining operational, two with the Northern Fleet at Saida Guba and five with the Pacific Fleet. A stretched version, *K 433*, with a 164 ft long plug inserted in the central section, is engaged in underwater research.

The 'Delta IVs' have acoustic coating and fewer free flood holes than the earlier classes, making for quieter operations. They are now progressively being refitted, beginning with *K 51* in 1999, indicating a pressing need to preserve their operational integrity because of continuing delays to build the latest Russian SSBN, the 'Borey' class.

Their SLBMs, the SS-N-23, have considerably improved accuracy over the 'Delta III's SS-N-18.

	Delta IV	Delta III	Delta I
Length (ft)	544.6 oa	524.9 oa	459.3 oa
Beam (ft)	39.4	39.4	30.4
Displacement (tons)			
Surfaced	10,800	10,550	8,700
Submerged	13,500	13,250	10,200
Speed (kts)			
Surfaced	14	14	19
Dived	24	24	25
Armament			
	16 SS-N-23 Skiff SLBM	16 SS-N-18 Stingray SLBM	12 SS-N-8 Sawfly
	4-10 MIRVed 100 kT warheads	3-7 MIRVed or single warhead	with 2 MIRVed
		100kT - 450kT	500kT warheads
	SS-N-15 Starfish ASW weapon	-	
	with 200kT depth-charge or Type 40 torpedo		
	4 x 21" torpedo tubes	4 x 21" and 2 x 400mm torpedo tubes	4 x 21" and 2 x 16" torpedo tubes
		10 reloads	
Engines			
	2 PWR nuclear reactors, 180 MW output	2 PWR nuclear reactors, 180 MW output	2 PWR nuclear reactors, 155 MW output
	2 x 612 hp emergency diesel	2 x 612 hp emergency diesel	2 turbines
	2 shafts	2 shafts	2 shafts
Diving depth	1,000 ft	1,000 ft	1,000 ft
Complement	135	130	120

Left: Delta I SSBN, showing missile tube structure and continuous acoustic coating on the outer casing.

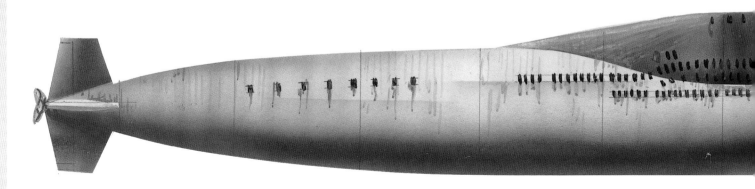

Below: Delta I SSBNs have a raised structure to accomodate the SS-N-8 Sawfly submarine launched ballistic missile.

Left and Below: The missile compartment abaft the sail is the best recognition feature to distinguish between the versions of the Delta class. The Delta IV (below) has a distinctive hump at the rear of the compartment, compared to the Delta III (left).

UK's *Vanguard* class SSBNs

Despite the fitting of British designed Chevaline A3TK versions of Polaris strategic nuclear weapons in the *Resolution* class SSBNs in 1982-1986, it was clear the missile system and the elderly boats could not maintain the effectiveness of the UK's national strategic deterrent. After toying with the notion of deploying cruise missiles, the British government finally decided on the US Trident C4 missile system on July 15 1980, upgrading the missile to the D5 version on March 11 1982.

The *Vanguard* design is smaller than the US *Ohio* class Trident boats, carrying 16 missile launch tubes instead of the American 24. Hull diameter, dictated by the size of the missile, remains the same. The forward hydroplanes are positioned in the bows rather than the sail, which is tapered and faired into the hull. The class is fitted with a British-designed shrouded propulsor, consisting of an aerodynamically-profiled rotor and stator housed within a duct to control water-flow through the unit. This greatly improves acoustic performance as well as providing lower shaft speeds.

Vanguard began sea trials in October 1992, with the first UK test firing of the D5 down the US Atlantic range on May 26 1994. First operational patrol was in early 1995 as the boats progressively replaced the *Resolution* class.

The Marconi/Plessey Type 2054 composite multi-frequency sonar suite includes the Type 2046 towed array, the Type 2043 hull-mounted active/passive search and the Type 2082 passive intercept and ranging sonar.

Length	491.8
Beam (ft)	42
Displacement (tons)	
Surfaced	N/K
Submerged	15,900
Speed (kts)	
Surfaced	12
Dived	25
Armament	
	16 Trident D5 SLBM with up to 8 British MIRVed (100-125 kT) nuclear warheads. Range: 6,500 nm.*
	4 x 21" torpedo tubes, Spearfish torpedoes
Engines	
	1 Rolls-Royce PWR nuclear reactor,
	2 turbines, 27,500 hp.
	1 pumpjet propulsor
	2 auxiliary motors
	1 shaft
Diving depth	?800 ft
Complement	135

* Under a British Government decision announced in November 1993, each boat carried a maximum of 96 warheads, which reduced to 48 in 1999. Single low-yield tactical nuclear warheads fitted to some missiles from 1996 to replace the air-dropped WE 177 nuclear weapon.

Right: HMS *Vanguard*, the second of the class.

UK's *Vanguard* class SSBNs

UK's *Vanguard* class SSBNs

UK Vanguard Class SSBNS

Boat	Builder	Laid down	Commissioned	Status
Vanguard	Vickers Shipbuilding, Barrow-in-Furness	03-09-1986	14-08-1993	In service
Victorious	Vickers Shipbuilding, Barrow-in-Furness	03-12-1987	07-01-1995	In service
Vigilant	Vickers Shipbuilding, Barrow-in-Furness	16-02-1991	02-11-1996	In service
Vengeance	Vickers Shipbuilding, Barrow-in-Furness	01-02-1993	27-11-1999	In service

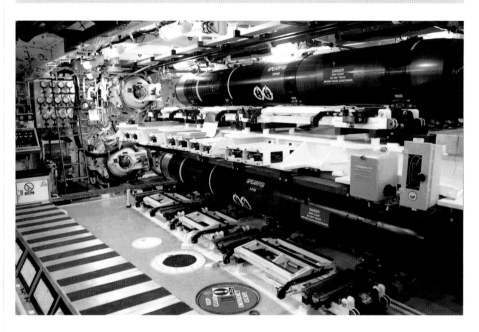

Above: The Torpedo compartment on HMS Vanguard, with two advanced 21-inch Spearfish torpedoes visible. (API)

Left: HMS *Vigilant.*

Le Triomphant - France's new SSBN/SNLE-NG

France's new *Le Triomphant* SSBN class - or *Sous-marins Nucléaires Lanceurs d'Engins-Nouvelle Génération* - entered service with first of class on March 21 1997 as successor to the six boat *Le Redoubtable/L'Inflexible*[1] class. The new boats, built of HY 130 steel to provide extraordinary hull strength and deep operational depth, are said to be 1,000 times quieter than their predecessors.

Six were originally planned to replace the earlier class on a one-for-one basis but the end of the Cold War brought new perceptions of threat and building was reduced to four.

First of class, *Le Triomphant*, was ordered on March 10 1986, but development of the planned missile fit, the M5, was cancelled and the cheaper M51 version substituted, beginning with the fourth boat in 2008. This missile will be retrofitted in the other three boats. A new warhead will replace the TN 75 by 2015.

Sensor suite includes the DMUX 80 multi-function passive and flank arrays, passive ranging and intercept and a very low frequency towed array.

Sea trials of *Le Triomphant* began on April 15 1994, with the first submerged launch of the M45 missile on February 15 1995. She was commissioned on March 21 1997.

Length (ft)	453
Beam (ft)	41
Displacement (tons)	
Surfaced	12,640
Submerged	14,120
Speed (kts)	
Surfaced	12
Dived	25
Armament	
	16 T45/TN 75 SLBM with six MIRVed
	150kT nuclear warheads.
	Range: 2,860 nm.
	SM 39 Exocet anti-ship missile, range 27 nm.
	4 x 21" torpedo tubes,
	ECAN L5 Mod 3, 10 reloads
Engines	
	1 PWR Type K 15 nuclear reactor
	with 150 MW output
	2 diesel auxiliary motors
	1 emergency motor
	pump jet propulsor
	1 shaft
Diving depth	1,640 ft
Complement	111

France's Le Triomphant Class SSBN (SNLE-NG)

Boat	Builder	Launched	Commissioned	Status
Le Triomphant (S 616)	DCN Cherbourg	13-07-1993	21-03-1997	In service.
Le Téméraire (S 617)	DCN Cherbourg	08-08-1997	23-12-1999	In service.
Le Vigilant (S 618)	DCN Cherbourg	03-2002 07	-2004	Building. Trials planned 2003.
Le Terrible (S 619)	DCN Cherbourg	11-2005 07	-2008	Ordered 2000.

1 LE REDOUTABLE WAS DECOMMISSIONED IN DECEMBER, 1991 AND IS ON DISPLAY AT A NEW MUSEUM AT CHERBOURG FROM SUMMER, 2001. OF THIS CLASS, LE TERRIBLE DECOMMISSIONED IN 1996, LE FOUDROYANT IN 1997 AND LE TONNANT IN 1998. L'INDOMPTABLE AND L'INFLEXIBLE REMAIN IN SERVICE UNTIL PAYING OFF IN JULY 2004 AND JULY 2006 RESPECTIVELY, ALTHOUGH THE LATTER MAY BE EXTENDED TO 2010. ACTIVE BOATS ARE ARMED WITH M4/TN 71 SLBMS, ALTHOUGH M45/TN 75 MISSILES ARE TO ARM L'INDOMPTABLE BY 2002.

Below: The Triomphant class will be phased into service until 2008, allowing the predecessor class to be gradually taken out of service by around 2010.

Le Triomphant - France's new SSBN/SNLE-NG

Chinese 'Xia' class SSBN

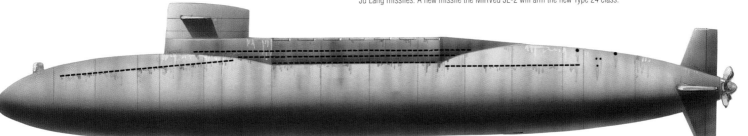

Below: After a lengthy refit, *Xia* eventually re-emerged in January 2001 and is now back at sea with an interim SLBM, the JL-1A. China's single operational SSBN, *Xia* (406) is armed with 12 improved Ju Lang missiles. A new missile the MIRVed JL-2 will arm the new Type 24 class.

China's only SSBN, *Xia*, was launched at the Huludao Shipyard in the Yellow Sea on April 30 1981, and was first commissioned in 1987. The boat went into an extensive refit in 1995, possibly to include an interim improved missile, and entered service in 2000. There are persistent reports of a second of class, launched in 1981, that was lost in an accident, possibly involving its reactor, in 1985.

Both the lengthy construction and missile trials were troubled, with the first firing trial of the JL-1 from *Xia* failing in 1985. It was almost three years later, on September 27 1988, that the first successful launch was staged.

Xia will continue in service until the first boat of a class of four new SSBNs, the Type 094, comes into service around 2005, fitted with 16 tubes to launch the new MIRVed JL-2 missile, now being trialled by the elderly single 'Golf' submarine.

Length (ft)	393.6 oa
Beam (ft)	33
Displacement (tons)	
Surfaced	N/K
Submerged	6,500
Speed (kts)	
Surfaced	10
Dived	22
Armament	
	12 Ju Lang-1 SLBM with 1 single 250 kT*
	warhead, with 1,160 nm range.
	6 x 21" bow tubes with SET-65E torpedoes.
Engines	
	1 PWR nuclear reactor with 90 MW output.
	1 auxiliary diesel.
	1 shaft.
Range	
Surfaced	6,000 nm at 7 kts (snorting)
Submerged	400 nm at 3 kts.
Diving depth	787 ft (985 ft max)
Complement	140

* Improved JL-1A has increased range and accuracy.

Right: Xia has been plagued by poor reliability of her nuclear power plants.

Russia's Typhoon - Monster of the Deep

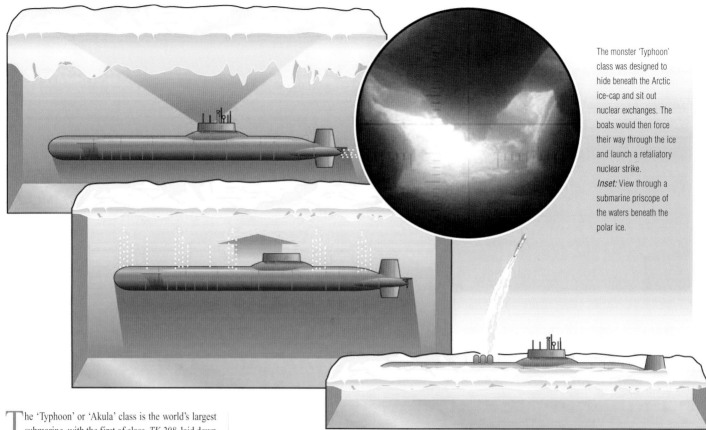

The monster 'Typhoon' class was designed to hide beneath the Arctic ice-cap and sit out nuclear exchanges. The boats would then force their way through the ice and launch a retaliatory nuclear strike.

Inset: View through a submarine priscope of the waters beneath the polar ice.

The 'Typhoon' or 'Akula' class is the world's largest submarine, with the first of class, *TK 208*, laid down on March 3 1977, at the Severodvinsk shipyard, and the last, *TK 20*, commissioned on September 4 1989. Only this boat, and *TK 17*, now remain in service.

The role for the class was to preserve a survivable nuclear retaliatory strike capability for the Russian leadership by sitting out any nuclear exchanges beneath the Arctic Ocean. Hence, the boats were configured for under ice-operations with the fin strengthened and shaped to break through the Arctic ice-cap up to 12 ft thick. The retractable forward hydroplanes were also designed for these conditions, as was the VLF navigation system.

The 'Typhoon' design provides considerable protection against attacking torpedoes with two 27.5 ft diameter hulls within the outer free-flood hull, separated by 4.6 ft. Each contains a missile section forward of the fin and a propulsion section aft. Three further 22.9 ft diameter pressure hulls at the fore-ends and fin house the torpedo tubes and anti-submarine missiles, the command, control and communications centre and the steering gear respectively.

All six boats were originally based at the Russian Northern Fleet base at Nerpichya but the survivors are now home-ported at Litsa Guba. It is clear that they proved unsatisfactory in service, and were expensive to maintain and operate.

TK 17 was damaged by fire during an accident loading a missile in 1992, but was repaired. *TK 208* went into refit in 1994 to take the new SS-N-28 SLBM; however this programme has been cancelled after test failures and it seems unlikely that the boat will re-emerge. The other hulls, *TK 202, TK 13* and *TK 14* have been paid off and the US has promised funds and technical assistance to decommission the reactors and break up the hulls.

The surviving two boats are likely to be taken out of service as they come up for re-fuelling.

Below: The Typhoon sail was strengthened and shaped for breaking through the Arctic ice-cap.

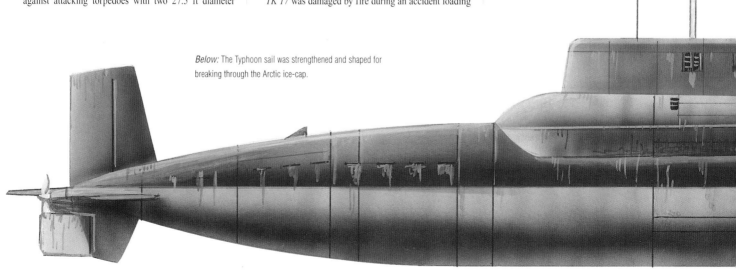

Length	562.6 oa
Beam (ft)	80.7
Displacement (tons)	
Surfaced	18,500
Submerged	26,500
Speed (kts)	
Surfaced	12
Dived	26
Armament	
	20 SS-N-20 Sturgeon SLBM with
	10 MIRVed 200kT warheads and
	range of 4,500 nm.
	SS-N-15 Starfish anti-submarine weapon
	with 200kT depth charge warhead
	or Type 40 torpedo.
	6 x 21" torpedo tubes.
	SA-N-8 shoulder-launched
	SAM missile (surfaced).
Engines	
	2 PWR nuclear reactor with 380 MW output
	2x517 hp emergency diesel
	2 shafts
Diving depth	1,200 ft
Complement	175

Russia's new class of SSBN, the 'Borey' (Type 955) is under construction at Severodvinsk. The hull of *Yuri Dolgoruky*, 17,000 tons dived and 12,500 tons surface displacement, was laid down on November 2 1996. Some of the design features of the new class of SSN, the *Severodvinsk* have been incorporated, but economic problems, as well as uncertainties over the SLBM missile to be utilised, have caused delays. The new SSBN is unlikely to be commissioned before 2009, probably armed with 12 marinised versions of the new SS-27 Topol ICBMs now entering service with the Strategic Rocket Forces. These will be held in four groups of three tubes abaft a well-forward fin. Surface speed is estimated at 17 kts and submerged, 29 kts. Diving depth: 1,200 ft.

Right: Unusually, the Typhoon missile tubes are located forward of the sail. The missiles' range of 4,500nm enables a strike at targets anywhere in the world.

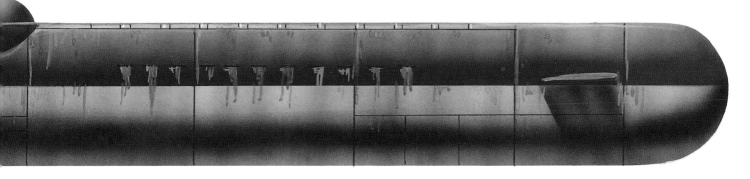

'Ohio' class - USA's main strategic nuclear force

The massive 'Ohio' class SSBMs, the world's most powerful submarine weapons platform, was designed to spend 66% of their time at sea, and is now the main US strategic deterrent, following reductions in silo-based and bomber carried missiles. The D5 version of Trident provides an accuracy of 90 metres.

Under original plans, 24 of the giant boats were to be built, but this was later reduced to 18. All were built by the General Dynamics Electric Boat Division at Groton, Connecticut. First of class, *Ohio*, was laid down on April 10 1976, commissioning on November 11 1981. Its first operational patrol ran from October 1 to December 10 1982. Hull life has now been lengthened to 42 years.

The size of the class was driven by the 24 vertical launch tubes for the missiles - 50% up on previous US SSBNs - and the larger reactor, which employs a circulation system that enjoys quieter operation through the avoidance of pumps. Nuclear core life is around 15 years between refuellings.

The sonar fit includes the AN/BQS-13 bow-mounted spherical hydrophone array for the passive search BQQ-6 and the AN/BQR-15 passive towed array, designed to detect targets astern. The AN/BQS-15 active/passive high frequency sonar, located in the leading edge of the sail, picks up close contacts, particularly under ice.

Countermeasures include the ADC Mk 2 Mod 1, an 8cm diameter, vertically-hovering device dispensed through eight launchers to decoy attacking acoustic torpedoes. The WLY-1 acoustic intercept system, an automatic response system to defend against torpedo attack, is now being fitted.

First eight boats, (*Ohio* to *Nevada*) are armed with the shorter-range, less accurate C4 version of the Trident SLBM, which first entered service in converted 'Lafayette' class SSBNs in 1979. The larger D5 missiles equip the remaining 10 boats and with its greater accuracy, provides the first 'hard kill' capability for the US Navy SSBNs. Four of the C4 hulls are being upgraded to take D5, beginning with *Alaska* and *Nevada* in May 2000 and February 2001. *Henry M Jackson* and *Alabama* will follow in 2005/6. *Ohio, Michigan, Florida* and *Georgia* may have their launch silos reduced to 22 to launch up to 154 non-nuclear Tomahawk land attack missiles.

The second Strategic Arms Reduction Treaty cut the size of the US SSBN force to 14 boats, now with effect from 2007.

Length	560
Beam (ft)	42
Displacement (tons)	
Surfaced	16,600
Submerged	18,750
Speed (kts)	
Surfaced	12
Dived	24
Armament	
	24 Trident C4 (Pacific-based boats) SLBM with up to eight MIRVed 100kT W76 nuclear warheads. Range: 4,000 nm.
	24 Trident D5 (Atlantic boats) SLBM with up to 12 MIRVed W76 or W88 (300-475 kT) nuclear warheads. Range: 6,500 nm.
	4x21" bow torpedo tubes
Engines	
	1 PWR nuclear reactor with 44.8 MW output
	1 x 325 hp auxiliary motor
	1 shaft
Diving depth	800 ft
Complement	155

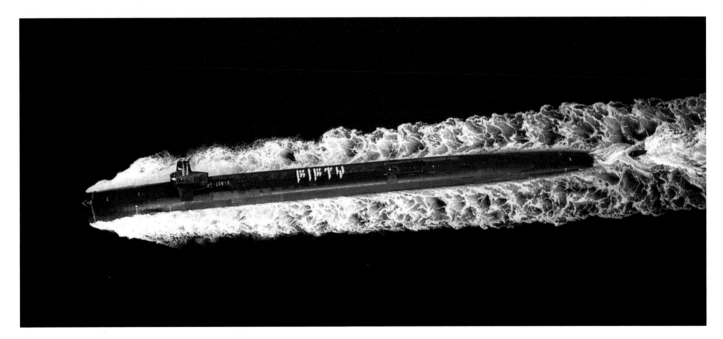

Left: USS *Pennsylvania* SSBN 735, armed with 24 Trident D5 missiles, is assigned to the Atlantic fleet.

Above: Members of *Ohio* (SSBN 726) Blue crew commemorate the completion of an historic 50th strategic patrol by spelling out fifty on deck as the submarine returns to Bangor, on March 12, 1998.

Right: An unusual view of a Los Angeles class attack submarine gliding past three incomplete Ohio boats.

US Ohio Class SSBNS

Boat	Builder	Launched	Commissioned	Fate
Ohio (SSBN 726)	General Dynamics Electric Boat, Groton, Connecticut	07-04-1979	11-11-1981	Trident C4. Pacific Fleet.
Michigan (SSBN 727)	General Dynamics Electric Boat, Groton, Connecticut	26-04-1980	11-09-1982	Trident C4. Pacific Fleet
Florida (SSBN 729)	General Dynamics Electric Boat, Groton, Connecticut	14-11-1981	18-06-1983	Trident C4. Pacific Fleet.
Georgia (SSBN 729)	General Dynamics Electric Boat, Groton, Connecticut	06-11-1982	11-02-1984	Trident C4. Pacific Fleet.
Henry M Jackson (SSBN 730)	General Dynamics Electric Boat, Groton, Connecticut	15-10-1983	06-10-1984	Trident C4. Pacific Fleet. Conversion to D5 FY 2005/6.
Alabama (SSBN 731)	General Dynamics Electric Boat, Groton, Connecticut	19-05-1984	25-05-1985	Trident C4. Pacific Fleet. Conversion to D5, FY 2005/6.
Alaska (SSBN 732)	General Dynamics Electric Boat, Groton, Connecticut	12-01-1985	25-01-1986	Trident C4. Pacific Fleet. Conversion to D5. FY 2000.
Nevada (SSBN 733)	General Dynamics Electric Boat, Groton, Connecticut	14-09-1985	16-08-1986	Trident C4. Pacific Fleet. Conversion to D5, FY 2000.
Tennessee (SSBN 734)	General Dynamics Electric Boat, Groton, Connecticut	13-12-1986	17-12-1988	Trident D5. Atlantic Fleet.
Pennsylvania (SSBN 735)	General Dynamics Electric Boat, Groton, Connecticut	23-04-1988	09-09-1989	Trident D5. Atlantic Fleet.
West Virginia (SSBN 736)	General Dynamics Electric Boat, Groton, Connecticut	14-10-1989	20-10-1990	Trident D5. Atlantic Fleet.
Kentucky (SSBN 737)	General Dynamics Electric Boat, Groton, Connecticut	11-08-1990	13-07-1991	Trident D5. Atlantic Fleet.
Maryland (SSBN 738)	General Dynamics Electric Boat, Groton, Connecticut	10-08-1991	13-06-1992	Trident D5. Atlantic Fleet.
Nebraska (SSBN 739)	General Dynamics Electric Boat, Groton, Connecticut	15-08-1992	10-07-1993	Trident D5. Atlantic Fleet.
Rhode Island (SSBN 740)	General Dynamics Electric Boat, Groton, Connecticut	16-07-1993	09-07-1994	Trident D5. Atlantic Fleet.
Maine (SSBN 741)	General Dynamics Electric Boat, Groton, Connecticut	16-07-1994	29-07-1995	Trident D5. Atlantic Fleet.
Wyoming (SSBN 742)	General Dynamics Electric Boat, Groton, Connecticut	15-07-1995	13-07-1996	Trident D5. Atlantic Fleet.
Louisana (SSBN 743)	General Dynamics Electric Boat, Groton, Connecticut	27-07-1996	06-09-1997	Trident D5. Atlantic Fleet.

Cold War at Sea: Boomers and Battle Groups

The Cold War beneath the waves was not a shooting conflict, but was nonetheless waged by both sides with a frightening intensity for four decades in the most hostile sea environments. Two potential Soviet submarine threats constantly galvanised Western naval planners. These were the expanding and ever-more capable Russian strategic missile boats and the prospect of SSN/SSGNs breaking out into the Atlantic to hunt down and destroy carrier battle groups, therefore causing havoc amongst wartime convoys bringing American reinforcements and war *materiel* to Europe.

The process began soon after the end of World War 2. In May 1948, the US submarine *Sea Dog* staged covert reconnaissance patrols along the Siberian coast.

The advent of Soviet strategic missile firing submarines with the Project 667 Yankee I SSBNs in the 1960s established the doctrinal priority of defending the homeland against missile attack. Two strategic options were exercised: the forward deployment of US submarines in the Barents Sea to track, and if necessary

destroy, Soviet SSBNs before missile launch, and the establishment of a secret chain of fixed sonar arrays by 1960, positioned off the USA coast and later extended into the Atlantic and the Pacific.

SOSUS (Sound Surveillance Systems) consisted of hundreds of sensitive hydrophones mounted on huge scaffolding-like structures, sunk at strategic points in the ocean. Cables carried data back to shore processing centres. A strategic barrier was erected across submarine transit areas like the Greenland-Iceland-UK gap - the entry point for Soviet submarines to the North Atlantic - with terminals at Norfolk, Virginia and Brawdy, Wales. Very soon a library of acoustic signatures of Soviet submarines by individual hull was built up, augmented by sonar data derived from covert patrols by American and British submarines off the Soviet bases in the Kola Peninsula and during Soviet naval exercises.

It was the Pacific SOSUS arm that picked up the sinking of the 'Golf' class diesel-powered ballistic missile submarine *K-129* NW of Hawaii in 1968 after an

explosion, with the system recording the hull crushing.

In the 1970s, the development of longer-range submarine-launched nuclear ballistic missiles enabled the Soviet Navy to evolve the 'bastion' strategy to defend its SSBNs. While their Western counterparts patrol entirely separately from other naval units, the Soviets placed their SBBNs in areas close to home, protected by SSNs. The only exception was the massive *Typhoon* SSBNs, which were built to survive earlier strategic nuclear exchanges, hidden beneath the Arctic polar ice and to launch a second or third strike with their missiles at Western targets. Inevitably, British and American SSNs were tasked, in wartime, in penetrating these bastions and destroying both boomers and protecting submarines.

In the Cold War environment, both sides played cat and mouse in the cold waters of the Barents Sea and in the Sea of Okhotsk, off the other Russian SSBN base at Vladivostock, gathering intelligence on tactics, equipment capabilities and failings, intentions and determination. In 1969, the US SSN, *Lapon* (*SSN 661*) tailed a Soviet

Right: A rare view of the 'business end' of a Trident missile submarine.

Below: A Russian crewman about to undertake the unenviable task of retrieving a sonobuoy from a NATO patrol aircraft in 1980. The boat is a Soviet Foxtrot.

Cold War at Sea: Boomers and Battle Groups

Below: Vaunting its tremendous underwater endurance capability, the USS *Guarnard* surfaces through the ice at the North Pole.

Cold War at Sea: Boomers and Battle Groups

submarine for 40 days without being detected. Small wonder that accidents happened - 11 since 1967 have involved Russian, American and British boats.

In June, 1970, the American boat *Tautog* (*SSN 639*) was reported damaged in a collision with the Soviet 'Echo II' cruise missile boat *K 108* in the northern Pacific when the Russian suddenly doubled back and hit the American's sail. The Russian boat flooded and sank. In 1986, the *Los Angeles* class SSN *Augusta* (*SSN 710*) reportedly was in collision with a Russian nuclear boat in the North Atlantic, and on February 11 1992, sister boat *Baton Rouge* (*SSN 689*) was badly damaged in a collision with a Russian 'Sierra' class SSN, the *Barracuda.* Two British nuclear submarines also reportedly had near misses, one with marks of Russian propeller blades remaining on her bows.

NATO naval strategy was fixed firmly on forward deployment, and included the use of carrier battle groups to suppress the wartime activities of Soviet Naval Aviation over the Atlantic. It is not surprising then, that a key part of Soviet submarine deployment was to break through the Greenland-Iceland-UK gap (GIUK) and to neutralise this threat as far away from Russia as possible. Indeed, the 'Oscar' class cruise missile boats were designed to attack large surface combatants, particularly carrier battle groups.

NATO's response would have been to deploy surface anti-submarine warfare ships along the GIUK gap and aided by barriers of air-dropped sonar buoys, prevent any break-out into the Atlantic.

In the later years of the Cold War, interdiction of allied convoys assumed a lower priority within Soviet naval thinking although the West expected attacks still to be concentrated at origins and destinations of sea lines of communications (SLOC). The Pentagon publicly declared as late as 1989 that in the event of hostilities, "a total Soviet interdiction effort would probably include attacks on NATO ports of embarkation and debarkation, mining of close-in transit routes and harbour approaches as well as attacks against merchant shipping in coastal and open area."

Above: Soviet submarine movements were constantly tracked by NATO units. This Victor was found passing through the Straights of Malacca in 1974 by a US Navy P-3.

Left: The legacy of the end of the Cold War: a Yankee class submarine being broken up for scrap near Severodvinsk in the mid 1990s.

Today, covert surveillance continues, although with straitened financial resources, the Russian Navy is no longer able to mount so many patrols. Qualitatively, their submarines have become much quieter, sometimes through the acquisition of commercially available Western technology, and the new classes of SSN and SSBN, if they ever are completed, are expected to almost equal Western counterparts.

Left: The layout of the diving controls on a typical nuclear powered submarine, as shown in a museum.

Below: USS *Abraham Lincoln* heading out for a lengthy deterrence patrol in the 1970s.

Right: Even aboard a large nuclear-powered submarine conditions are cramped. The ever increasing need for better detection equipment leaves little room for crew comfort.

MIDGET SUBMARINES: THE NEW UNDERWATER MENACE

MIDGET SUBMARINES ENJOYED A BRIEF VOGUE IN WORLD WAR II
with varying levels of success. In the 21st Century, they have returned,
particularly in some developing nations, as an efficient method
of inserting special forces or as diver vehicles to mount
mine attacks on larger naval targets.

Midget submarines - the new underwater menace

During World War Two, Axis forces developed or deployed a series of midget or miniature submarines to attack high value Allied naval targets, both to stem the tide of the war then flowing against them but also because of the high propaganda benefits such attacks could hold.

AXIS POWERS

The Japanese Navy began to develop midget submarines in the early 1930s with the Type A class, 78.5-feet long, displacing 46 tons submerged, armed with two 18-inch torpedoes and carrying a two-man crew. The class, with a tiny conning tower, could produce a surface speed of 23 kts and submerged, a startling 19 kts, powered by a 600 hp electric motor. Five of the class took part in the Japanese attack on Pearl Harbor on December 7 1941, precipitating the USA's entry into the war - but none hit

Above: One of the two-man midget submarines used in the attack against Pearl Harbour, after it was raised by the US Navy in January 1942.

Right: After the surrender of the Italian fleet in 1943, the Allies were able to take a more detailed look at one of their adversaries more 'exotic' weapons.

any targets and *HA-19* ran aground on a coral reef and was captured.[1]

The Italians were next in the development of this most covert of submarine weapons with the *Maiale* or 'pig', a 23-feet long torpedo-shaped vehicle that carried two

Below: The Italian Maiale 'human torpedo' carried two divers and were responsible for sinking two British battleships in Alekandria harbour.

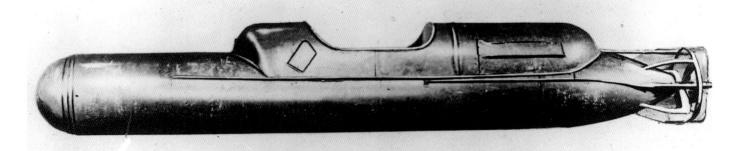

1 *HA-19,* LAUNCHED IN 1938 AT KURE NAVAL DOCKYARD, IS ON DISPLAY AT THE NATIONAL MUSEUM OF THE PACIFIC WAR AT FREDERICKSBURG, TEXAS. ANOTHER, *HA-8,* IS AT THE SUBMARINE FORCE MUSEUM AT GROTON, CONNECTICUT.

divers who controlled it with a joystick.[2] With a 2 hp electric motor generating at most 4 kts, it was designed to penetrate enemy harbours and destroy shipping by attaching the 300 kg explosive charge carried in its nose to the keel of the target. Three *Maiales* attacked British warships in Alexandria harbour, sinking the battleships *Valiant,* and *Queen Elizabeth* and a destroyer. The British, impressed by the capability of the weapon, built their own - the so-called human chariot.

But it was in the latter stages of the war when, faced with amphibious landings, the midget submarine came into its own in Germany and Japan. Germany launched a massive programme of development and construction, building six different classes, totalling 1,755 units, not all commissioned.

Most numerous was the one-man *Marder,* which entered service in July 1944, with about 500 built. In reality it was a three-ton manned torpedo, with a plastic dome covering the control cockpit. Slung beneath the slim cigar-shaped hull was a torpedo. Attacks were mounted against allied shipping off invasion beaches in Normandy in France but in two such attacks, 67 out of the 100 that set out, failed to return. They sank one 7,200 ton liberty ship, a minesweeper and the British destroyer

Quorn in Seine Bay. One prototype larger version, the *Hai* or 'shark,' was built with greater battery capacity and a speed of 20 kts but this was abandoned after unsatisfactory trials.

The most successful of the German midgets was the Type 127 *Seehund* class, with at least 138 commissioned out of 285 built. These craft, displacing 17 tons submerged, carried two underslung G7 torpedoes and a crew of two, and were capable of 7 kts on the surface. They were used in attacks on shipping off the East Coast of England, mounting more than 140 sorties in 1945,

Above: Armed British naval officer, with Danish and German officers, inspecting a Marder 'human torpedo' at Fort Lynaes, Denmark in May 1945.

Below: The conning tower of a German *Seehund* midget submarine being trialled by the Royal Navy after capture in 1945. The two-man *Seehund* carried two torpedoes slung under the hull.

2 One is on display at the Submarine Force Museum, Groton, Connecticut.

197

Midget submarines - the new underwater menace

Above: A sapper from the Royal Engineers inspecting a German Biber after Allied forces captured Kiel .

Below: The Biber was designed to carry two torpedoes alongside the hull, but stability problems required them to be fired whilst the boat was surfaced.

Above: A bow view of a Biber type midget submarine high and dry after capture.

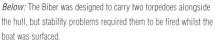

3 On display at the Submarine Memorial Association, Hackensack, New Jersey.

sinking eight ships totalling 17,000 tons, but losing 35 boats in the process.[3]

Two further one-man boats with underslung torpedoes were developed, which together sank only seven small Allied ships in return for losing 70 craft in more than 100 missions in 1945. One of then, the 324-strong *Biber* class displaced 6.5 tons, had a surface range of 130 nm at 6 kts but because of depth-keeping problems, was forced to launch its torpedoes on the surface. The other class, the larger *Molch*, displaced 11 tons and were expended fruitlessly in attacks against allied forces in the landings in the South of France in September 1944.

Two hundred of another class, the *Mohr* were built in 1944. These were again used against Allied shipping off the Normandy invasion beaches and sank two minesweepers, HMS *Magic* and *Cato* on July 6 1944, in Seine Bay and three days later, the Free Polish cruiser *Dragon* and British minesweeper *Pylades* off Juno Beach. In the former attack, only nine out of 26 survived.

The largest German midget submarines were the 53 three-man Type XXVII *Hecht,* originally conceived to attach magnetic limpet mines to the hulls of enemy

warships, but in practice were only used for training.

Prototypes of three different designs were also built. The first was the 2.5 ton one-man *Delphin* designed to attain high underwater speeds of above 17 kts, of which three were built in late 1944. The second was the *Schwertwal*, a cigar-shaped hull, powered by a Walter hydrogen peroxide turbine, designed to reach 30 kts underwater and the third was the curious two-man *Seeteufel*, 46-feet long, equipped with tracks with which to crawl on the seabed. Its designers claimed an operating depth of 70-feet and an underwater speed of 8 kts, although it was hardly streamlined. The only prototype, displacing 35 tons, was blown up near Lübeck in May 1945.

It was the Japanese who deployed midget submarines, or more properly manned torpedoes on a large-scale against the hard-fought amphibious landings in the Pacific Islands. After the re-taking of the Philippines in 1944, the Japanese Navy produced their 'Special Attack' tactics of adapting Type 93 'Long Lance' 24" torpedoes, lengthened by inserting a plug in the central section holding the craft's pilot, into the 'Kaiten' midget submarine.

Two types were developed. Type 1 displaced 8.3 tons, was powered by two Type 93 oxygen-kerosene 1,500 hp torpedo motors, with an operational radius of 78 nm at 12 kts. Top speeds of 30 kts could be achieved. Up to six Kaitens would be carried into range of their targets, piggy-backed on the casing of a conventional mother submarine and then released, leaving the tiny boat to manoeuvre to within 550 yards of its target before diving

Below: A British officer inspects the interior of a Molch type midget in August 1945.

Midget submarines - the new underwater menace

Midget submarines - the new underwater menace

Midget submarines - the new underwater menace

to around 13-feet for the attack run. The craft, of which 400 were built, suffered from a propensity to catch fire and a series of mechanical problems.

Type 2, was considerably larger at 18.4 tons, with a two-man crew, and could reach 40 kts in the right conditions. It was not deployed operationally. Both carried 3,960 lbs of explosives in their noses. The chances of any crewmen coming back alive were practically nil - indeed 100 died during operations in the closing months of the Pacific War which sank only three US ships. No escape hatch was provided.[4]

ALLIED FORCES

Britain meanwhile was pursuing the Italian concept of stealthy penetration into tightly guarded port facilities to destroy high value targets. The 'X' class midget submarine was conceived, with the 43.4-feet long prototype displacing 22 tons surfaced, 30 tons submerged, and capable of 5.5 kts underwater. This proved successful, so the 'X' class was built, displacing 27 tons surfaced, 35 submerged, with a crew of four and

Above and left: The British X and XE classes accomplished a number of successful missions in Europe and the Far East.

Above: A British XE at sea in calm conditions. Conning the vessel on the surface in rough weather must have been an alarming experience.

Below: A Swedish Spiggen II midget submarine on trials in the 1990s.

role is the clandestine insertion of agents in hostile territory. One of the class grounded at Kangnung, 100 miles east of Seoul, South Korea, and was captured by South Korean forces on September 18 1996. The crew committed suicide.

North Korea also operates 36 'Yugo' and 'P4' midget submarines built locally since the early 1960s. The later version, being built since 1987, displaces 90 tons, surfaced and 110 divided, and has a crew of four, plus up to seven divers. The earlier P4 class operated from eight mother merchant ships. Two P4 were exported to Vietnam in 1997.

Yugoslavia herself operates five *Una* class midget submarines, built between 1983-88, the last commissioning in 1989. The 61.7-feet long boats have a crew of six and can accommodate six divers plus four swimmer delivery vehicles and limpet mines. Diving depth is reportedly 394-feet.

4 KAITENS ARE DISPLAYED AT THE USS *BOWFIN* MUSEUM IN HONOLULU AND AT THE SUBMARINE MEMORIAL ASSOCIATION, HACKENSACK, NEW JERSEY.

5 *TIRPITZ* WAS KNOCKED OUT OF ACTION FOR NINE MONTHS.

the slightly larger '*XE*' class, 30 tons, surfaced.

The '*X*' class, towed by conventional diesel-electric submarines, mounted attacks on the German battleship *Tirpitz* , sheltering in Altenfjord, Norway, on September 22, 1943. Of the six that set out in the operation, two were lost on passage, one was sunk, another abandoned the attack after navigation problems. Of the two remaining, *X7* placed her two side charges of two tons of explosive each under *Tirpitz* but became caught in anti-submarine nets while trying to escape and was damaged when her charges blew. The final midget boat, *X 10*, had been tasked to attack *Scharnhorst* but the heavy warship had already sailed. She was recovered by her mother submarine but sank on tow, returning to England.[5]

Another operation, this time in the Far East, was mounted by the later *XE* class boats. *XE3* and *XE 1* sank the Japanese cruiser *Takao,* 9,850 tons, in the Johore Strait, off Singapore, on July 31, 1945, and on the same day *XE4* and *XE5* cut seabed telegraph cables connecting Saigon, Hong Kong, and Singapore off Hong Kong.

POST-WAR DEVELOPMENTS

With the end of World War II, interest in midget submarines did not disappear. In modern times, Iran built a boat, based on Japanese and German wartime designs, but later acquired two more displacing 76 tons surfaced and 90 divided, possibly of North Korean design. The boats, based at Bandar Abbas, have an operating depth of around 328 feet and are armed with side cargoes of explosives.

North Korea itself has developed an indigenous class of 28 midget boats, beginning in 1991, based on Yugoslav designs. The *Sang-O* class displaces 256 tons surfaced, 277 dived, and carries a crew of 19. Although armed with two or four 21-inch torpedoes or 16 mines, their primary

Appendix 1: Order of Battle of the World's Submarines

Above: The Argentinian Santa Cruz (TR 1700).

ALGERIA

SSK - 2 KILO (TYPE 877E) CLASS
Rais Hadj Mubarek, El Hadj Slimane
Displacement (tons): 2,325 surfaced, 3,076 dived.
Speed (kts) 17 dived, 10 surfaced.
Diving depth: 790 ft.
Armament: 6x21" tubes.12 reloads. Minelaying
configuration: 24 replace torpedoes.

ARGENTINA

SSK - 2 'SANTA CRUZ' (TR 1700) CLASS.
1 'SALTA' (209 TYPE 1200) CLASS
'SANTA CRUZ' CLASS
Santa Cruz, San Juan
Displacement (tons) 2,116 surfaced, 2,264 dived.
Speed (kts): 25 dived, 15 surfaced.
Diving depth: 890 ft.
Armament: 6x21" bow tubes. Can carry 34 mines.
'SALTA' CLASS
Salta
Displacement (tons) 1,248 surfaced, 1,440 dived.
Speed (kts): 22 dived, 10 surfaced.
Diving depth: 820 ft.
Armament: 8x21" bow tubes. Can carry mines.

AUSTRALIA

SSK - 6 'COLLINS' CLASS
*Collins, Farncomb, Waller, Dechaineux, Sheenan,
Rankin*
Displacement (tons) 3,051 surfaced, 3,353 dived.
Speed (kts): 20 dived, 10 surfaced.
Diving depth: 984 ft.
Armament: 6x21" bow tubes. Sub Harpoon anti-ship
missiles.
Minelaying configuration: 44 replace torpedoes.

BRAZIL

SSK - 4 'TUPI' (209 TYPE 1400) CLASS;
1 'HUMAITÁ' ('OBERON') CLASS, PLUS
1 'TIKUNA' CLASS (BUILDING)
'TUPI' CLASS
Tupi, Tamoio, Timbira, Tapajó (ex-Tapajós)
Displacement (tons) 1,400 surfaced, 1,550 dived.
Speed (kts): 21.5 dived, 11 surfaced.
Diving depth: 820 ft.
Armament: 8x21" bow tubes. 8 reloads.

'HUMAITÁ' CLASS
Tonetero
Displacement (tons) 2,030 surfaced, 2,410 dived.
Speed (kts): 17 dived, 12 surfaced.
Diving depth: 600 ft.
Armament: 8x21" (6 bow, 2 stern) tubes. 16 reloads.

'TIKUNA' CLASS
Tikuna(ex-*Tocantins*)*
Displacement (tons) 1,850 surfaced, 2,425 dived.
Speed (kts): 22 dived, 11 surfaced.
Diving depth: 985 ft.
Armament: 8x21" bow tubes. Exocet or Sub Harpoon
anti-ship missiles.
* Commissioning 2003.

BULGARIA

SS - 1 'ROMEO' CLASS
Slava
Displacement (tons) 1,475 surfaced, 1,830 dived.
Speed (kts): 13 dived, 16 surfaced.
Diving depth: 165 ft.
Armament: 8x21" bow tubes. 6 reloads. Minelaying
configuration: 28 replace torpedoes.

CANADA

SSK - 4 'VICTORIA' ('UPHOLDER') CLASS
Chicoutimi (ex-*Upholder*), *Cornerbrook* (ex-*Ursula*),
Victoria (ex-*Unseen*),*Windsor* (ex-*Unicorn*)
Displacement (tons) 2,168 surfaced, 2,455 dived.
Speed (kts): 20 dived, 12 surfaced.
Diving depth: 675 ft.
Armament: 6x21" bow tubes. 12 reloads.

CHILE

**SSK - 2 'THOMSON' (209 TYPE 1300) CLASS;
2 'OBERON' CLASS**

'THOMSON' CLASS
Thomson, Simpson
Displacement (tons) 1, 260 surfaced, 1,390 dived.
Speed (kts): 21.5 dived, 11 surfaced.
Diving depth: 800 ft.
Armament: 8x21" bow tubes. 8 reloads.

'OBERON' CLASS
O'Brien, Hyatt (ex-Condell)
Displacement (tons) 2.030 surfaced, 2,410 dived.
Speed (kts): 17 dived, 12 surfaced.
Diving depth: 600 ft.
Armament: 8x21" (6 bow, 2 stern tubes.) Stern tubes
    sealed. 14 reloads. To be deleted when
    2 'Scorpene' commission in 2004/6.

CHINA

SSBN - 1 'XIA' (TYPE 092)
Xia
Displacement (tons) 6,500 dived.
Speed (kts): 22 dived, 11 surfaced.
Diving depth: 985 ft.
Armament: 12 JL-1A (CSS-N-3)
    SLBM. 6x21" bow tubes.

SSB - 1 'GOLF' CLASS
200
Displacement (tons) 2,350 surfaced, 2,950 dived.
Speed (kts): 13 dived, 17 surfaced.
Diving depth: 750 ft.
Armament: 1 JL 2 SLBM. (Trials boat). 10x21"
    tubes. (6 bow, 4 stern) 8 reloads.

**SSN - 5 'HAN' (TYPE 091) CLASS PLUS
2 TYPE 093 CLASS (BUILDING)**
HAN CLASS *401-405*
Displacement (tons) 4,500 surfaced, 5,550 dived.
Speed (kts): 25 dived, 12 surfaced.
Diving depth: 980 ft.
Armament: YJ-82 (C-801) anti-ship missile. 6x21"
    bow tubes. 14 reloads. 36 mines instead of
    torpedoes.

SSG - 3 'SONG' (TYPE 039) CLASS PLUS 1 BUILDING
320-323
Displacement (tons) 1,700 surfaced, 2,250 dived.
Speed (kts): 22 dived, 15 surfaced.
Diving depth: 820 ft.
Armament: YJ-82 (C-801_ anti-ship missile. 6x21"
    bow tubes. Minelaying configuration:
    Mines replace torpedoes.

SSK - 4 'KILO' (TYPE 877EKM/636) CLASS
364-367
Displacement (tons) 2,325 surfaced, 3,076 dived.

Speed (kts): 17 dived, 10 surfaced.
Diving depth: 790ft.
Armament: 6 x21" tubes. 12 reloads.
    Minelaying configuration: 24 replace torpedoes.

**SS - 18 'MING' (TYPE 035) CLASS,
32 'ROMEO' (TYPE 033) CLASS**

'MING' CLASS
232, 342, 352-354, 356-363, 305-309
Displacement (tons) 1,584 surfaced, 2,113 dived.
Speed (kts): 18 dived, 15 surfaced.
Diving depth: 790 ft.
Armament: 8x21" tubes. Minelaying configuration:
    32 replace torpedoes.

'ROMEO' CLASS
*256-260, 268-272, 275-280, 286-287, 291-304,
    343-349,355.*
Displacement (tons): 1,475 surfaced, 1,850 dived.
Speed (kts) 12 dived, 14 surfaced.
Diving depth: 650 ft.
Armament: 8x21" tubes. (6 bow, 2 stern) 6 reloads.
    Minelaying configuration: 28 replace torpedoes.

COLUMBIA

SS - 2 'PIJAO' (209 TYPE 1200) CLASS
Pijao, Tayrona
Displacement (tons): 1,180 surfaced, 1,285 dived.
Speed (kts) 22 dived, 11 surfaced.
Diving depth: 820 ft.
Armament: 8x21" tubes. 7 reloads.
MIDGET SUBMARINES: 2 'INTREPIDO' CLASS
Intrepido, Indomable
Displacement (tons): 58 surfaced, 70 dived.
Speed (kts) 6 dived, 11 surfaced.

Below: Ecuador: The Type 209 Huancavilca.

Diving depth: N/K
Armament:
    Minelaying configuration: 6 Mk 21 or 8 Mk 50.

CROATIA

MIDGET SUBMARINES: 2 MODIFIED 'UNA' CLASS
VELEBIT (EX-SOCA) PLUS 1 AS YET UN-NAMED.
Displacement (tons): 88 surfaced, 99 dived.
Speed (kts) 7 dived, 6 surfaced.
Diving depth: 395 ft.
Swimmer delivery with mining capability.

DENMARK

**SSK 3 'TUMLEREN' ('KOBBEN' TYPE 207) CLASS AND
2 'NARHVALEN' CLASS**

'TUMLEREN' CLASS
*Tumleren (ex-Utvaer), Saelen (ex-Uthaug),
    Springeren (ex-Kya)*
Displacement (tons): 459 surfaced, 524 dived.
Speed (kts) 18 dived, 12 surfaced.
Diving depth: >550 ft.
Armament: 8x21" bow tubes. 12 reloads.

'NARHVALEN' CLASS
Narhvalen, Nordkaperen
Displacement (tons): 420 surfaced, 450 dived.
Speed (kts) 17 dived, 12 surfaced.
Diving depth: >500 ft.
Armament: 8 x21" bow tubes.

ECUADOR

SSK - 2 'SHYRI' (209 TYPE 1300) CLASS
Shyri, Huancavilca
Displacement (tons): 1,285 surfaced, 1,390 dived.
Speed (kts) 21.5 dived, 11 surfaced.
Diving depth: 800 ft.
Armament: 8x21" bow tubes. 6 reloads.
    Minelaying configuration: 24 replace torpedoes.

Appendix 1: Order of Battle of the World's Submarines

Left: France: The leading boat of the Rubis class.

EGYPT

SSK - 4 'IMPROVED ROMEO' (TYPE 033) CLASS
849, 852, 855, 858
Displacement (tons): 1,475 surfaced, 1,830 dived.
Speed (kts) 13 dived, 16 surfaced.
Diving depth: 600 ft.
Armament: Sub Harpoon anti-ship missile.
8x21" tubes.(4 bow, 2 stern) 6 reloads.
Minelaying configuration: 28 replace torpedoes.

FRANCE

SSBN - 2 'L'INDOMPTABLE' M4 CLASS,
2 'LE TRIOMPHANT' CLASS PLUS ONE BUILDING
'LE TRIOMPHANT' CLASS
Le Triomphant, Le Téméraire, Le Vigilant (building)
Displacement (tons): 12,640 surfaced, 14,120 dived.
Speed (kts) 25 dived, 20 surfaced.
Diving depth: 1,640 ft.
Armament: 16 M45/TN 75 SLBM. SM 39 Exocet
anti-ship missiles. 4x21" tubes. 12 reloads.

'L'INDOMPTABLE' CLASS
L'Indomptable, L'Inflexible
Displacement (tons): 8,080 surfaced, 8,920 dived.
Speed (kts) 25 dived, 20 surfaced.
Diving depth: 820 ft.
Armament: 16 M4/TN 71 SLBM. SM 39 Exocet
anti-ship missiles. 4x21" tubes. 14 reloads.

SSN - 6 'RUBIS' CLASS
Rubis, Saphir, Casabianca, Émeraude, Améthyste, Perle
Displacement (tons): 2,410 surfaced, 2,670 dived.
Speed (kts) 25 dived, 20 surfaced.
Diving depth: 984 ft.
Armament: SM 39 Exocet anri-ship missile.
4x21" tubes. 10 reloads.
Minelaying configuration: 32 replace torpedoes.

SSK - 1 'AGOSTA' CLASS
*La Praya**
Displacement (tons): 1,510 surfaced, 1,760 dived.
Speed (kts) 20 dived, 12 surfaced.
Diving depth: 1,050 ft.
Armament: SM 39 Exocet anti-ship missile 4x21"
tubes. 16 reloads. Minelaying configuration:
36 replace torpedoes.
*Test platform for new SSN equipment.

GERMANY

SSK - 12 TYPE 206A
U 15-18, U-22-26, U28-30
Displacement (tons): 450 surfaced, 498 dived.
Speed (kts) 17 dived, 10 surfaced.
Diving depth: >500 ft.
Armament: 8x21" bow tubes. Minelaying containers
outside hull with 24. Additional 16 instead of
torpedoes.

SSA - 2 TYPE 205
U 11-12
Displacement (tons): 419 surfaced, 450 dived.
Speed (kts) 17 dived, 10 surfaced.
Diving depth: 500 ft.
Armament: 8x21" tubes.

Below: Germany: U 30, a type 206A submarine.

Appendix 1: Order of Battle of the World's Submarines

GREECE

***SSK* - 8 'Glavkos' class (209, Type 1100/1200)**

Glavkos, Nereus, Triton, Proteus, Poseidon,
Amphitrite, Okeanos, Pontos
Displacement (tons): 1,100 surfaced, 1.285 dived.
Speed (kts) 22 dived, 12 surfaced.
Diving depth: 820 ft.
Armament: Sub Harpoon anti-ship missile.
8x21" tubes. 4 reloads.

INDIA

***SSK* - 4 'Shishumar' (209, Type 1500) class,**
10 'Sindhughosh' ('Kilo', Type 877EM636) class

'Shishumar' class
Shishumar, Shankush, Shalki, Shankul
Displacement (tons): 1,660 surfaced, 1,850 dived.
Speed (kts) 22 dived, 12 surfaced.
Diving depth: 855 ft.
Armament: 8x21" tubes. 6 reloads. 24 mines in
external containers.

'Sindhughosh' class
Sindhughosh, Sindhudhvaj, Sindhuraj, Sindhuvir,
Sindhuratna, Sindhukesari, Sindhukirti,
Sindhuvijay, Sindhurakshak, Sindhushastra
Displacement (tons): 2,325 surfaced, 3,076 dived.
Speed (kts) 17 dived, 10 surfaced.
Diving depth: 985 ft.
Armament: SS-N-27 SLCM. SA-N-8 portable SAM
6x21" tubes. 12 reloads.
Minelaying configuration: 24 replace torpedoes.

SS - 4 'Foxtrot' (Type 641) class
Kursura, Karanj, Vela, Vagli
Displacement (tons): 1,952 surfaced, 2,475 dived.
Speed (kts) 15 dived, 16 surfaced.
Diving depth: >750 ft.
Armament: 10x21" tubes. 12 reloads.
Minelaying configuration: 44 replace torpedoes.

INDONESIA

***SSK* - 2 'Cakra' (209, Type 1300) class**

Above: India: INS Sindhurakshak.

Cakra, Nanggala
Displacement (tons): 1,285 surfaced, 1,390 dived.
Speed (kts) 22 dived, 11 surfaced.
Diving depth: 790 ft.
Armament: 8x21" tubes. 6 reloads.

IRAN

***SSK* - 3 'Kilo' (Type 877EKM) class**

Tareq, Noor, Yunes
Displacement (tons): 2,356 surfaced, 3,076 dived.
Speed (kts) 17 dived, 10 surfaced.
Diving depth: 790 ft.
Armament: 6x21" tubes. 12 reloads.
Minelaying configuration: 24 replace torpedoes.

Above: Israel: The first boat of the Dolphin class.

Armament: 6x21" tubes. 12 reloads.
　　Minelaying configuration: 24 replace torpedoes.

Midget submarines - 3
Displacement (tons): 76 surfaced, 90 dived.
Speed (kts) 8 dived, 12 surfaced.
Diving depth: 330 ft.

ISRAEL
SSK -3 'DOLPHIN' (TYPE 800) CLASS

Dolphin, Leviathan, Tekuma
Displacement (tons): 1,640 surfaced 1,900 dived
Speed (kts) 20 dived, 10 surfaced.
Diving depth: 1,150 ft.
Armament: Sub Harpoon anti-ship missile.
　　4x25.6" and 6x21" tubes. 4 reloads.

ITALY
SSK 4 'IMPROVED SAURO'
4 'SAURO' (TYPE 1081) CLASSES

'IMPROVED SAURO' CLASS
*Salvatore Pelosi, Giuliano Prini, Prime Longobardo,
　Gianfranco Gazzana Piraroggia*

Displacement (tons): 1,476 surfaced, 1,662 dived.
Speed (kts) 19 dived, 11 surfaced.
Diving depth: 985 ft.
Armament: 6x21" bow tubes. 6 reloads.

'SAURO' CLASS
*Nazario Sauro, Fecia di Cossato, Leonardo da Vinci,
　Guglielmo Marconi*
Displacement (tons): 1,456 surfaced, 1,631 dived.
Speed (kts) 19 dived, 11 surfaced.
Diving depth: 820 ft.
Armament: 6x21" bow tubes. 6 reloads.

JAPAN
SSK - 4 'OYASHIO' CLASS,
7 'HARUSHIO' CLASS, 8 'YUUSHIO' CLASS

'OYASHIO' CLASS
Oyashio, Michishio, Uzushio, Makishio
Displacement (tons): 2,700 surfaced, 3,000 dived.
Speed (kts) 20 dived, 12 surfaced.
Diving depth: 1,150 ft.
Armament: Sub Harpoon anti-ship missile.
　　6x21" tubes. 12 reloads.

'HARUSHIO' CLASS
*Harushio, Natsushio, Hayashio, Arashio, Wakashio,
　Fuyushio, Asashio*
Displacement (tons): 2,450 surfaced, 2,750 dived.
Speed (kts) 20 dived, 12 surfaced.
Diving depth: 1,150 ft.
Armament: Sub Harpoon anti-ship missile 6x21"

Below: Italy: Gianfranco Gazzana Piraroggia.

Appendix 1: Order of Battle of the World's Submarines

Above: North Korea: Romeo class.

'YUUSHIO' CLASS
Setoshio, Okishio, Nadashio, Hamashio, Akishio,
Takeshio, Yukishio, Sachishio
Displacement (tons): 2,200 surfaced, 2,450 dived.
Speed (kts) 20 dived, 12 surfaced.
Diving depth: 900 ft.
Armament: Sub Harpoon anti-ship missile 6x21"
amidships tubes. 12 reloads.

KOREA, NORTH
SS - 22 'ROMEO' (TYPE 033) CLASS
Displacement (tons): 1,475 surfaced, 1,830 dived.
Speed (kts) 13 dived, 15 surfaced.
Diving depth: >500 ft.
Armament: 8x21" tubes. 6 reloads.
Minelaying configuration: 28 replace torpedoes.

SSC - 28 'SANG-O' CLASS
Displacement (tons): 256 surfaced, 277 dived.
Speed (kts) 9 dived, 7 surfaced.

Diving depth: 590 ft.
Armament: 4x21" tubes.
Minelaying configuration: 16 replace torpedoes.

MIDGET SUBMARINES - 36 'YUGO' CLASS
Displacement (tons): 90 surfaced, 110 dived.
Speed (kts) 8 dived, 10 surfaced.
Diving depth: N/K
Armament: 2 torpedo tubes.

KOREA, SOUTH
SSK - 8 'CHANG BOGO' (209, TYPE 1200) CLASS
Chang Bogo, Yi Chon, Choi Muson, Pakui,
Nadaeyong, Lee Sunsin, Jeongun, Lee Jongmu
Displacement (tons): 1,100 surfaced, 1,285 dived.
Speed (kts) 22 dived, 10 surfaced.
Diving depth: 820 ft.
Armament: 8x21" tubes. 6 reloads.
Minelaying configuration: 28 replace torpedoes.

LIBYA
SS - 2 'FOXTROT' (TYPE 641) CLASS
Al Khyber, Al Hunain
Displacement (tons): 1,950 surfaced, 2,475 dived.
Speed (kts) 15 dived, 16 surfaced.

Diving depth: >500 ft.
Armament: 10x21" tubes. (6 bow, 4 stern) 12 reloads.
Minelaying configuration: 44 replace torpedoes.

NETHERLANDS
SSK - 4 'Walrus' class
Walrus, Bruinvis, Zeeleeuw, Dolfijn
Displacement (tons): 2,465 surfaced, 2,800 dived.
Speed (kts) 20 dived, 12 surfaced.
Diving depth: 985 ft.
Armament: Sub Harpoon anti-ship missile 4x21"
tubes. Minelaying configuration: 40 replace
torpedoes.

NORWAY
SSK - 6 'ULA' CLASS,
6 MODERNISED 'KOBBEN' (TYPE 207) CLASS

'ULA' CLASS
Ula, Uredd, Utvaer, Uthaug, Utstein, Utsira
Displacement (tons): 1,040 surfaced, 1,150 dived.
Speed (kts) 23 dived, 11 surfaced.
Diving depth: 820 ft.
Armament: 8x21" tubes. 6 reloads.

Ula, Uredd, Utvaer, Uthaug, Utstein, Utsira
Displacement (tons): 1,040 surfaced, 1,150 dived.
Speed (kts) 23 dived, 11 surfaced.
Diving depth: 820 ft.
Armament: 8x21" tubes. 6 reloads.

MODERNISED 'KOBBEN'
Sklinna, Skolpen, Stord, Svenner, Kunna, Kobben
Displacement (tons): 459 surfaced, 524 dived.
Speed (kts) 18 dived, 12 surfaced.
Diving depth: 650 ft.
Armament: 8x21" tubes.

PAKISTAN

SSK - 2 'KHALID' (AGOSTA 90B) CLASS
    (PLUS 1 BUILDING),
2 'HASHMAT' (AGOSTA) CLASS,
4 'HANGOR' (DAPHNÉ) CLASS

'KHALID' CLASS
    Khalid, Saad, Ghazi (building)
    Displacement (tons): 1,510 surfaced, 1,760 dived.
    Speed (kts) 20 dived, 12 surfaced.
    Diving depth: 1,050 ft.
    Armament: SM 39 Exocet anti-ship missile.
        4x21" bow tubes. 12 reloads.

'HASHMAT' CLASS
    Hashmat (ex-Astrant), Hurmat (ex-Adventurous)
    Displacement (tons): 1,490 surfaced, 1,740 dived.
    Speed (kts) 20 dived, 12 surfaced.
    Diving depth: 985 ft.
    Armament: Sub Harpoon anti-ship missile.
        4x21" tubes. 16 reloads.

'HANGOR' CLASS
    Hangor, Shushuk, Ghazi (ex-Cachalote), Mangro
    Displacement (tons): 700 surfaced, 1,043 dived.
    Speed (kts) 15 dived, 13 surfaced.
    Diving depth: 985 ft.
    Armament: Sub Harpoon anti-ship missile.
        12x21.7" tubes. No reloads.

MIDGET SUBMARINES - 3

Displacement (tons): 80 surfaced, 118 dived.
Speed (kts) 7 dived, 5 surfaced.
Diving depth: N/K
Armament: 2x21" tubes. No reloads. 12 limpet mines.

PERU

SSK - 6 'CASMA' (209, TYPE 1200)
    Casma, Antofagasta, Pisagua, Chipana, Islay, Arica
    Displacement (tons): 1,185 surfaced, 1,290 dived.
    Speed (kts) 21 dived, 12 surfaced.
    Diving depth: 820 ft.
    Armament: 8x21" tubes. 6 reloads.

SS - 2 'ABTAO' CLASS
    Abtao (ex-Tiburon), Dos de Mayo (ex-Lobo)
    Displacement (tons): 825 surfaced, 1,400 dived.
    Speed (kts) 10 dived, 16 surfaced.
    Diving depth: >450? ft.
    Armament: 6x21" tubes. 1x5" gun.

POLAND

SSK - 1 'KILO' (TYPE 877E) CLASS
    Orzel
    Displacement (tons): 2,325 surfaced, 3,076 dived.
    Speed (kts) 17 dived, 10 surfaced.
    Diving depth: 790 ft.
    Armament: 6x21" tubes. 12 reloads.
        Minelaying configuration: 24 replace torpedoes.

SS - 2 'FOXTROT' (TYPE 641) CLASS
    Wilk, Dzik
    Displacement (tons): 1,952 surfaced, 2,475 dived.
    Speed (kts) 15 dived, 16 surfaced.
    Diving depth: 820 ft.
    Armament: 10x21" tubes. 12 reloads.
        Minelaying configuration: 32 replace torpedoes.

PORTUGAL

SSK - 3 'ALBACORA' ('DAPHNÉ') CLASS
    Albacora, Barracuda, Delfim

Displacement (tons): 869 surfaced, 1,043 dived.
Speed (kts) 16 dived, 13 surfaced.
Diving depth: 984 ft.
Armament: 12 x21.7" tubes. No reloads.

ROMANIA

SSK - 'KILO' (TYPE 877E) CLASS
    Delfinul
    Displacement (tons): 2,325 surfaced, 3,076 dived.
    Speed (kts) 20 dived, 10 surfaced.
    Diving depth: 790 ft.
    Armament: 6x21" tubes. 12 reloads.
        Minelaying configuration: 24 replace torpedoes.

RUSSIA

SSBN - 2 TYPHOON ('AKULA') CLASS;
7 DELTA IV ('DELFIN') CLASS,
7 DELTA III ('KALMAR') CLASS,

'TYPHOON' CLASS
    TK 17, TK 20
    Displacement (tons): 18, 500 surfaced, 26, 500 dived.
    Speed (kts) 25 dived, 12 surfaced.
    Diving depth: 1,000 ft.
    Armament: 20 SS-N-20 SLBM. SS-N-15 Starfish
        anti-submarine weapon with nuclear warhead;
        6x21" torpedo tubes. 16 reloads.

'DELTA IV' CLASS
    K 51, K 84, K 64, K 18, K 114, K 117, K 407
    Displacement (tons): 10,800 surfaced, 13,500 dived.
    Speed (kts) 24 dived, 14 surfaced.
    Diving depth: 1,000 ft.
    Armament: 16 SS-N-23 SLBM. SS-N-15 Starfish
        anti-submarine weapon with nuclear warhead.
        4 x21" torpedo tubes.

'DELTA III' CLASS

Below: Russia: a Kilo class boat, en-route to its
new owners in Iran.

Appendix 1: Order of Battle of the World's Submarines

SSN - 2 'SIERRA II' CLASS,
8 'OSCAR' CLASS, 2 'AKULA II',
8 'AKULA I' CLASS PLUS 1 BUILDING,
7 'VICTOR III' CLASS

'SIERRA II' (KONDOR) CLASS
Pskow, Nizny-Novgorod
Displacement (tons): 7, 600 surfaced, 9,100 dived.
Speed (kts) 32 dived, 10 surfaced.
Diving depth: 2,450 ft.
Armament: SS-N-21 Sampson SLCM.
    SS-N-15 Starfish, SS-N-16 Stallion nuclear
    anti-submarine weapons. 4x25.6", 4x21" tubes.
    Minelaying configuration: 42 replace torpedoes.

'OSCAR II' (ANTYEY) CLASS
Veronesh, Smolensk, Celjabinsk, Omsk,
    St. George the Victorious (ex-*Tomsk*), *Belgorod,*
    Wiliuczinsk (ex-*Kasatka*), *Orel* (ex-*Severodvinsk*)
Displacement (tons): 13,900 surfaced, 18,300 dived.
Speed (kts) 28 dived, 15 surfaced.
Diving depth: 1,200 ft.
Armament: 24 SS-N-19 anti-ship missiles;
    SS-N-15 Starfish, SS-N-16 Stallion nuclear
    anti-submarine weapons, 4x21", 2x26" tubes.
    Minelaying configuration: 32.

'AKULA I' (BARS) CLASS
Dolphin, Kit, Narwhal, Wolf, Cougar, Leopard,
    Tiger, Dragon.

'IMPROVED AKULA'
Cougar, Leopard, Tiger, Dragon, Nerpa (building)
Displacement (tons): 7,500 surfaced, 9,100 dived.
Speed (kts) 28 dived, 10 surfaced.
Diving depth: 1,300 ft.
Armament: SS-N-21 Sampson SLCM,
    SS-N-15 Starfish, SS-N-16 Stallim nuclear
    anti-submarine weapons. 4x21", 4x25.6" tubes.

'AKULA II' CLASS
Viper, Gepard
Displacement (tons): 7,500 surfaced, 9,500 dived.
Speed (kts) 28 dived, 10 surfaced.
Diving depth: 1,475 ft.
Armament: SS-N-21 Sampson SLCM,
    SS-N-15 Starfish and SS-N-16 Stallion nuclear
    anti-submarine weapons. 4x21", 4x25.6" tubes.

'VICTOR III' (SCHUKA) CLASS
K 138, K 255, K 388, K 502, K 507, K 524, K 527
Displacement (tons): 4,850 surfaced, 6,300 dived.
Speed (kts) 30 dived, 10 surfaced.
Diving depth: 1,300 ft.
Armament: SS-N-21 Sampson SLCM,
    SS-N-15 Starfish, SS-N-16 Stallion nuclear
    anti-submarine weapons. 4x21", 2x25.6" tubes.
    Minelaying configuration: 36 replace torpedoes.

SSK - 6 'KILO' AND 6 'KILO B' CLASS,
4 'TANGO' CLASS

'KILO' (VASHAVYANKA) CLASS
Displacement (tons): 2,325 surfaced, 3,076 dived.
Speed (kts) 18 dived, 10 surfaced.
Diving depth: 790 ft.
Armament: 6x21" tubes. 12 reloads. Minelaying
configuration: 24 replace torpedoes.

'TANGO' (SOM) CLASS
Displacement (tons): 3,100 surfaced, 3,800 dived.
Speed (kts) 16 dived, 12 surfaced.
Diving depth: 820 ft.
Armament: 6x21" bow tubes. 18 reloads.

SINGAPORE
SSK - 3 'SJÖORMEN' CLASS
Challenger (ex-*Sjöbjönen*), *Centurion* (ex-*Sjöörmen*),
    Conqueror, (ex-*Sjölejonet*)
Displacement (tons): 1,130 surfaced, 1,210 dived.
Speed (kts) 20 dived, 12 surfaced.
Diving depth: 490 ft.
Armament: 4x21" bow tubes, 6 reloads. 2x16" tubes.
    2 reloads.

SOUTH AFRICA
SSK - 2 'DAPHNÉ' CLASS
Umkhonto (ex-*Emily Hobhouse*),
    Assegaai (ex-*Johanna van der Merwe*)
Displacement (tons): 869 surfaced, 1,043 dived.
Speed (kts) 16 dived, 12 surfaced.
Diving depth: 985 ft.
Armament: 12x21.7" (8 bow, 4 stern) tubes.
    No reloads.

SPAIN
SSK - 4 'GALERNA' (AGOSTA) CLASS;
4 'DELFÍN' (DAPHNÉ) CLASS

'GALERNA' CLASS
Galerna, Tramontana, Siroco, Mistral
Displacement (tons): 1,490 surfaced, 1,740 dived.
Speed (kts) 20 dived, 12 surfaced.
Diving depth: 790 ft.
Armament: 4x21" tubes. 16 reloads. Minelaying
    configuration: 19 with reduced torpedo reloads.

'DELFÍN' CLASS
Delfín, Tonina, Narval, Marsopa.
Displacement (tons): 869 surfaced, 1,043 dived.
Speed (kts) 16 dived, 13 surfaced.
Diving depth: 985 ft.
Armament: 12x21.7" (8 bow, 4 stern) tubes.
    No reloads. Minelaying configuration:
    12 replace torpedoes.

SWEDEN
SSK - 4 'VÄSTERGÖTLAND' CLASS, 3 'GOTLAND', 2
'NÄCKEN' CLASS.

'VÄSTERGÖTLAND' CLASS
Västergötland, Hälsingland, Södermanland,
    Östergötland
Displacement (tons): 1,070 surfaced, 1,143 dived.
Speed (kts) 20 dived, 10 surfaced.
Diving depth: 985 ft.
Armament: 6x21" tubes. 6 reloads.

Below: Sweden: Gotland class

Displacement (tons): 1,070 surfaced, 1,143 dived.
Speed (kts) 20 dived, 10 surfaced.
Diving depth: 985 ft.
Armament: 6x21" tubes. 6 reloads.

'GOTLAND' CLASS
Gotland, Halland, Uppland
Displacement (tons): 1,240 surfaced, 1,494 dived.
Speed (kts) 20 dived, 11 surfaced.
Diving depth: 1,050 ft.
Armament: 4x2" bow tubes. 8 reloads.
  2x15.75" bow tubes. 4 reloads.
  Minelaying configuration: 12 replace torpedoes
  plus 48 in external container.

'NÄCKEN' CLASS
Näcken, Najad.
Displacement (tons): 1.015 surfaced, 1,085 dived.
Speed (kts) 20 dived, 10 surfaced.
Diving depth: 790 ft.
Armament: 6x21" tubes. 2 reloads. 2x15.75" tubes.
  2 reloads. Minelaying capability.

TAIWAN
SSK - 2 'HAI LUNG' CLASS, 2 'GUPPY II' CLASS

'HAI LUNG' CLASS
Hai Lung, Hai Hu.
Displacement (tons): 2,376 surfaced, 2,660 dived.
Speed (kts) 20 dived, 12 surfaced.
Diving depth: 985 ft.
Armament: 6x21" bow tubes. 14 reloads.

'GUPPY II' CLASS
Hai Shih (ex-*Cutlass*), *Hai Bao* (ex-*Tusk*)
Displacement (tons): 1,870 surfaced, 2,420 dived.
Speed (kts) 15 dived, 18 surfaced.
Diving depth: 500 ft.
Armament: 10x21" tubes.

TURKEY
SSK - 4 'PREVEZE' (209, TYPE 1400) CLASS, (PLUS 2
BUILDING), 6 'ATILAY' CLASS (209, TYPE 1200),

'PREVEZE' CLASS
Preveze, Sakarya, Anafartalar, 18 Mart,
  Gür (building), *Çanakkale* (building)
Displacement (tons): 1,454 surfaced, 1,576 dived.
Speed (kts) 21 dived, 10 surfaced.
Diving depth: 820 ft.
Armament: Sub Harpoon anti-ship missile.
  8x21" tubes. 5 reloads.

'ATILAY' CLASS
Atilay, Saldiray, Batiray, Yildiray, Doganay, Dolunay.
Displacement (tons): 980 surfaced, 1,185 dived.
Speed (kts) 22 dived, 10 surfaced.
Diving depth: 820 ft.
Armament: 8x21" tubes. 6 reloads.

SS - 2 'GUPPY IIA' CLASS; 2 'TANG' CLASS
'GUPPY IIA' CLASS
Muratreis (ex-*Razorback*), *Uluçalireis* (ex-*Thornback*)
Displacement (tons): 1,848 surfaced, 2, 440 dived.
Speed (kts) 14 dived, 16 surfaced.
Diving depth: 20 ft. (periscope depth)
Armament: 10x21" (6 bow, 4 stern) tubes. 11 reloads.
  Minelaying configuration: 40 replace torpedoes.

'TANG' CLASS
Hizirreis (ex-*Gudgeon*) *Pirireis* (ex-*Tang*)
Displacement (tons): 2,100 surfaced, 2,700 dived.
Speed (kts) 16 dived, 16 surfaced.
Diving depth: 600 ft.
Armament: 8x21" tubes. 13 reloads.

UKRAINE
SSK - 1 'FOXTROT' CLASS
Zaporizya
Displacement (tons): 1,952 surfaced, 2,475 dived.
Speed (kts) 15 dived, 13 surfaced.
Diving depth: 700 ft.
Armament: 10x21" tubes. 11 reloads.
  Minelaying configuration: 44 replace torpedoes.

UNITED KINGDOM
SSBN - 4 'VANGUARD' CLASS
Vanguard, Victorious, Vigilant, Vengeance
Displacement (tons): 15,900 dived.
Speed (kts) 25 dived, 12 surfaced.
Diving depth: N/K.
Armament: 16 Trident 2 (D5) SLBM. 4x21" tubes.

SSN - 7 'TRAFALGAR' CLASS,
5 'SWIFTSURE' CLASS,
3 'ASTUTE' CLASS (BUILDING)

'TRAFALGAR' CLASS
Trafalgar, Turbulent, Tireless, Torbay, Trenchant,

Above: Saldiroy, one of Turkey's *Atilay* class of SSK, equipped
with very high capacity batteries.

Talent, Triumph.
Displacement (tons): 4, 740 surfaced, 5,208 dived.
Speed (kts) 32 dived, 12 surfaced.
Diving depth: 1,000 ft.
Armament: Tomahawk Block IIIC SLCM.
  Sub Harpoon anti-ship missile. 5x21" bow tubes.
  20 reloads. Minelaying configuration: 24 replace
  torpedoes.

'SWIFTSURE' CLASS
Sovereign, Superb, Sceptre, Spartan, Splendid.
Displacement (tons): 4,400 surfaced, 4,900 dived.
Speed (kts) 32 dived, 12 surfaced.
Diving depth: N/K
Armament: Tomahawk Block III SLCM. Sub Harpoon
  anti-ship missile 5x21" bow tubes. 20 reloads.

'ASTUTE' CLASS (ALL BUILDING).
Astute, Ambush, Artful.
Displacement (tons): 6,500 surfaced, 7,200 dived.
Speed (kts) 29 dived, 12 surfaced.
Diving depth:N/K.
Armament: Tomahawk SLCM.
  Sub Harpoon anti-ship missile. 6x21" tubes.

UNITED STATES OF AMERICA
SSBN - 18 'OHIO' CLASS
Ohio, Michigan, Florida, Georgia, Henry M Jackson,
  Alabama, Alaska, Nevada, Tennessee,
  Pennsylvania, West Virginia, Kentucky, Maryland,
  Nebraska, Rhode Island, Maine, Wyoming,
  Louisiana.
Displacement (tons): 16,600 surfaced, 18,750 dived.
Speed (kts) 24 dived, 12 surfaced.
Diving depth: 790 ft.

Appendix 1: Order of Battle of the World's Submarines

'LOS ANGELES' CLASS

Los Angeles, Philadelphia, Memphis, Bremerton, Jacksonville, Dallas, La Jolla, City of Corpus Christi, Albuquerque, Portsmouth, Minneapolis-Saint Paul, Hyman G Rickover, Augusta, San Francisco, Houston, Norfolk, Buffalo, Salt Lake City, Olympia, Honolulu, Providence, Pittsburgh, Chicago, Key West, Oklahoma City, Louisville, Helena, Newport News, San Juan, Pasadena, Albany, Topeka, Miami, Scranton, Alexandria, Asheville, Jefferson City, Annapolis, Springfield, Columbus, Santa Fe, Boise, Montpelier, Charlotte, Hampton, Hartford, Toledo, Tucson, Columbia, Greeneville, Cheyenne

Displacement (tons): 6,082 surfaced, 6,927 dived.
Speed (kts) 32 dived, 12 surfaced.
Diving depth: 1,475 ft.
Armament: Tomahawk Block III land attack SLCM. Tomahawk and Sub Harpoon anti-ship missiles. 4x21" midships tubes. 10 reloads.

'SEAWOLF' CLASS

Seawolf, Connecticut, Jimmy Carter.
Displacement (tons): 8,060 surfaced, 9,142 dived.
Speed (kts) 39 dived, 13 surfaced.
Diving depth: 1,925 ft.
Armament: Tomahawk Block III land attack SLCM. Tomahawk anti-ship missiles. 8x26" tubes. Minelaying configuration: 100 replace torpedoes.

'VIRGINIA' CLASS

Virginia, Texas, Hawaii.
Displacement (tons): 7,800 dived.
Speed (kts) 34 dived, 14 surfaced.
Diving depth: 1,600 ft.
Armament: Tomahawk land attack SLCM. Anti-ship cruise missiles. 4x21" tubes.

VENEZUELA

SSK - 2 'SÁBALO (209, TYPE 1300) CLASS

Sábaolo, Caribe.
Displacement (tons): 1,285 surfaced, 1,600 dived.
Speed (kts) 22 dived, 10 surfaced.
Diving depth: 800 ft.
Armament: 8x21" bow tubes. 6 reloads.

VIETNAM

MIDGET SUBMARINES - 2 'YUGO' CLASS

Displacement (tons): 90 surfaced, 110 dived.
Speed (kts) 8 dived, 12 surfaced.
Diving depth: N/K
Armament: None. Swimmer delivery.

YUGOSLAVIA

SS - 1 'SAVA' CLASS,
1 'HEROJ' CLASS.

SAVA

Displacement (tons): 830 surfaced, 960 dived.
Speed (kts) 16 dived, 10 surfaced.
Diving depth: 950 ft.
Armament: 6x21" midships tubes. 4 reloads. Minelaying configuration: 20 replace torpedoes.

HEROJ

Displacement (tons): 615 surfaced, 705 dived.
Speed (kts) 15 dived, 10 surfaced.
Diving depth: 375 ft.
Armament: 4x21" midships tubes. 2 reloads. Minelaying configuration: 12 replace torpedoes.

MIDGET SUBMARINES - 5 'UNA' CLASS

Displacement (tons): 76 surfaced, 88 dived.
Speed (kts) 7 dived, 6 surfaced.
Diving depth: N/K
Armament: Swimmer delivery

Below: USS *Los Angeles* (SSN 688) alongside at Changi Naval Base, Singapore seventh annual Cooperation Afloat Readiness and Training (CARAT) 2001 exercise. CARAT is a series of exercises which take place throughout the Western Pacific each summer to increase regional cooperation and promote interoperability between participating countries. Countries taking part included Indonesia, Singapore, Philippines, Thailand, Malaysia and Brunei.

Appendix 2: Submarine Accidents 1905-2000

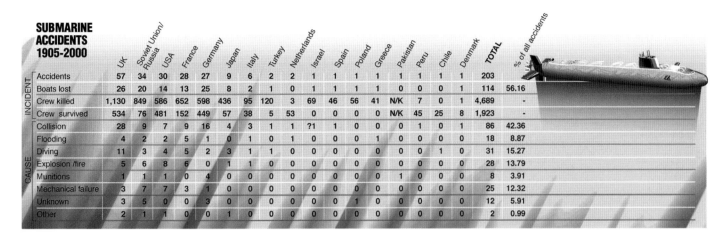

SUBMARINE ACCIDENTS 1905-2000

		UK	Soviet Union/ Russia	USA	France	Germany	Japan	Italy	Turkey	Netherlands	Israel	Spain	Poland	Greece	Pakistan	Peru	Chile	Denmark	TOTAL	% of all accidents
INCIDENT	Accidents	57	34	30	28	27	9	6	2	2	1	1	1	1	1	1	1	1	203	
	Boats lost	26	20	14	13	25	8	2	1	0	1	1	1	1	0	0	0	1	114	56.16
	Crew killed	1,130	849	586	652	598	436	95	120	3	69	46	56	41	N/K	7	0	1	4,689	-
	Crew survived	534	76	481	152	449	57	38	5	53	0	0	0	0	N/K	45	25	8	1,923	-
CAUSE	Collision	28	9	7	9	16	4	3	1	1	?1	1	0	0	0	1	0	1	86	42.36
	Flooding	4	2	2	5	1	0	1	0	1	0	0	0	1	0	0	0	0	18	8.87
	Diving	11	3	4	5	2	3	1	1	0	0	0	0	0	0	0	1	0	31	15.27
	Explosion /fire	5	6	8	6	0	1	1	0	0	0	0	0	0	0	0	0	0	28	13.79
	Munitions	1	1	1	0	4	0	0	0	0	0	0	0	0	1	0	0	0	8	3.91
	Mechanical failure	3	7	7	3	1	0	0	0	0	0	0	0	0	0	0	0	0	25	12.32
	Unknown	3	5	0	0	3	0	0	0	0	0	0	1	0	0	0	0	0	12	5.91
	Other	2	1	1	0	0	1	0	0	0	0	0	0	0	0	0	0	0	2	0.99

Right: The salvaged US submarine S-51 in dock at Brooklyn Navy Yard. 25 lives were lost following a collision with a surface vessel. Note the impact mark on the starboard side.

Below: HMS Sidon in Portland harbour after being raised. 13 men died after the vessel sank following a torpedo explosion aboard in 1955.

Below right: June 1939. The stern of HMS Thetis remain visible as engineers attempt to cut their way into the hull to rescue any survivors still trapped aboard. Only four crewmen survived. She was re-commissioned as HMS Thunderbolt.

Appendix 2: Submarine Accidents 1905-2000

Above: HMS Affray was lost on April 17th 1951 in a diving accident that has never been fully explained. The Royal Navy located the boat 59 days after she went missing in an epic search that involved the investigation of 161 wrecks before she was found.

Below: The French submarine Sibylle being taken over from the Royal Navy in 1952. She foundered during a dive off Toulon, France a few months later. The cause of the accident is not known. 46 officers and crew were killed.

Right: The Portuguese submarine Barracuda was damaged after colliding with a merchant vessel during exercises off the UK in 1995.

Above: So interested in the technology aboard Soviet submarines during the Cold War, the US built a massive salvage barge (HMB-1) under the codename Project Jennifer to retrieve a sunken example, intact, from the ocean bed. Few official details are publicly available on this audacious plan.

Left: In April, 1989, the nuclear submarine K-278, Komsomolets, (Project 685 - Mike Class) sank in the Norwegian Sea following a fire.

217

Appendix 2: Submarine Accidents 1905-2000

Above: Soviet Victor I class SNN lying alongside a repair ship of the Oskol Class at Hammamet, Tunisia. The sub was damaged in a collision with a Soviet tanker while exiting the Straits of Gibraltar whilst submerged.

Below: The fire aboard this Soviet Echo I killed nine crewmen and injured three others 100 miles east of Okinawa, Japan.

Right: The Soviet fleet did not have the best of safety records. This Yankee class boat was disabled after a fire in one of its missile compartments.